AFTER THE FACT

❖

The Art of Historical Detection

VOLUME I

James West Davidson

Mark Hamilton Lytle
Bard College

 Alfred A. Knopf   New York

For
Gretchen, Mike, and Rug
(first readers)
and Jesse and Kate
(future prospects)

First Edition   98765432   *Copyright © 1982 by Alfred A. Knopf, Inc.*

Published in the United States by Alfred A. Knopf, Inc.,
and simultaneously in Canada by Random House of Canada Limited, Toronto.

Library of Congress Cataloging in Publication Data

Davidson, James West.
   After the fact.

   Includes index.
   1. United States—Historiography—Addresses,
essays, lectures. 2. United States—History—
Addresses, essays, lectures. I. Lytle, Mark H.
II. Title
E175.D38 1981b   973'.072   81-13747
ISBN 0-394-32129-4 (v. 1)   AACR2

Manufactured in the United States of America
Composed by Haddon Craftsmen, Inc. Scranton, Pennsylvania.   Printed and bound by
R. R. Donnelley & Sons Company, Harrisonburg, Virginia.

Cover design and photo: Doug Fornuff
Authors' photographs: John Rugge

PHOTO CREDITS

xvi, xxix, 5, 7, 23, 63, 64, 93, 97, 102, 107, 123, 126, 127, 128, 129, 140, 143,
144, 146, 160, 163, 170, 175, 199—Library of Congress;
61, 184, 192—National Archives;
xxv, 44—Sterling Memorial Library, Yale University;
122—The Beinecke Rare Art and Manuscript Library, Yale University;
131, 132—The Warner Collection of Gulf States Paper Corporation;
86—(left) Collection of the University of Wisconsin - Madison Library,
(right) The Huntington Library, San Marino, California.

INTRODUCTION

This book began as an attempt to bring more life to the reading and learning of history. As young historians we have been troubled by a growing disinterest in or even animosity toward the study of the past. How is it that when we and other historians have found so much that excites curiosity, other people find history irrelevant and boring? Perhaps, we thought, if lay readers and students understood better how historians go about their work—how they examine evidence, how they pose questions, and how they reach answers—history would engage them as it does us.

As often happens, it took a mundane event to focus and clarify our preoccupations. One day while working on another project, we went outside to watch a neighboring farmer cut down a large old hemlock that had become diseased. As his saw cut deeper into the tree, we joked that it had now bit into history as far back as the Depression. *"Depression?"* grunted our friend. "I thought you fellas were historians. I'm deep enough now, so's Hoover wasn't even a gleam in his father's eye."

With the tree down, the three of us examined the stump. Our woodcutter surprised us with what he saw.

"Here's when my folks moved into this place," he said, pointing to a ring. "1922."

"How do you know without counting the rings?" we asked.

"Oh, *well*," he said, as if the answer were obvious. "Look at the core, here. The rings are all bunched up tight. I bet there's sixty or seventy —and all within a couple inches. Those came when the place was still forest. Then, you notice, the rings start getting fatter all of a sudden. That's when my dad cleared behind the house—in '22—and the tree started getting a lot more light. And look further out, here—see how the rings set together again for a couple years? That's from loopers."

"Loopers?" we asked cautiously.

"Sure—*loopers*. You know. The ones with only front legs and back." His hand imitated a looping, hopping crawl across the log. "Inchworms. They damn near killed the tree. That was sometime after the war—'49 or '50." As his fingers traced back and forth among the concentric circles, he spoke of other events from years gone by. Before we returned home, we had learned a good deal about past doings in the area.

Now, it occurs to us that our neighbor had a pretty good knack for putting together history. The evidence of the past, like the tree rings, comes easily enough to hand. But we still need to be taught how to see it, read it, and explain it before it can be turned into a story. Even more to the point, the explanations and interpretations *behind* the story often turn out to be as interesting as the story itself. After all, the fascination in our neighbor's account came from the way he traced his tale out of those silent tree rings.

Unfortunately, most readers first encounter history in school textbooks, and these omit the explanations and interpretations—the detective work, if you will. Textbooks, by their nature, seek to summarize knowledge. They have little interest and less space for looking at how that knowledge was gained. Yet the challenge of doing history, not just reading it, is what attracts so many historians. Couldn't some of that challenge be communicated in a concrete way? That was our first goal.

We also felt that the writing of history has suffered in recent years because some historians have been overly eager to convert their discipline into an unadulterated social science. Undeniably, history would lose much of its claim to contemporary relevance without the methods and theories it has borrowed from anthropology, psychology, political science, economics, sociology, and other fields. Indeed, such theories make an important contribution to these pages. Yet history is rooted in the narrative tradition. As much as it seeks to generalize from past events, as do the sciences, it also remains dedicated to capturing the uniqueness of a situation. When historians neglect the literary aspect of their discipline—when they forget that good history begins with a good story—they risk losing the wider audience that all great historians have addressed. They end up, sadly, talking to themselves.

Our second goal, then, was to discuss the methods of American historians in a way that would give proper due to both the humanistic and scientific sides of history. In taking this approach, we have tried to examine many of the methodologies that allow historians to unearth new evidence or to shed new light on old issues. At the same time, we selected topics that we felt were inherently interesting as stories.

Thus our book employs what might be called an apprentice approach to history rather than the synthetic approach of textbooks. A text strives to be comprehensive and broad. It presents its findings in as rational and programmatic a manner as possible. By contrast, apprentices are much less likely to receive such a formal presentation. They learn their profession from artisans who take their daily trade as it comes through the front door. A pewter pot is ordered? Very well, the pot is fashioned. Along the way, an apprentice is shown how to pour the mold. An engraving is needed? Then the apprentice receives his first taste of etching. While this method of teaching communicates a broad range of knowledge over the long run, it does so by focusing on specific situations.

So also this book. Our discussion of methods is set in the context of specific problems historians have encountered over the years. In piecing the individual stories together, we try to pause as an artisan might, and point out problems of evidence, historical perspective, or logical inference. Sometimes, we focus on problems that all historians must face, whatever their subjects. These include such matters as the selection of evidence, historical perspective, the analysis of a document, and the use of broader historical theory. In other cases, we explore problems not encountered by all historians, but characteristic of specific historical fields. These include the use of pictorial evidence, questions of psychohistory, problems encountered analyzing oral interviews, the value of decision-making models in political history, and so on. In each case, we have tried to provide the reader with some sense of vicarious participation—the savor of doing history as well as of reading it.

Given our approach, the ultimate success of this book can be best measured in functional terms—how well it works for the apprentices and artisans. We hope that the artisans, our fellow historians, will find the volume's implicit as well as explicit definitions of good history worth considering. In choosing our examples, we have naturally gravitated toward the work of those historians we most respect. At the same time we have drawn upon our own original research in many of the topics discussed; hopefully those findings also may be of use to scholars.

As for the apprentices, we admit to being only modest proselytizers. We recognize that, of all the people who read this, only a few will go on to become professional historians. That is only natural. We do hope, however, that even casual readers will come to appreciate the complexity and excitement that go into the study of the past. History is not something that is simply brought out of the archives, dusted off, and displayed as "the way things really were." It is a painstaking construction, held together only with the help of assumptions, hypotheses, and inferences. Readers of history who push dutifully onward, unaware of all the backstage work, miss the essence of the discipline. They miss the opportunity to question and to judge their reading critically. Most of all, they miss the chance to learn how enjoyable it can be to go out and do a bit of digging themselves.

ACKNOWLEDGMENTS

Because this book is as much about doing history as about history itself, we have drawn heavily on the research and methods of those scholars we most respect and whose history seems to us to provide excellent working models for any apprentice. These historians, past and present, demonstrate how exciting the pursuit of history can and ought to be. Because our narrative is written for lay readers and students as much as for professional scholars, we have omitted extensive footnotes and instead tried to acknowledge our many specific debts in the bibliographical essays that follow each chapter. These essays should provide scholars with the data needed to track down any specific points or issues of interest, as well as direct general readers and students to the primary and secondary sources needed for beginning their own investigations.

For the lay reader or student who comes to history only to sample the discipline or to fulfill distribution requirements, a confession of sorts is in order. Neither of us entered college with the idea of majoring in history, much less making a profession out of it. In the end it was good teachers who lured us into the vineyard. We had the fortune as undergraduates to study under some unusually exciting historians. At Cornell University, Donald Kagan made the ancient world come alive in a way that convinced Mark Lytle that history offered an indispensable way of organizing human knowledge. Walter LaFeber persuaded him that historians could have deep convictions, a powerful grasp of critical issues, and basic human decency. David Davis and Michael Kammen astonished him with the breadth and depth of their intellectual interests.

Jim Davidson's undergraduate years at Haverford College brought him the guidance and friendship of Wallace MacCaffery, whose judicious and eloquent lectures served as models not only for the department but for the rest of the college. In American history, Roger Lane's insights were by turns laconic (Vermont-style) and oratorical (the Irish mode), but always keenly analytical. And then there was William Smith—a colonial historian unaccountably serving in the English department and refusing to be digested by it. He taught unsuspecting freshmen the art of expository prose, a job he performed with more hard-nosed rigor (and consequent effect) than most of his suspicious colleagues.

Graduate school brought the authors together under the tutelage of many exceptional historians. To Edmund S. Morgan, David Davis, John Blum, Gaddis Smith, David Hall, Sydney Ahlstrom, Lawrence Chisolm,

Donald Kagan, Firuz Kazemzadeh, Steven Ozment, C. Vann Woodward, and others who taught at Yale, we owe our belief that historians can adopt all manner of methodologies and still write with precision and eloquence. They demonstrated the value of imaginative approaches to evidence, at the same time insisting that history ought to be literate as well as accurate. To the extent that we have followed their precepts, we owe them our gratitude. Where we have not succeeded in following, we can at least say that the spirit was willing, if the flesh a little weak.

We have been fortunate, too, to have had graduate school friends who researched, wrote, kibitzed, and shared lunches along the way. Glenn May, Sherm Cochran, Alan Williams, Bill Gienapp, Jon Clark, Marie Caskey, Allan Winkler, Alexis Pogerlskin, Jim Crisp, Steve Wiberley, Ellen Dwyer, Hal Williams, Rick Warch, and Elsa Dixler have now scattered across the nation, but they all contributed to the authors' present respect for the teaching and writing of history. Among our present colleagues, friends, and wife (only one of the latter), we would like to thank Gretchen Lytle, Mike Stoff, Mary Keller, John Rugge, Avi Soifer, Christine Stansell, James Lytle, Tom Frost, Geoff Linburn, Eric Berger, Doug Baz, Sam Kauffmann, Irene Solet, Ellen Boyce, Ken Ludwig, Adrienne George, Robert Koblitz, Stephen Andors, David Pierce, Peter Skiff, John Fout, and Fred Crane. All of them responded generously with advice and comment, sharpened the authors' focus, lampooned their pretensions, and generated ideas and criticism that have kept this book alive. To them all we say, *wea culpa* but thanks.

To Angus Cameron, editor at Alfred Knopf, goes our gratitude for early and continuing interest in the project. Professor Jack Wilson of Smith College provided many perceptive comments that improved the final draft substantially. He is one of those rare critics who not only pinpoints the flaws in a manuscript but also comes up with concrete and creative remedies. At the College Department, David Follmer and Marilyn Miller of Alfred Knopf patiently superintended the manuscript through the hurdles of writing, editing, and production. At Bard College, Ann McTigue and Curt Crane found time, amidst the mounting requests for "yesterday if not sooner," to type and retype the many drafts of chapters.

There are many names here. But then, history has not proved a lonely business. For that, too, we remain grateful.

JIM DAVIDSON
MARK LYTLE

June 1981

CONTENTS

Volume I

The Strange Death of Silas Deane

The writing of history is one of the most familiar ways of organizing human knowledge. And yet, if familiarity has not always bred contempt, it has at least encouraged a good deal of misunderstanding. All of us meet history long before we have heard of any of the social science disciplines, at a tender age when tales of the past easily blend with heroic myths of the culture. In Golden Books, Abe Lincoln looms every bit as large as Paul Bunyan, while George Washington's cherry tree gets chopped down yearly with almost as much ritual as St. Nick's Christmas tree goes up. Despite this long familiarity, or perhaps because of it, most students absorb the required facts about the past without any real conception of what history is. Even worse, most think they do know and never get around to discovering what they missed.

"History is what happened in the past." That is the everyday view of the matter. It supposes that historians must return to the past through the surviving records and bring it back to the present to display as "what really happened." The everyday view recognizes that this task is often difficult. But historians are said to succeed if they bring back the facts without distorting them or forcing a new perspective on them. In effect, historians are seen as couriers between the past and present. Like all good couriers, they are expected simply to deliver messages without adding to them.

This everyday view of history is profoundly misleading. In order to demonstrate how it is misleading, we would like to examine in detail an event that "happened in the past"—the death of Silas Deane. Deane does not appear in most American history texts, and rightly so. He served as a distinctly second-rate diplomat for the United States during the years of the American Revolution. Yet the story of Deane's death is an excellent example of an event that cannot be understood merely by transporting it, courier-like, to the present. In short, it illustrates the important difference between "what happened in the past" and what history really is.

AN UNTIMELY DEATH

Silas Deane's career began with one of those rags-to-riches stories so much appreciated in American folklore. In fact, Deane might have made a lasting place for himself in the history texts, except that his career ended with an equally dramatic riches-to-rags story.

He began life as the son of a humble blacksmith in Groton, Connecticut. The blacksmith had aspirations for his boy and sent him to Yale College, where Silas was quick to take advantage of his opportunities. After studying law, Deane opened a practice near Hartford; then continued his climb up the social ladder by marrying a well-to-do widow, whose inheritance included the business of her late husband, a merchant. Conveniently, Deane became a merchant. After his first wife died, he married the granddaughter of a former governor of Connecticut.

Not content to remain a prospering businessman, Deane entered politics. He served on Connecticut's Committee of Correspondence and later as a delegate to the first and second Continental Congresses, where he attracted the attention of prominent leaders, including Benjamin Franklin, Robert Morris, and John Jay. In 1776 Congress sent Deane to France as the first American to represent the united colonies abroad. His mission was to purchase badly needed military supplies for the Revolutionary cause. A few months later Benjamin Franklin and Arthur Lee joined him in an attempt to arrange a formal treaty of alliance with France. The American commissioners concluded the alliance in March 1778.

Deane worked hard to progress from the son of a blacksmith all the way to Minister Plenipotentiary from the United States to the Court of France. Most observers described him as ambitious: someone who thoroughly enjoyed fame, honor, and wealth. "You know his ambition —" wrote John Adams to one correspondent, "his desire of making a Fortune. . . . You also know his Art and Enterprise. Such Characters are often useful, altho always to be carefully watched and contracted, specially in such a government as ours." One man in particular suspected Deane enough to watch him: Arthur Lee, the third member of the

American mission. Lee accused Deane of taking unfair advantage of his official position to make a private fortune—as much as fifty thousand pounds, some said. Deane stoutly denied the accusations and Congress engaged in a heated debate over his conduct. In 1778 it voted to recall its Minister Plenipotentiary, although none of the charges had been conclusively proved.

Deane embroiled himself in further controversy in 1781, having written friends to recommend that America sue for peace and patch up the quarrel with England. His letters were intercepted, and copies of them turned up in a New York Tory newspaper just after Cornwallis surrendered to Washington at Yorktown. For Deane, the timing could not have been worse. With American victory complete, anyone advocating that the United States rejoin Britain was considered as much a traitor as Benedict Arnold. So Deane suddenly found himself adrift. He could not return to America, for no one would have him. Nor could he go to England without confirming his reputation as a traitor. And he could not stay in France, where he had injudiciously accused Louis XVI of aiding the Americans for purely selfish reasons. Rejected on all sides, Deane took refuge in Flanders.

The next few years of his life were spent unhappily. Without friends and with little money, he continued in Flanders until 1783, when the controversy had died down enough for him to move to England. There he lived in obscurity, took to drink, and wound up boarding at the house of an unsavory prostitute. The only friend who remained faithful to him was Edward Bancroft, another Connecticut Yankee who, as a boy, had been Deane's pupil and later his personal secretary during the Paris negotiations for the alliance. Although Bancroft's position as a secretary seemed innocent enough, members of the Continental Congress knew that Bancroft was also acting as a spy for the Americans, using his connections in England to secure information about the British ministry's war plans. With the war concluded, Bancroft was back in London. Out of kindness, he provided Deane with living money from time to time.

Finally, Deane decided he could no longer live in London and in 1789 booked passage on a ship sailing for the United States. When Thomas Jefferson heard the news, he wrote his friend James Madison: "Silas Deane is coming over to finish his days in America, not having one *sou* to subsist on elsewhere. He is a wretched monument of the consequences of a departure from right."

The rest of the sad story could be gotten from the obituaries. Deane

S. Deane.

Drawn from the life by Du Simitier at Philadelphia.   Engraved by B. L. Prevost at Paris

"You know his ambition—his desire of making a Fortune. . . . You also know his Art and Enterprise. Such
Characters are often useful, altho always to be carefully
watched and contracted, specially in such a government
as ours."   —John Adams on Silas Deane

boarded the *Boston Packet* in mid-September, and it sailed out of London
down the estuary of the Thames. A storm came up, however, and on
September 19 the ship lost both its anchors and beat a course for safer
shelter, where it could wait out the storm. On September 22, while
walking the quarter deck with the ship's captain, Deane suddenly "com-

plain'd of a dizziness in his head, and an oppression at his stomach." The captain immediately put him to bed. Deane's condition worsened; twice he tried to say something, but no one was able to make out his words. A "drowsiness and insensibility continually incroached upon his faculties," and only four hours after the first signs of illness he breathed his last.

Such, in outline, was the rise and fall of the ambitious Silas Deane. The story itself seems pretty clear, although certainly people might interpret it in different ways. Thomas Jefferson thought Deane's unhappy career demonstrated "the consequences of a departure from right," whereas one English newspaper more sympathetically attributed his downfall to the mistake of "placing confidence in his [American] Compatriots, and doing them service before he had got his compensation, of which no well-bred Politician was before him ever guilty." Yet either way, the basic story remains the same—the same, that is, until the historian begins putting together a more complete account of Deane's life. Then some of the basic facts become clouded.

For example, a researcher familiar with the correspondence of Americans in Europe during 1789 would realize that a rumor had been making its way around London in the weeks following Deane's death. According to certain people, Deane had become depressed by his poverty, ill-health, and low reputation, and consequently had committed suicide. John Cutting, a New England merchant and friend of Jefferson, wrote of the rumor that Deane "had predetermin'd to take a sufficient quantity of Laudanum [a form of opium] to ensure his dissolution" before the boat could sail for America. John Quincy Adams heard that "every probability" of the situation suggested Deane's death was "voluntary and self-administered." And Tom Paine, the famous pamphleteer, also reported the gossip: "Cutting told me he took poison."

At this point we face a substantial problem. Obviously, historians cannot rest content with the facts that come most easily to hand. They must search the odd corners of libraries and letter collections in order to put together a complete story. But how do historians know when their research is "complete?" How do they know to search one collection of letters rather than another? These questions point up the misconception at the heart of the everyday view of history. History is not "what happened in the past;" rather, it is *the act of selecting, analyzing, and writing about the past.* It is something that is done, that is constructed, rather than an inert body of data that lies scattered through the archives.

The distinction is important. It allows us to recognize the confusion in the question of whether a history of something is "complete." If history were merely "what happened in the past," there would never be a "complete" history of Silas Deane—or even a complete history of the last day of his life. The past holds an infinite number of facts about those last days, and they could never all be included in a historical account.

The truth is, no historian would *want* to include all the facts. Here, for example, is a list of items from the past which might form part of a history of Silas Deane. Which ones should be included?

Deane is sent to Paris to help conclude a treaty of alliance.
Arthur Lee accuses him of cheating his country to make a private profit.
Deane writes letters which make him unpopular in America.
He goes into exile and nearly starves.
Helped out by a gentleman friend, he buys passage on a ship for America as his last chance to redeem himself.
He takes ill and dies before the ship can leave; rumors suggest he may have committed suicide.

      •   •   •

Ben Franklin and Arthur Lee are members of the delegation to Paris.
Edward Bancroft is Deane's private secretary and an American spy.
Men who know Deane say he is talented but ambitious, and ought to be watched.

      •   •   •

Before Deane leaves, he visits an American artist, John Trumbull.
The *Boston Packet* is delayed for several days by a storm.
On the last day of his life, Deane gets out of bed in the morning.
He puts on his clothes and buckles his shoes.
He eats breakfast.
When he takes ill, he tries to speak twice.
He is buried several days later.

Even this short list of facts demonstrates the impossibility of including all of them. For behind each one lie hundreds more. You might mention that Deane put on his clothes and ate breakfast, but consider also: What color were his clothes? When did he get up that morning? What did he have for breakfast? When did he leave the table? All these things "happened in the past," but only a comparatively small number of them can appear in a history of Silas Deane.

It may be objected that we are placing too much emphasis on this process of selection. Surely, a certain amount of good judgment will suggest which facts are important. Who needs to know what color Deane's clothes were or when he got up from the breakfast table?

Admittedly this objection has some merit, as the list of facts about

Deane demonstrates. The list is divided into three groups, roughly according to the way common sense might rank them in importance. The first group contains facts which every historian would be likely to include. The second group contains less important information, which could either be included or left out. (It might be useful, for instance, to know who Arthur Lee and Edward Bancroft were, but not essential.) The last group contains information that appears either too detailed or else unnecessary. Deane may have visited John Trumbull, but then, he surely visited other people as well—why include any of that? Knowing that the *Boston Packet* was delayed by a storm reveals little about Silas Deane. And readers will assume without being told that Deane rose in the morning, put on his clothes, and had breakfast.

But if common sense helps to select evidence, it also produces a good deal of pedestrian history. The fact is, the straightforward account of Silas Deane we have just presented has actually managed to miss the most fascinating parts of the story.

Fortunately, one enterprising historian named Julian Boyd was not satisfied with the traditional account of the matter. He examined the known facts of Deane's career and put them together in ways common sense had not suggested. Take, for example, two items on our list: (1) Deane was down on his luck and left in desperation for America; and (2) he visited John Trumbull. One fact is from the "important" items on the list and the other from items that seem incidental. How do they fit together?

To answer that, we have to know the source of information about the visit to Trumbull's, which is the letter from John Cutting informing Jefferson of Deane's rumored suicide.

> A subscription had been made here chiefly by Americans to defray the expense of getting [Deane] out of this country. . . . Dr. Bancroft with great humanity and equal discretion undertook the management of the *man* and his *business.* Accordingly his passage was engaged, comfortable cloaths and stores for his voyage were laid in, and apparently without much reluctance he embarked. . . . I happen'd to see him a few days since at the lodging of Mr. Trumbull and thought I had never seen him look better.

We are now in a better position to see how our two items fit together. And as Julian Boyd has pointed out, they don't fit. According to the first, Deane was depressed, dejected, almost starving. According to the second, he had "never looked better." An alert historian begins to get nervous when he sees contradictions like that, so he hunts around a little more. And finds, among the collection of papers published by the Connecticut and New York historical societies, that Deane had been writing letters of his own.

One went to his brother-in-law in America, who had agreed to help pay Deane's transportation over and to receive him when he arrived— something that nobody had been willing to do for years. Other letters reveal that Deane had plans for what he would do when he finally returned home. He had seen models in England of the new steam engines, which he hoped might operate gristmills in America. He had talked to friends about getting a canal built from Lake Champlain in New York to the St. Lawrence River, in order to promote trade. These were not offhand dreams. As early as 1785, Deane had been at work drumming up support for his canal project. He had even laboriously calculated the cost of the canal's construction. ("Suppose a labourer to dig and remove six feet deep and eight feet square in one day. . . . 2,933 days of labour will dig one mile in length, twenty feet wide and eight feet deep. . . .") Obviously, Deane looked forward to a promising future.

Lastly, Deane appeared to believe that the controversy surrounding his French mission had finally abated. As he wrote an American friend,

> It is now almost ten years since I have solicited for an impartial inquiry [into the dispute over my conduct]. . . . that justice might be done to my fortune and my character. . . . You can sufficiently imagine, without my attempting to describe, what I must have suffered on every account during so long a period of anxiety and distress. I hope that it is now drawing to a close.

Other letters went to George Washington and John Jay, reiterating Deane's innocence.

All this makes the two items on our list even more puzzling. If Deane was depressed and discouraged, why was he so enthusiastic about coming back to build canals and gristmills? If he really believed that his time of "anxiety and distress" was "drawing to a close," why did he commit suicide? Of course, Deane might have been subject to dramatic shifts in mood. Perhaps hope for the future alternated with despair about his chances for success. Perhaps a sudden fit of depression caused him to take his life.

But another piece of "unimportant" information, way down on our third list, makes this hypothesis difficult to accept. After Deane's ship left London, it was delayed offshore for more than a week. Suppose Deane did decide to commit suicide by taking an overdose of laudanum. Where did he get the drug? Surely not by walking up to the ship's surgeon and asking for it. He must have purchased it in London, before he left. Yet he remained on shipboard for more than a week. If Deane bought the laudanum during a temporary "fit" of depression, why did he wait a week before taking it? And if his depression was not just a sudden fit, how do we explain the optimistic letters to America?

This close look at three apparently unrelated facts indicates that perhaps Deane's story has more to it than meets the eye. It would be well, then, to reserve judgment about our first reconstruction of Silas Deane's career, and try to find as much information about the man as possible— regardless of whether it seems relevant at first. That means investigating not only Deane himself but also his friends and associates, like Ben Franklin, Arthur Lee, and Edward Bancroft. Since it is impossible in this prologue to look closely at all of Deane's acquaintances, for purpose of example we will take only one: his friend Bancroft.

SILAS DEANE'S FRIEND

Edward Bancroft was born in Westfield, Massachusetts, where his stepfather presided over a respectable tavern, the *Bunch of Grapes*. Bancroft was a clever fellow, and his father soon apprenticed him to a physician. Like many boys before him, Edward did not fancy his position and so ran away to sea. Unlike many boys, he managed to make the most of his situation. His ship landed in the Barbadoes, and there Bancroft signed on as the surgeon for a plantation in Surinam. The plantation owner, Paul Wentworth, liked the young man and let him use his private library for study. In addition, Bancroft met another doctor who taught him much about the area's exotic tropical plants and animals. When Bancroft returned to New England in 1766 and continued on to London the following year, he knew enough about Surinam's wildlife to publish a book entitled *An Essay on the Natural History of Guiana in South America*. It was well received by knowledgeable scholars and, among other things, established that an electric eel's shock was actually caused by electricity, a fact not previously recognized.

A young American bright enough to publish a book at age twenty-five and to experiment with electric eels attracted the attention of another electrical experimenter then in London, Ben Franklin. Franklin befriended Bancroft and introduced him to many influential colleagues, not only learned philosophers but also the politicians with whom Franklin worked as colonial agent for Pennsylvania. A second trip to Surinam produced more research on plants used in making color dyes; research so successful that Bancroft soon found himself elected to the prestigious Royal Society of Medicine. At the same time, Franklin led Bancroft into the political arena, both public and private. On the public side, Bancroft published a favorable review of Thomas Jefferson's pamphlet, *A Summary View of the Rights of British America;* privately, he joined Franklin and other investors in an attempt to gain a charter for land along the banks of the Ohio River.

Up to this point it has been possible to sketch Bancroft's career without once mentioning the name of Silas Deane. Common sense would suggest that the information about Bancroft's early travels, his scientific studies, his friends in Surinam, tell us little about Deane, and that the story ought to begin with a certain letter Bancroft received from Deane in June 1776. (Common sense is again wrong, but we must wait a little to discover why.)

The letter, which came to Bancroft in 1776, informed him that his old friend Silas Deane was coming to France as a merchant engaged in private business. Would Bancroft be interested in crossing over from England to meet Deane at Calais to catch up on news for old time's sake? An invitation like that would very likely have attracted Bancroft's curiosity. He did know Deane, who had been his teacher in 1758, but not very well. Why would Deane now write and suggest a meeting? Bancroft may have guessed the rest, or he may have known it from other contacts; in any case, he wrote his "old friend" that he would make all possible haste for Calais.

The truth of the matter, as we know, was that Deane had come to France to secure military supplies for the colonies. Franklin, who was back in Philadelphia, had suggested to Congress's Committee of Secret Correspondence that Deane contact Bancroft as a good source of information about British war plans. Bancroft could easily continue his friendship with English officials, because he did not have the reputation of being a hot-headed American patriot. So Deane met Bancroft at Calais in July and the two concluded their arrangements. Bancroft would be Deane's "private secretary" when needed in Paris and a spy for the Americans when in England.

It turned out that Deane's arrangement worked well—perhaps a little too well. Legally, Deane was permitted to collect a commission on all the supplies he purchased for Congress, but he went beyond that. He and Bancroft used their official connections in France to conduct a highly profitable private trade of their own. Deane, for instance, sometimes sent ships from France without declaring whether they were loaded with private or public goods. Then if the ships arrived safely, he would declare that the cargo was private, his own. But if the English navy captured the goods on the high seas, he labelled it government merchandise and the public absorbed the loss.

Deane used Bancroft to take advantage of his official position in other ways. Both men speculated in the London insurance markets, which were the eighteenth-century equivalent of gambling parlors. Anyone who wished could take out "insurance" against a particular event which might happen in the future. An insurer, for example, might quote odds on the chances of France going to war with England within the year. The insured would pay whatever premium he wished, say £1,000, and if France did go to war, and the odds had been five-to-one against it, the insured would receive £5,000. Wagers were made on almost any public event: which armies would win which battles, which politicians would fall from power, and even on whether a particular lord would die before the year was out.

Obviously, someone who had access to inside information—someone who knew in advance, for instance, that France was going to war with England—could win a fortune. That was exactly what Bancroft and Deane decided to do. Deane was in charge of concluding the French alliance, and he knew that if he succeeded Britain would be forced to declare war on France. Bancroft hurried across to London as soon as the treaty had been concluded and took out the proper insurance before the news went public. The profits shared by the two men from this and other similar ventures amounted to approximately ten thousand pounds. Like most gamblers, however, Deane also lost wagers. In the end, he netted little for his troubles.

Historians know these facts because they now have access to the papers of Deane, Bancroft, and others. Acquaintances of the two men lacked this advantage, but they suspected shady dealings anyway. Arthur Lee publicly accused Deane and Bancroft of playing the London insurance game. (Deane shot back that Lee was doing the same thing.) And the moralistic John Adams found Bancroft's conduct distasteful. Bancroft, according to Adams, was

> a meddler in stocks as well as reviews, and frequently went into the alley, and into the deepest and darkest retirements and recesses of the brokers and jobbers . . . and found amusement as well, perhaps, as profit, by listening to all the news and anecdotes, true or false, that were there whispered or more boldly pronounced. . . . This man had with him in France, a woman with whom he lives, and who by the French was called La Femme de Monsieur Bancroft. At tables he would season his foods with

such enormous quantities of cayenne pepper which assisted by generous
burgundy would set his tongue a running in the most licentious way both
at table and after dinner. . . .

Yet for all Bancroft's dubious habits, and for all the suspicions of men
like Lee and Adams, there was one thing that almost no one at the time
suspected, and that not even historians discovered until the records of
certain British officials were opened to the public more than a century
later. Edward Bancroft was a double agent.

At the end of July 1776, after he had arranged to be Deane's secretary,
Bancroft returned to England and met with Paul Wentworth, his friend
from Surinam, who was then working in London for Britain's intelligence organization. Immediately Wentworth realized how valuable Bancroft would be as a spy and introduced him to two Secretaries of State.
They in turn persuaded Bancroft to submit reports on the American
negotiations in France. For his services, he received a lifetime pension
of £200 a year—a figure the British were only too happy to pay for such
good information. So quick was Bancroft's reporting that the Secretaries
of State knew about the American mission to France even before the
United States Congress could confirm that Deane had arrived safely!

Eventually, Bancroft discovered that he could pass his information
directly to the British ambassador at the French court. To do so, he wrote
innocent letters on the subject of "gallantry" and signed them
"B. Edwards." On the same paper would go another note written in
invisible ink, to appear only when the letter was dipped in a special
developer held by Lord Stormont, the British ambassador. Bancroft left
his letters every Tuesday morning in a sealed bottle in a hole near the
trunk of a tree on the south terrace of the Tuileries, the royal palace.
Lord Stormont's secretary would put any return information near another tree on the same terrace. With this system in operation Stormont
could receive intelligence without having to wait for it to filter back from
England.

Did any Americans suspect Bancroft of double dealing? Arthur Lee
once claimed he had evidence to charge Bancroft with treason, but he
never produced it. In any case, Lee had a reputation for suspecting
everybody of everything. Franklin, for his part, shared lodgings with
Deane and Bancroft during their stays in Paris. He had reason to guess
that someone close to the American mission was leaking secrets—especially when Lord Stormont and the British newspapers made embarrass-
ingly accurate accusations about French aid. The French wished to keep
their assistance secret in order to avoid war with England as long as
possible, but of course Franklin knew America would fare better with

The Tuileries, much as it appeared when Bancroft and Lord Stormont used the south terrace as a drop for their secret correspondence. The royal palace overlooks a magnificent formal garden which, as a modern observer has noted, "seems so large, so full of surprising hidden corners and unexpected stairways, that its strict ground plan—sixteen carefully spaced and shaped gardens of trees, separated by arrow-straight walks—is not immediately discernable."

France fighting, so he did little to stop the leaks. "If I was sure," he remarked, "that my *valet de place* was a spy, as he probably is, I think I should not discharge him for that, if in other respects I liked him." So the French would tell Franklin he *really* ought to guard his papers more closely, and Franklin would say yes, yes, he really would have to do something about that; and the secrets continued to leak. Perhaps Franklin suspected Deane and Bancroft of playing the London insurance markets, but there is no evidence that he knew Bancroft was a double agent.

What about Deane, who was closer to Bancroft than anyone else? We have no proof that he shared the double agent's secret, but his alliance with Bancroft in other intrigues tells against him. Furthermore, one published leak pointed to a source so close to the American commissioners that Franklin began to investigate. As Julian Boyd has pointed out, Deane immediately directed suspicion toward a man he knew perfectly well was not a spy. We can only conclude he did so to help throw suspicion away from Bancroft. Very likely, if Bancroft was willing to help Deane play his games with the London insurers, Deane was willing to assist Bancroft in his game with British intelligence.

Of the two, Bancroft seems to have made out better. While Deane suffered reproach and exile for his conduct, Bancroft returned to England still respected by both the Americans and the British. Not that he had been without narrow escapes. Some of the British ministry (the king especially) did not trust him, and he once came close to being hung for treason when his superiors rightly suspected that he had associated with John the Painter, a notorious incendiarist who tried to set England's navy ablaze. But Bancroft left for Paris at the first opportunity, waited until the storm blew over, and returned to London at the end of the war with his lifetime pension raised to £1,000 a year. At the time of Deane's death, he was doing more of his scientific experiments, in hopes that Parliament would grant him a profitable monopoly on a new process for making dyes.

DEANE'S DEATH: A SECOND LOOK

So we finally arrive, the long way around, back where the story began: September 1789 and Deane's death. But now we have at hand a much larger store of information out of which to construct a narrative. Since writing history involves the acts of analyzing and selecting, let us review the results of our investigation.

We know that Deane was indeed engaged in dubious private ventures; ventures Congress would have condemned as unethical. We also have reason to suspect that Deane knew Bancroft was a spy for the British. Combining that evidence with what we already know about Deane's death, we might theorize that Deane committed suicide because, underneath all his claims to innocence, he knew he was guilty as Congress charged. The additional evidence, in other words, reveals a possible new motive for Deane's suicide.

Yet this theory presents definite problems. In the first place, Deane never admitted any wrongdoing to anyone—not in all the letters he wrote, not in any of his surviving papers. That does not mean he was innocent, nor even that he believed himself innocent. But often it is easier for a person to lie to himself than to his friends. Perhaps Deane actually convinced himself that he was blameless; that he had a right to make a little extra money from his influential position; that he did no more than anyone would in his situation. Certainly his personal papers point to that conclusion. And if Deane believed himself innocent—correctly or not—would he have any obvious motive for suicide? Furthermore, the theory does not explain the puzzle that started this investigation. If Deane felt guilty enough about his conduct to commit suicide, why did that guilt increase ten years after the fact? If he did feel suddenly guilty, why wait a week aboard ship before taking the fatal dose of laudanum? For that matter, why go up and chat with the captain when death was about to strike?

No, things still do not set quite right, so we must question the theory. What proof do we have that Deane committed suicide? Rumors about London. Tom Paine heard it from Cutting, the merchant. And Cutting reports in his letter to Jefferson that Deane's suicide was "the suspicion of Dr. Bancroft." How do we know the circumstances of Deane's death? The captain made a report, but for some reason it was not preserved. The one account that did survive was written by Bancroft, at the request of a friend. Then there were the anonymous obituaries in the newspapers. Who wrote them? Very likely Bancroft composed at least one; certainly, he was known as Silas Deane's closest friend and would have been consulted by any interested parties. There are a lot of strings here, which, when pulled hard enough, all run back to the affable Dr. Bancroft. What do we know about *his* situation in 1789?

We know Bancroft is dependent upon a pension of £1,000 a year, given him for his faithful service as a British spy. We know he is hoping Parliament will grant him a monopoly for making color dyes. Suddenly his old associate Deane, who has been leading a dissolute life in London, decides to return to America, vindicate himself to his former friends, and start a new life. Put yourself in Bancroft's place. Would you be just a little nervous about that idea? Here is a man down on his luck, now picking up and going to America to clear his reputation. What would Deane do to clear it? Tell everything he knew about his life in Paris? Submit his record books to Congress, as he had been asked to do so many years before? If Deane knew Bancroft was a double agent, would he say so? And if Deane's records mentioned the affair of John the Painter (as indeed they did), what would happen if knowledge of Bancroft's role in the plot reached England? Ten years earlier, Bancroft would have been hung. True, memories had faded, but even if he were spared death, would Parliament grant a monopoly on color dyes to a known traitor? Would Parliament continue the £1,000 pension? It was one thing to have Deane living in London, where Bancroft could watch him; it would be quite another to have him all the way across the Atlantic Ocean, ready to tell—who knows what?

Admit it: if you were Bancroft, wouldn't you be just a little nervous?

We are forced to consider, however reluctantly, that Deane was not expecting to die as he walked the deck of the *Boston Packet*. Yet if Bancroft did murder Deane, how? He was not aboard ship when death came and had not seen Deane for more than a week. That is a good alibi, but then, Bancroft was a clever man. We know (once again from the letters of John Cutting) that Bancroft was the person who "with great humanity and equal discretion undertook the management of the *man* and the *business*" of getting Deane ready to leave for America. Bancroft himself wrote Jefferson that he had been visiting Deane often "to assist him with advice, medicins, and money for his subsistence." If Deane were a laudanum addict, as Bancroft hinted to Cutting, might not the good doctor who helped with "medicins" also have procured the laudanum? And having done that, might he not easily slip some other deadly chemical into the mixture, knowing full well that Deane would not use it until he was on shipboard and safely off to America? That is only conjecture. We have no direct evidence to suggest this is what happened.

But there is one other fact we do know for sure; and in light of our latest theory, it is an interesting one. Undeniably, Edward Bancroft was an expert on poisons.

He did not advertise that knowledge, of course; few people in London at the time of Deane's death would have been likely to remember the fact. But twenty years earlier, the historian may recall, Bancroft wrote a book on the natural history of Guiana. At that time, he not only investigated electric eels and color dyes, but also the poisons of the area, particularly curare (or "Woowara" as Bancroft called it). He investigated it so well, in fact, that when he returned to England he brought samples of curare with him which (he announced in the book) he had deposited with the publishers so that any gentleman of "unimpeachable" character might use the samples for scientific study.

Furthermore, Bancroft seemed to be a remarkably good observer not only of the poisons but also of those who used them. His book described in ample detail the natives' ability to prepare poisons which, given in the smallest quantities, produce a very slow but inevitable death, particularly a composition which resembles wheat-flour, which they sometimes use to revenge past injuries, that have been long neglected, and are thought forgotten. On these occasions they always feign an insensibility of the injury which they intend to revenge, and even repay it with services and acts of friendship, until they have destroyed all distrust and apprehension of danger in the destined victim of the vengeance. When this is effected, they meet at some festival, and engage him to drink with them, drinking first themselves to obviate suspicion, and afterwards secretly dropping the poison, ready concealed under their nails, which are usually long, into the drink.

Twenty years later Bancroft was busy at work with the color dyes he had brought back from Surinam. Had he, by any chance, also held onto any of those poisons?

Unless new evidence comes to light, we will probably never know for sure. Historians are generally forced to deal with probabilities, not certainties, and we leave you to draw your own conclusions about the death of Silas Deane.

What does seem certain is that whatever "really happened" to Deane 200 years ago cannot be determined today without the active participation of the historian. Being courier to the past is not enough. For better or worse, historians inescapably leave an imprint as they go about their business: asking interesting questions about apparently dull facts, seeing connections between subjects that had not seemed related before, shifting and rearranging evidence until it assumes a coherent pattern. The past is not history; only the raw material of it. How those raw materials come to be fashioned and shaped is the central concern of the rest of this book.

* As the Author has brought a confiderable quantity of this Poifon to *England*, any Gentleman, whofe genius may incline him to profecute thefe experiments, and whofe character will warrant us to confide in his hands a preparation, capable of perpetrating the moft fecret and fatal villainy, may be fupplied with a fufficient quantity of the *Woo-rara*, by applying to Mr. *Becket*, in the *Strand*.

—from *An Essay on the Natural History of Guiana in South America,* by Edward Bancroft

Additional Reading

The historian responsible for the brilliant detective work exposing the possibility of foul play on the *Boston Packet* is Julian Boyd. He makes his case, in much greater detail than can be summarized here, in a series of three articles entitled "Silas Deane: Death by a Kindly Teacher of Treason?" *William and Mary Quarterly,* 3rd Ser., XVI (1959), 165–187, 319–342, and 515–550. For additional background on Silas Deane, see the entry in the *Dictionary of American Biography* (New York, 1946). (The *DAB,* incidentally, is a good starting point for those seeking biographical details of American figures. It provides short sketches as well as further bibliographical references.) For details on additional intrigue surrounding the American mission to France, see Samuel F. Bemis, "The British Secret Service and the French-American Alliance," *American Historical Review,* XXIX (1923–1924), 474–495.

We have pointed out that no evidence in the historical record conclusively links Edward Bancroft with Silas Deane's death. In an eminently fair-minded manner, we left you to draw your own conclusions. Yet, as the lesson of this chapter makes clear, every historical narrative is bound to select facts in shaping its story—including this narrative. Given our limitations of space, we chose to concentrate on the evidence and arguments which illuminated Boyd's hypothesis most forcibly. So we suspect that most readers, if left to draw their "own" conclusions, will tend to find Bancroft guilty as charged.

Boyd's case strikes us as impressive too, but it certainly can be questioned. How sound, for instance, is the hypothesis about Deane's depression (or lack of it)? Many people who have contemplated suicide, it could be argued, do so over an extended period of time, and their moods of depression may alternate with happier periods. Perhaps Deane toyed with the idea, put it away, then returned to it in the gloomy confines of the *Boston Packet.* If Deane were a laudanum addict and had a large quantity of the drug on hand, might he not easily take an overdose during a sudden return of severe depression?

In another area, William Stinchcombe has suggested that, contrary to Julian Boyd's suggestion, Deane did not face any really hopeful prospects for success in America. If Deane continued to be destitute and down on his luck when he departed for America, then the suicide theory again becomes more probable. Stinchcombe's article, "A Note on Silas Deane's Death," may be found in the *William and Mary Quarterly,* 3rd Ser., XXXII (1975), 619–624. Another hypothesis is suggested by Lewis Einstein in *Divided Loyalties* (New York, 1933). Einstein argues that Deane never suspected Bancroft's treachery and that the British Secret Service contrived Bancroft's "near miss" in the affair of John the Painter so that Bancroft would have an excuse for "fleeing" to Paris, where he could work full-time spying for England. Although Einstein published his conclusions long before Boyd's article appeared, his theory still merits consideration.

Those who wish to examine some of the primary documents in the case may do so easily enough. Much of Deane's correspondence is available in *The Deane Papers,* published as part of the New York Historical Society's *Collections,* XIX–XXIII (New York, 1887–1891) and in *The Deane Papers: Correspondence between Silas Deane, His Brothers . . . 1771–1795,* Connecticut Historical Society *Collections,* XXIII (Hartford, Conn., 1930). These volumes shed helpful light on Deane's state of mind during his London years. The London obituary notices are reprinted in the *American Mercury* (Hartford, Conn., December 28, 1789), the *Gazette of the United States* (Philadelphia, Pa., December 12, 1789), and other newspapers in New York and Boston. See also the *Gentleman's Magazine* of London, LIX, Pt. ii (September 1789), 866. American colonial newspapers are available in many libraries on microprint, published by the Readex Microprint Corporation in conjunction with the American Antiquarian Society.

Edward Bancroft's role as double agent was not established conclusively until the private papers of William Eden (Lord Auckland) were made public in the 1890s. As director of the British Secret Service during the Revolution, Eden and his right-hand man, Paul Wentworth, were in close touch with Bancroft. The details of the Bancroft-Wentworth-Eden connection are spelled out in Paul L. Ford, *Edward Bancroft's Narrative of the Objects and Proceedings of Silas Deane* (Brooklyn, N.Y., 1891). Further information on Bancroft may be found in Sir Arthur S. MacNalty, "Edward Bancroft, M.D., F.R.S. and the War of American Independence," Royal Society of Medicine *Proceedings,* XXXVIII (1944), 7–15. The Historical Society of Pennsylvania, in Philadelphia, has a collection of Bancroft's papers. And further background may be gained, of course, from the good doctor's own writings, chief among them the *Essay on the Natural History of Guiana in South America . . .* (London, 1769).

AFTER
THE
FACT

The Art of
Historical
Detection

Serving Time in Virginia

As has become clear, the historian's simple act of selection irrevocably separates "history" from "the past." The reconstruction of an event is quite clearly different from the event itself. Yet selection is only one in a series of interpretive acts that historians perform as they proceed about their business. Even during the preliminary stages of research, when the historian is still gathering information, interpretation and analysis are necessary. That is because the significance of any piece of evidence is seldom apparent at first glance. The historian quickly learns that the words *evidence* and *evident* rarely mean the same thing.

For historians attempting to reconstruct an accurate picture of the first English settlements in Virginia, the difficulty of taking any document at face value becomes quickly apparent. The early Virginians were, by and large, an enterprising lot. They gave America its first representative assembly, gave England a new and fashionable vice, tobacco, and helped establish slavery as a labor system in the New World. These actions raise perplexing and important questions for historians, and yet the answers to them cannot be readily found in the surviving source materials without out a good deal of work.

The difficulty does not arise entirely from lack of information. Indeed, some Virginians were enterprising enough to write history as well as make it, not the least of them being Captain John Smith. Captain Smith wrote an account of the young colony entitled *A Generall Historie of Virginia,* published in 1624. Much of his history is based on eyewitness, firsthand knowledge. At a vigorous age twenty-seven, he joined the expedition sent to Virginia in 1606 by the Virginia Company of London.

Once there, he played a crucial role in directing the affairs of the inex-
perienced Jamestown colony.

Yet Smith's evidence cannot be accepted without making some basic
interpretive judgments. Simplest and most obvious—is he telling the
truth? If we are to believe his own accounts, the young captain led a
remarkably swashbuckling life. Before joining the Virginia expedition,
he had plunged as a soldier of fortune into a string of complicated
intrigues in central Europe. There he waged desperate and brave warfare on behalf of the Hungarian nobility before being taken prisoner by
the infidel Turk. Once a prisoner, he likely would have spent the remain-
der of his years as a slave had he not won the affections (so he relates)
of a Greek princess with the romantic name of Charatza Trabiganza. The
smitten princess helped Smith make his escape, and he subsequently
worked his way back to England in time to join the expedition to Virginia in 1606.

In Virginia the adventures came nearly as thick and fast as in Hungary.
While the colony's governing council quarrelled at Jamestown, Captain
Smith went off on an exploring and food-gathering mission. He estab-
lished the first European contact with many of the Indian tribes around
Chesapeake Bay, succeeded in buying needed corn from them, and
when captured by Chief Powhatan, once again managed to get himself
rescued by a beautiful princess—this one, the chief's young daughter
Pocahontas.

How much of this romantic adventure story do we believe? The tone
of Captain Smith's narrative makes it reasonably apparent that he was not
the sort of man to hide his light under a bushel. Indeed, several nineteenth-century scholars, including Henry Adams, challenged Smith's
account of his Indian rescue. Adams pointed out that the Pocahontas
story did not appear in Smith's earliest published descriptions of the
Virginia colony. Only in 1624, when the *Generall Historie* was issued, did
the public first read of the Indian maiden's timely devotion. Captain
Smith, Adams argued, probably invented the story out of wholecloth, in
order to enhance his reputation.

We can, of course, look for independent evidence that would corrobo-
rate Smith's claims. But in the case of the Pocahontas story no independent records survive. Yet recent historians have defended Smith, Philip
Barbour prime among them. Barbour has checked Smith's tales against
available records in both Hungary and England and found them generally accurate as to names, places, and dates. Smith claimed, for example,
that he used an ingenious system of torch signals to coordinate a night-
time attack by his Austrian friends, "Lord Ebersbaught" and "Baron
Kisell." No other records mention Smith's role, but we do know such

The Country wee now call Virginia beginneth at Cape Henry distant from Roanoack 60 miles, where was Sr. Walter Raleigh's plantation: and because the people differ very little from them of Powhatan in any thing, I have inserted those figures in this place because of the conveniency.

King Powhatan comands C: Smith to be slaine, his daughter Pokahontas begns his life his thankfullnes and how he subiected 39 of their kings. reade ye histor

printed by James Reeve

"Their clubs were raised, and in another moment I should have been dead, when Pocahontas, the King's dearest daughter, a child of ten years old, finding no entreaties could prevail to save me, darted forward, and taking my head in her arms, laid her own upon it, and thus prevented my death." In Robert Vaughan's illustration for the *Generall Historie* (1624), Pocahontas apparently is pictured twice, once at Smith's side, and again, larger than life, pleading for mercy.

an attack was launched—and that it was led by two Austrians named Sigismund Eibiswald and Jakob Khissl. Similarly, although the records show no Greek princess named Charatza Trabiganza, that seems to have been Smith's fractured pronunciation of the Greek *koritsi* [girl] *Trapedzoûndos* [from Trebizond]. Quite possibly, when he asked his captors the

identity of his saviour, they merely replied, *"koritsi Trapedzoûndos"*—a
"girl from Trebizond."

Yet even if we grant Smith the virtue of honesty, significant problems
remain when using his account; problems common to all historical evidence. To say that Smith is truthful is only to say that he reported events
as he saw them. The qualification is not small. Like every observer, Smith
viewed events from his own perspective. When he set out to describe
the customs of the Chesapeake Indians, for instance, he did so as a
seventeenth-century Englishman. Behind each observation he made,
stood a whole constellation of presuppositions, attitudes, and opinions
that he took for granted without ever mentioning them. His descriptions
were thus necessarily limited by the experience and education—or lack
of it—that he brought with him.

The seriousness of these limitations becomes clearer if we take a
hypothetical example of what might happen were Captain Smith to set
down a history, not of Indian tribal customs, but of a baseball game
between the Boston Red Sox and the New York Yankees:

> Not long after, they tooke me to one of their greate Counsells, where
> many of the generalitie were gathered in greater number than ever I
> had seen before. And they being assembled about a great field of open
> grass, a score of their greatest men ran out upon the field, adorned each
> in brightly hued jackets and breeches, with letters cunningly woven
> upon their Chestes, and wearinge hats uppon their heades, of a sort I
> know not what. One of their chiefs stood in the midst and would at his
> pleasure hurl a white ball at another chief, whose attire was of a different
> colour, and whether by chance or artyfice I know not the ball flew ex-
> ceeding close to the man yet never injured him, but sometimes he
> would strike att it with a wooden club and so giveing it a hard blow
> would throw down his club and run away. Such actions proceeded in
> like manner at length too tedious to mention, but the generalitie waxed
> wroth, with greate groaning and shoutinge, and seemed withall much
> pleased.

Before concluding any more than that Smith would make a terrible
writer for the *New York Post* (we don't even know if the Yankees
won!), compare the description of the baseball game with one by the
real Smith, of Chesapeake Indian life:

> In this place commonly are resident seaven [7] Priests. The chiefe
> differed from the rest in his ornaments, but inferior Priests could hardly
> be knowne from the common people, but that they had not so many holes
> in their eares to hang their jewels at.

The ornaments of the chiefe Priest were certaine attires for his head made thus. They tooke a dosen, or 16, or more snakes skins and stuffed them with mosse; and of Weesels and other Vermines skins a good many. All these they tie by their tailes, so as all their tailes meete in the toppe of their head, like a great Tassell. Round about this Tassell is as it were a crown of feathers, the skins hang round about his head, necke, and shoulders, and in a manner cover his face.

The faces of all their Priests are painted as ugly as they can devise, in their hands they had every one his Rattle, some base, some smaller. Their devotion was most in songs, which the chiefe Priest beginneth and the rest followed him: sometimes he maketh invocations with broken sentences, by starts and strange passions; and at every pause, the rest give a short groane.

Without having read the account of the baseball game first, it would not be anywhere near as obvious just how little Smith has told us about

"In this place commonly are resident seaven [7] Priests. . . . The faces of all their Priests are painted as ugly as they can devise, in their hands they had every one his Rattle, some base, some smaller." Presumably, the dark figure to the right of Captain Smith is the chief priest with his headdress of snakeskins stuffed with moss. Illustration by Robert Vaughan.

the Indian rituals. Indeed, anyone who reads the *Generall Historie* or any
of the Captain's writings will be impressed by their freshness, their
wealth of detail, and their perceptiveness. But that is because we, like
Smith, are unfamiliar with the rituals of the seventeenth-century Chesapeake Indians. Quite naturally—almost instinctively—we adopt Smith's
point of view as our own.

Furthermore, the perspective that is embedded in Captain Smith's
description unconsciously diverts us from asking questions to which
Smith does not have the answer. What, after all, is the point of the
communal ritual? the significance of the fur tassels covering the priest's
face? Is *priest* even the right word to use? Or is Smith choosing an English
term that distorts the Indian's status from the beginning? In addition, the
Captain's very presence has added a new dimension to the ceremony.
What effect will English culture have on Indian social structures and
belief systems? How much will the traditional tribal authority of the
"priests" be undermined by the arrival of a technologically superior
culture? These and many other questions remain unanswered or, more
to the point, unasked. They are beyond Smith's interest, his competence,
or his ken. If historians are to answer them, they must make a conscious
effort to raise the questions in the first place.

It is easy enough to see how a point of view is embedded in the facts
of an eloquent narration. Smith is, after all, not only headstrong and
unabashed, but he is also consciously writing for a wider public. He
intends his book to be read and, in being read, to convince. But consider
for a moment evidence recorded by one of the pedestrian clerks whose
jottings constitute the great bulk of history's raw material. The following
excerpts are taken from the records of Virginia's General Assembly and
the proclamations of the Governor:

> We will and require you, Mr. Abraham Persey, Cape Marchant, from this
> daye forwarde to take notice, that . . . you are bounde to accepte of the
> Tobacco of the Colony, either for commodities or upon billes, at three
> shillings the beste and the second sorte at 18*d* the punde, and this shalbe
> your sufficient dischardge.
> Every man to sett 2 acres corn (Except Tradesmen following their trades)
> penalty forfeiture of corn & Tobacco & be a Slave a year to the Colony.
> No man to take hay to sweat Tobacco because it robs the poor beasts of
> their fodder and sweating Tobacco does it little good as found by
> Experience.

Here we face the opposite of Smith's description: small bits of information dependent on a great deal of assumed knowledge. Whereas Smith
attempted to describe the Indian ceremony in some detail because it

was new to him, Virginia's General Assembly knows all too much about tobacco prices and the planting of corn. Policy is stated without any explanation, just as the scorebox in the paper lists the single line, "Yankees 10, Red Sox 3." In each case the notations are so terse, the "narratives" so brief, that the novice historian is likely to assume they contain no point of view at all, only the bare facts. But the truth is, each statement has a definite point of view that can be summed up as simple questions: (1) Did the Yankees win and if so by how much? (2) Should the price of tobacco be three shillings or eighteen pence or how much? (3) What should colonists use hay for? And so on. These viewpoints are so obvious, they would not bear mentioning—except that, unconsciously, we are led to accept them as the only way to think about the facts. Since the obvious perspective often appears irrelevant, we tend to reject the information as not worth our attention.

But suppose a fact is stripped of its point of view—suppose we ask, in effect, a completely different question of it? Historians looking back on twentieth-century America would undoubtedly learn little from baseball box scores, but at least by comparing the standings of the 1950s with those of the 1970s, they would soon discover that the Giants of New York had become the Giants of San Francisco and that the Brooklyn Dodgers had moved to Los Angeles. If they knew a bit more than Captain Smith about the economic implications of major league franchises, they could infer a relative improvement in the economic and cultural status of the West coast. Similarly, by refusing to accept the evidence of tobacco prices or corn planting at its face value, historians might make inferences about economic and cultural conditions in seventeenth-century Virginia.

In adopting a perspective different from any held by the historical participants, we are employing one of the most basic tactics of sociology. Sociologists have long recognized that every society functions, in part, through structures and devices that remain unperceived by its members. "To live in society means to exist under the domination of society's logic," notes sociologist Peter Berger. "Very often men act by this logic without knowing it. To discover this inner dynamic of society, therefore, the sociologist must frequently disregard the answers that the social actors themselves would give to his questions and look for explanations that are hidden from their own awareness."

Using that approach, recent historians have taken documents from colonial Virginia, stripped them of their original perspectives, and reconstructed a striking picture of Virginia society. Their research reveals that life in the young colony was more volatile, acquisitive, rowdy, raw—and deadly—than most traditional accounts have assumed. Between the high ideals of the colony's London investors and the disembarkation points along the Chesapeake, something went wrong. The society that was designed to be a productive and diversified settlement in the wilderness soon developed into a world where the singleminded pursuit of one crop, tobacco, made life as nasty, brutish, and short as anywhere in the hemisphere. And the colony that had hoped to pattern itself on the free and enlightened customs of England instead found itself establishing something which the government of England had never thought to introduce at home: the institution of human slavery.

A COLONY ON THE EDGE OF RUIN

None of the English colonial ventures found it easy to establish successful and independent settlements along the Atlantic coast, but for the Virginia colony, the going was particularly rough. In the first ten years of the colony's existence, £75,000 had been invested to send around 2,000 settlers across the ocean to what Captain Smith described as a "fruitfull and delightsome land" where "heaven and earth never agreed better to frame a place for mans habitation." Yet at the end of that time, the attempt to colonize Virginia could be judged nothing less than unmitigated disaster.

Certainly most members of the Virginia Company viewed it that way. In 1606 King James had granted a charter to a group of London merchants who became formally known as "The Treasurer and Company of Adventurers and Planters of the City of London for the First Colony in Virginia." The Virginia Company, as it was more commonly called, allowed merchants and gentlemen of quality to "adventure" money in a joint stock arrangement, pooling their resources to support an expedition to Virginia. The expedition would plant a colony and extract the riches of the new country, such as gold or iron, and also begin cultivating crops that would yield a high return, such as grapes for the production of wine or mulberry trees for the production of silk. King James, a silkworm buff, even donated some of his own specially bred worms. The proceeds would repay the company's expenses, the investors (or "adventurers") would reap handsome profits, the colonists themselves would prosper, and England would gain a strategic foothold in the New World. So the theory went.

As might be expected, the practice ran rather differently. After four difficult months at sea, only 105 of the original 144 settlers reached Chesapeake Bay in April of 1607. The site chosen at Jamestown for a fort was swampy, its water unhealthy, and the Indians less than friendly. By the end of the first hot and humid summer, 46 more settlers had perished. When the first supply ship delivered 120 new recruits the following January, it found only 38 men still alive.

The Company correctly blamed part of the failure on the colony's original system of government. A president led a council of 13 men, but in name only. Council members refused to take direction and continually bickered among themselves. In 1609 the company obtained a new charter providing for centralized control in a governor, but when it sent another 600 settlers across, the results were even worse. Because a hurricane scattered the fleet on its way over, only 400 settlers arrived, leaderless, in September of 1609. Captain Smith, the one old hand who had acted decisively to pull the colony together, was sent packing on the first ship home, and as winter approached, the bickering began anew.

Nobody, it seemed, had planted enough corn to last through the winter, preferring to barter, bully, or steal supplies from the Indians. And the Indians knew that the English depended on them—knew that they could starve out the newcomers simply by moving away. When several soldiers took French leave to seek food from the natives, the other settlers discovered their comrades not long after, "slayne with their mowthes stopped full of Breade, being donn as it seemeth in Contempte and skorne thatt others might expect the Lyke when they shold come to seek for breade and reliefe amongst them."

As the winter wore on, the store of hogs, hens, goats, sheep, and horses were quickly consumed; the colonists then turned to "doggs Catts Ratts and myce." Those settlers who were healthy enough searched the woods for roots, nuts, and berries, while others resorted to boiling boot leather. Conditions became so desperate that one man "did kill his wife, powdered [i.e., salted] her, and had eaten part of her" before leaders discovered his villainy and had him executed. By May 1610, when Deputy Governor Thomas Gates and the rest of the original fleet limped in from Bermuda, only 60 settlers out of 500 had survived the winter, and these were "so Leane thatt they looked Lyke Anotamies Cryeing owtt we are starved We are starved."

Grim as such tales are, we have almost come to expect them in the first years of a new colony. The Virginia experiment broke new ground in a new land. Mistakes were inevitable. But as the years passed, the colonists seemed to have learned little. Ten years after the first landing yet another governor, Samuel Argall, arrived to find Jamestown hardly more than a slum in the wilderness: "but five or six houses [remaining standing], the Church downe, the Palizado's [stockade fence] broken, the Bridge in pieces, the Well of fresh water spoiled; the Storehouse they used for the Church; the market-place and streets, and all other spare places planted with Tobacco." Of the 2,000 or so settlers sent since 1607, only 400 remained alive and only 200 of them, Argall complained, were either trained or fit enough to farm. Even John Rolfe, who was usually willing to put as good a face on affairs as possible, could not help taking away with the left hand the praises he bestowed with the right. "Wee found the Colony (God be thanked) in good estate," he wrote home hopefully, "however in buildings, fortyfications, and of boats, much ruyned and greate want." All in all, it was not much of a progress report after ten years.

In England, Sir Edwin Sandys was one of the adventurers who watched with distress as the company's efforts came to naught. Sandys lacked the financial means of bigger investors like Thomas Smith, who had often presided as the company's treasurer. But that was precisely the point. Smith and the other big investors considered the Virginia enterprise just one venture among many: the East India Company, trading in the Levant, the Muscovy Company. If Virginia did not pay immediate dividends, they could afford to wait. Sandys and his followers, with less capital and less margin for error, pressed for immediate reform. By 1618 Smith had agreed to introduce significant changes into the colony's organization; the following year Sandys was elected treasurer of the company. With real power in his hands for the first time, he set out to reconstruct the failing colony from the bottom up.

BLUEPRINT FOR A VIRGINIA UTOPIA

Sandys knew that if his schemes for reform were to succeed, he would have to attract both new investors to the company and new settlers to the colony. Yet the Virginia Company was deeply in debt and the colony was literally falling apart. In order to entice both settlers and investors, Sandys offered the only commodity the company possessed in abundance —land.

In the first years of the colony, Virginia land had remained company land. Settlers who worked it might own shares in the company, but even so, they did not profit directly from their labor, since all proceeds went into the treasury to be divided only if there were any profits. There never were. In 1617 the company formally changed its policy. "Old Planters," those settlers who had arrived in Virginia before the spring of 1616, were each granted 100 acres of land. Freemen received their allotment immediately, while those settlers who were still company servants received their land when their terms of service expired.

Sandys lured new investors with the promise of property too. For every share they purchased, the company granted them 100 acres. More important, Sandys encouraged immigration to the colony by giving investors additional land if they would pay the ship passage of tenant laborers. For every new tenant an investor imported to Virginia, he received fifty additional acres. Such land grants were known as "headrights," since the land was apportioned per each "head" imported. Of course, if Old Planters wished to invest in the company, they too would receive 100 acres plus additional 50-acre headrights for every tenant whose passage they paid. Such incentives, Sandys believed, would attract needed funds to the company while also promoting immigration.

And so private property came to Virginia. This was the much-heralded event that every school child is called upon to recite as the salvation of the colony. "When our people were fed out of the common store and labored jointly together, glad was he could slip away from his labour, or slumber over his taske," noted Ralph Hamor. But "now for themselves they will doe in a day" what before they "would hardly take so much true paines in a weeke." It is important to understand, however, that the company still had its own common land and stock from which it hoped to profit. Thus a company shareholder had the prospect of making money in two ways: from any goods marketed by company servants working company lands, or directly from his newly granted private lands, also known as "Particular Plantations."

Sandys's administration provided still other openings for private investment. By 1616 the company had already granted certain merchants a four-year monopoly on providing supplies for the colony. The "Magazine," as it was called, sent supply ships to Virginia. There its agent, a man known as the Cape Merchant, sold the goods in return for produce. In 1620 the company removed the Magazine's monopoly and allowed other investors to send over supply ships.

Sandys and his friends also worked to make the colony a more pleasant place to live. Instead of being governed by martial law, as the colony had since 1609, the company instructed the new governor, George Yeardly, to create an assembly with the power to make laws. The laws would be binding so long as the company subsequently approved them. Inhabitants of the various company settlements as well as of the particular plantations were to choose two members each as their burgesses, or representatives. When the assembly convened in 1619 it became the first representative body in the English colonies.

Historians have emphasized the significance of this first step in the evolution of American democracy, and significant it was. But the colony's settlers may have considered it equally important that the company had figured out a way to avoid saddling them with high taxes to pay for their government. Once again, the answer was land, which the company used to pay officials' salaries. Thus the governor received a parcel of 3,000 acres plus 100 tenants to work it, the treasurer of the colony received 1,500 acres and 50 tenants, and so on. Everybody won, or so it seemed. The officers got their salaries without having to "prey upon the people"; the settlers were relieved "of all taxes and public burthens as much as may be"; and the sharecropping tenants, after splitting the profits with company officials for seven years, got to keep the land they worked. If the company carried out its policy, John Rolfe observed enthusiastically, "then we may truly say in Virginia, we are the most happy people in the world."

In 1619, with the reforms in place and Sandys in the treasurer's seat, the company moved into high gear. New investors sent scores of tenants over to work the particular plantations; the company sent servants to tend officers' lands; and lotteries throughout England provided income to recruit ironmongers, vine-tenders, and glassblowers for the New World. The records of the Virginia Company tell a story of immigration on a larger scale than ever before: over a thousand settlers in 1619, Sandys's first year, and equal numbers in the following three years. Historians who do a little searching and counting in company records will find that some 3,570 settlers were sent to join a population that stood, at the beginning of Sandys's program, around 700.

It would have been an impressive record, except that in 1622, three years later, the colony's population still totalled only about 700 people.

The figures are in the records; you can check the addition yourself. What it amounts to is that in 1622, there are 3,500 Virginians missing. No significant number returned to England; most, after all, could hardly afford passage over, let alone back. No significant number migrated to other colonies. We can account for the deaths of 347 colonists, slain in an Indian attack of 1622. But that leaves over 3,000 settlers and there seems to be only one way to do the accounting. Those immigrants died.

Who—or what—was responsible for the deaths of 3,000 Virginians? Something had gone terribly wrong with Sandys's plans. The magnitude of the failure was so great that the leaders of the company did not care to announce it openly. When the king got word of it, only after the company had virtually bankrupted itself in 1624, he revoked its charter. The historian who confronts the statistical outlines of this horror is forced to ask a few questions. Just what conditions would produce a society in which the death rate was in the neighborhood of 75 to 80 percent? A figure that high is simply staggering; for comparison, the death rate during the first (and worst) year at the Pilgrims' Plymouth colony stayed a little below 50 percent. During the severe plague epidemics that swept Britain in the fourteenth century, the death rate probably ranged from 20 to 45 or 50 percent.

Obvious answers suggest themselves. The colony could not sustain such an influx of new settlers, especially since Sandys, in his eagerness to increase the population, sent so many men unprepared. Immigrants often arrived with little or no food to tide them over until they could begin raising their own crops. Housing was inadequate; indeed, the records are replete with letters from the company in London begging the colony's governors to build temporary "guest houses" for the newcomers, while the governors' letters in return begged the company to send more adequate provisions with their recruits.

Disease took its toll. Colonists had discovered early on that Virginia was an unhealthy place to live. For newcomers, the first summer proved particularly deadly, so much so that it was called the "seasoning time." Those who survived the first summer significantly raised their chances of prospering. But dangers remained year round, especially for those weakened by the voyage or living on a poor diet. Contaminated wells most likely contributed to outbreaks of typhoid fever, and malaria claimed victims.

The obvious answers do much to explain the devastating death rates, but anomalies remain. Even granting the seriousness of typhoid and other diseases, why a death rate higher than the worst plague years? Virginia's population was made up of younger men primarily and lacked the older men and women who would have been more susceptible to disease. Even healthy men, of course, may be weakened by malnutrition and semistarvation, but that brings the problem right back to the question of why, after more than ten years, the Jamestown colony was not yet self-sufficient.

To be self-sufficient required that colonists raise their own food. And the principal food raised in the area was corn. So the historian asks a simple question. How much work did it take to grow corn? A quick look at the records confirms what might be suspected—that no Virginian in those first years bothered to leave behind a treatise on agriculture. But a closer search of letters and company records provides bits of data here and there. The Indians, Virginians discovered, spent only a few days out of the year tending corn, and they often produced surpluses that they traded to the Virginians. A minister in the colony reported that "in the idle hours of one week," he and three other men had planted enough corn to last for four months. Other estimates suggested that forty-eight hours' work would suffice to plant enough corn to last a whole year. Even allowing for exaggeration, it seems clear that comparatively little effort was needed to grow corn.

Yet if corn can be grown easily, and if it is needed to keep the colonists alive, what possible sense is the historian to make of a document we encountered earlier—Governor Argall's proclamation of 1618, requiring "Every man to sett 2 acres corn (Except Tradesmen following their trades). . . ." That year is not the last time the law appears on the books. It was re-entered in the 1620s and periodically up through the 1650s.

It is a puzzle. A law *requiring* Virginians to plant corn? The colony is continually running out of corn, people are starving, and planting and reaping take only a few weeks out of the year. Under these circumstances, the government has to *order* settlers to plant corn?

Yet the conclusion is backed up by other company records. Virginians had to be forced to grow corn. The reason becomes clearer if we re-examine Governor Argall's gloomy description of Jamestown when he stepped off the boat in 1617. The church is down, the palisades pulled apart, the bridge in pieces, the fresh water spoiled. Everything in the description indicates the colony is decrepit, falling apart, except for one paradoxical feature—the weeds in the street. The stockades and buildings may have languished from neglect, but it was not neglect that caused "the market-place and streets, and all other spare places" to be "planted with Tobacco." Unlike corn, tobacco required a great deal of attention to cultivate. It did not spring up in the streets by accident. Thus Governor Argall's description indicates that at the same time that settlers were willing to let the colony fall apart, they were energetically planting tobacco in all the "spare places" they could find.

Settlers had discovered as early as 1613 that tobacco was marketable, and they sent small quantities to England the following year. Soon shipments increased dramatically, from 2,500 pounds in 1616 to 18,-839 pounds in 1617 and 49,518 pounds in 1618. Some English buyers thought that tobacco could be used as a medicine, but most purchased it simply for the pleasure of smoking it. Sandys and many other gentlemen looked upon the "noxious weed" as a vice and did everything to discourage its planting. There had been "often letters from the Counsell" in London, he complained, "sent lately to the Governour for restraint of that immoderate following of Tobacco and to cause the people to apply themselves to other and better commodities." But his entreaties, as well as the corn laws, met with little success. Tobacco was in Virginia to stay.

VIRGINIA BOOM COUNTRY

The Virginia records are full of statistics like the tobacco export figures given in the last paragraph. Number of pounds shipped, price of the "better sort" of tobacco for the year 1619, number of settlers arriving on the *Bona Nova.* This is the sort of "linescore" evidence, recorded by pedestrian clerks for pedestrian reasons, that we noted earlier. Yet once the historian strips the facts of their pedestrian perspective and uses them for his own purposes, they begin to flesh out an astonishing picture of Virginia. Historian Edmund Morgan, in his own reconstruction of the situation, aptly labelled Virginia "the first American boom country."

For Virginia had indeed become a boom country. The commodity in demand—tobacco—was not as glamorous as gold or silver, but the social dynamics operated in similar fashion. The lure of making a fortune created a volatile society where wealth changed hands quickly, where an unbalanced economy centered on one get-rich-quick commodity, and where the values of stability and human dignity counted for little.

The implications of this boom-country society become clearer if we ask the same basic questions about tobacco that we asked about corn. Given the fact that Virginians seemed to be growing tobacco, just how much could one person grow in a year? If tobacco was being grown for profit, could Virginians expect to get rich doing it?

Spanish tobacco grown in the West Indies fetched 18 shillings a pound on the English market. Even the highest quality Virginia product was markedly inferior and sold for only 3 shillings. And that price fluctuated throughout the 1620s, dropping as low as 1 shilling. What that price range meant in terms of profits depended, naturally, on how much tobacco a planter could grow in a year. As with corn, the few available estimates are widely scattered. John Rolfe suggested 1,000 plants in one year. William Capps, another seasoned settler, estimated 2,000 and also noted that three of his boys, whose labor he equated with one and a half men, produced 3,000 plants. Fortunately Capps also noted that 2,000 plants made up about 500 "weight" (or pounds) of tobacco, which allows us to convert number of plants into number of pounds.

By comparing these figures with other estimates, it is possible to calculate roughly how much money a planter might receive for his crop. The chart below summarizes how many plants or pounds of tobacco one or more workers might harvest in a year. Extrapolating, the numbers in parentheses show the number of pounds harvested per worker and the income such a harvest would yield if tobacco were selling at either one or three shillings a pound.

TOBACCO PRODUCTION AND INCOME ESTIMATES*

Number of workers . . .	In one year produce. . . number of plants	number of lbs.	One man lbs/yr	Income, @ 1s	3s
1 (Rolfe)	1,000		(250)	£12	£37.5
1 (Capps)	2,000	500	(500)	25	75
3 boys (1½ men)	3,000		(500)	25	75
4 men		2,800	(930)	46.5	139.5
6–7 men	3,000–4,000		(540)	27	81

*Based on data presented in Morgan, *American Slavery, American Freedom* (New York, 1975)

These estimates indicate that the amount of tobacco one man could produce ranged from 250 to 930 pounds a year, an understandable variation given that some planters undoubtedly worked harder than others, some years provided better growing weather, and that, as time passed, Virginians developed ways to turn out bigger crops. Even by John Rolfe's estimate, made fairly early and therefore somewhat low, a man selling 250 pounds at 1 shilling a pound would receive £12 sterling for the year. On the high side, the estimates show a gross of £140 sterling, given good prices. Indeed, one letter tells of a settler who made £200 sterling after the good harvest of 1619. Such windfalls were rare, but considering that an average agricultural worker in England made from 30 to 50 shillings a year (less than £3), even the lower estimates look good.

They look particularly good for another reason—namely, because they indicate what a planter might do working *alone.* In a society where servants, tenants, and apprentices were commonplace, Virginians quickly discovered that if they could get other people to work for them, there were handsome profits to be made.

Back to the basic questions. How did an Englishman get others to work for him? In effect, he simply hired them and made an agreement, a bond indicating what he gave in return for their service and for how long the agreement was to run. The terms varied from servant to servant but fell into several general classes. Most favorable, from the worker's point of view, was the position of tenant. A landowner had fields that needed working; the tenant agreed to work them for a certain period of time, usually from four to seven years. In return, the tenant kept half of what he produced. From the master's point of view, a servant served the purpose better, since he was paid only room and board, plus his passage from England. In return he gave his master everything he produced. And then there were the apprentices, usually called "Duty boys" in Virginia, since the ship *Duty* brought many of them over. Apprentices served for seven years, then another seven as tenants. Again the master's cost was only transportation over and maintenance once in Virginia.

Little in the way of higher mathematics is required to discover that if it cost a master about £10 to £12 sterling to bring over a servant—as it did—and that if that master obtained the labor of several such servants for seven years, or even for two or three, he stood fair to make a tidy fortune. In the good harvest of 1619 one master with six servants managed a profit of £1,000 sterling. That was unusual perhaps, but by no means impossible. And Sandys's headright policies unwittingly played into the hands of the fortune-makers: every servant imported meant another fifty acres of land that could be used for tobacco.

The opportunities were too much to resist. Virginians began bending every resource in the colony toward growing tobacco. The historian can now appreciate the significance of the governor's proclamation (page 8) that no hay should be used to "sweat" or cure tobacco: obviously, colonists were diverting hay from livestock that desperately needed it ("it robs the poor beasts of their fodder"), thus upsetting Virginia's economy. The scramble for profits extended even to the artisans whom Sandys sent over to diversify the colony's exports. The ironmongers deserted in short order, having "turned good honest Tobaccoemongers;" and of similar well-intentioned projects, the report came back to London that "nothinge is done in anie of them but all is vanished into smoke (that is to say into Tobaccoe)." The boom in Virginia was on.

Planters were not the only people trying to make a fortune. The settler who raised tobacco had to get it to market in Europe somehow, had to buy corn if he neglected to raise any himself, and looked to supply himself with as many of the comforts of life as could be had. Other men stood ready to deal with such planters, and they had a sharp eye to their own profit.

The company, of course, sought to provide supplies through the magazine run by the Cape Merchant, Abraham Peirsey. And if we now return to the Virginia assembly's order, quoted earlier, requiring Peirsey to accept 3 shillings per pound for the "better sort" of tobacco, we can begin to understand why the assembly was upset enough to pass the regulation. Peirsey was charging exorbitant prices for his supplies. He collected his fees in tobacco because there was virtually no currency in Virginia. Tobacco had become the economic medium of exchange. If Peirsey counted a pound of the better sort of tobacco as worth only 2 shillings instead of 3, that was as good as raising his prices by fifty percent. As it happened, Peirsey charged two or three times the prices set by the investors in London. Further, he compounded injury with insult by failing to reimburse the company for their supplies that he sold. Sandys and the other investors never saw a cent of the magazine's profits.

Another hunt through the records indicates what Peirsey was doing with his ill-gotten gain: he ploughed it back into the most attractive investment of all, servants. We learn this not because Peirsey comes out and says so, but because the census of 1625 lists him as keeping thirty-nine servants, more than anyone else in the colony. At his death in 1628 he left behind him "the best Estate that was ever yett knowen in Virginia." When the company finally broke the magazine's monopoly in 1620, other investors moved in. They soon discovered that they could make more money selling alcohol than the necessities of life. So the Virginia boom enriched the merchants of "rotten Wynes" as well as the planters of tobacco, and settlers went hungry, in part, because liquor fetched a better return than food.

Given these conditions in Virginia—given the basic social and economic structures deduced from the historical record—put yourself in the place of an average tenant or servant. What would life be like for him under these conditions? What were his chances for success?

For servants, the prospect is bad indeed. First, they face the fierce mortality rate. Chances are they will not survive the first seasoning summer. Even if they do, their master is out to make a fortune by their labor. Any servant, poor as he is to begin with, is in no position to protect himself from abuse. In England the situation was different. Agricultural workers usually offered their services once a year at hiring fairs. Since their contracts lasted only a year, servants could switch to other employers if they became dissatisfied. But going to Virginia required the expense of a long voyage; masters would hire a person only if he signed on for four to seven years. Once in Virginia, what could a servant do if he became disillusioned? Go home? He had little enough money for the voyage over, and likely even less to get back.

Duty boys, the children, were least in a position to improve their lot. The orphans Sandys hoped to favor by taking them off the London streets faced a hard life in Virginia. They were additionally threatened by a law the Virginia labor barons put through the assembly declaring that an apprentice who committed a crime during his service had to begin his term all over again. What constituted a crime, of course, was left up to the governor's council. One Duty boy, Richard Hatch, appeared before the council because he had commented, in a private house, on the recent execution of a settler, one Richard Cornish, for sodomy. Hatch had remarked "that in his consyence he thought that the said Cornishe was put to death wrongfully." For this offense he was to be "whipt from the forte to the gallows and from thence be whipt back againe, and be sett uppon the Pillory and there to loose one of his eares." Although Hatch had nearly completed his term of service—to Governor George Yeardly, who also sat on the council—he was ordered to begin his term anew.

Tenants would seem to have been better off, but they too were subject to the demand for labor. If an immigrant could pay his passage over but was unable to feed himself upon arrival, he had little choice but to hire himself out as a servant. And if his master died before his term was up, there was virtually always another master ready to jump in and claim him, legally or not, as either a personal servant or as a company tenant due in payment of a salary. When George Sandys, Sir Edwin's brother, finished his term as colony treasurer, he dragged his tenants with him even though they had become free men. "He maketh us serve him whether wee will or noe," complained one, "and how to helpe it we doe not knowe for hee beareth all the sway."

Even independent small planters faced the threat of servitude if their crops failed or if Indian attacks made owning a small, isolated plantation too dangerous. William Capps, the small planter who recorded one of the tobacco production estimates, described his own precarious situation vividly. His plantation threatened by Indians, Capps proposed that the governor's council outfit him with an expedition against the neighboring tribes. The council refused, and the indignant Capps angrily suggested what was going through the wealthy planters' minds. "Take away one of my men," he imagines them saying,

there's 2000 Plantes gone, thates 500 waight of Tobacco, yea and what shall this man doe, runne after the Indians? soft, I have perhaps 10, perhaps 15, perhaps 20 men and am able to secure my owne Plantacion; how will they doe that are fewer? let them first be crusht alitle, and then perhaps they will themselves make up the Nomber for their owne safetie. Theis I doubt are the Cogitacions of some of our worthier men.

AND SLAVERY?

This reconstruction of Virginia society, from the Duty boy at the bottom to the richer planters at the top, indicates that all along the line labor had become a valuable and desperately sought commodity. Settlers who were not in a position to protect themselves found that the economy put constant pressure on them. Their status as free men was always in danger of debasement: planters bought, sold, and traded servants without their consent, and on occasion they even used them as stakes in gambling games. There had been "many complaints," acknowledged John Rolfe, "against the Governors, Captaines, and Officers in Virginia: for buying and selling men and boies," something that "was held in England a thing most intolerable." One Englishman put the indignity quite succinctly: "My Master Atkins hath sold me for a £150 sterling like a damnd slave."

Indeed, quite a few of the ingredients of slavery are there: the feverish economic boom that sparked an insatiable demand for human labor, the mortality rate that encouraged survivors to become callous about human life, the servants who were being bought and sold, treated as property; treated, almost, as slaves. If we were looking, in the abstract, to construct a society where social and economic pressures combined to encourage the development of human slavery, boom-town Virginia would fit the model neatly. Yet the actual records do not quite confirm the hypothesis.

The first record of blacks being imported to Virginia was John Rolfe's offhand report in 1619 that "About the last of August came in a dutch man of warre that sold us twenty Negars." Sold, yes. But sold as slaves or as servants? Rolfe doesn't say. Historians have combed the sparse records of early Virginia, looking at court records, inventories, letters, wills, church records—anything that might shed light on the way blacks were treated. Before 1640, there is virtually nothing in the surviving records; before 1660, bits and pieces of evidence do indicate that some blacks were held as slaves for life, but some definitely as servants. Other blacks were either given their freedom or were able to purchase it. Only during the 1660s did the Virginia assembly begin to pass legislation that separated blacks from whites, that defined slavery, legally, as an institution. Blacks, in other words, lived with white Virginians for over forty

"About the last of August came in a dutch man of warre that sold us twenty Negars." So wrote John Rolfe in 1619. Yet the status of these and other early blacks remains unclear. Court records indicate that in the 1640s at least some blacks had been freed and were purchasing their own land. One black, Anthony Johnson, even owned his own slave. The illustration is by Howard Pyle, a popular nineteenth-century artist whose meticulous research made his scenes accurate in terms of costume and setting.

years before their status had become fully and legally debased. The facts
in the records force us to turn the initial question around. If the 1620s
with its boom economy was such an appropriate time for slavery to have
developed, why *didn't* it?

Here, the talents of historians are stretched to their limits. They can
expect no obvious explanations from contemporaries like John Rolfe,
Captain Smith, or William Capps. The development of slavery was something that snuck up on Virginians. It was part of the "inner dynamic"
of the society, as sociologists would say—hidden from the awareness of
the social actors in the situation. Even the records left by the clerks of
society are scant help. The best that can be done is intelligent conjecture,
based on the kind of society that has been reconstructed.

Was it a matter of the simple availability of slaves? Perhaps. The
African slave trade was still in its infancy, and even if Virginians wanted
slaves, they may have found them hard to come by. During the time that
Virginia was experiencing its boom of the 1620s, the West Indian islands
like Barbadoes and St. Kitts were being settled. There, where the cultiva-
tion of sugar demanded even more intensive labor than tobacco, the
demand for slaves was extremely high, and slavery developed more
rapidly. If traders sailing from Africa could carry only so many slaves,
and if the market for them were better in the Barbadoes than in Virginia,
why sail all the way up to Chesapeake Bay? The slave traders may not
have found the effort worth it. That is the conjecture of one historian,
Richard Dunn.

Edmund Morgan has suggested another possibility, based on the continuing mortality rate in Virginia. Put yourself in the place of the planter
searching for labor. You can buy either servants or slaves. Servants come
cheaper than slaves, of course, but you only get to work them for seven
years before they receive their freedom. Slaves are more expensive, but
you get their labor for the rest of their lives, as well as the labor of any
offspring. In the long run, the more expensive slave would have been
the better buy. But in Virginia? Everyone is dying anyway. What are the
chances that either servants or slaves are going to live for more than
seven, five, even three years? The chances are not particularly good.
Wouldn't it make more sense to pay less and buy servants, on the
assumption that whoever is bought may die shortly anyway?

It is an ingenious conjecture, but it must remain that—for the present
at least. No plantation records or letters have been found indicating that
planters actually thought that way. Available evidence does suggest that
the high death rate in Virginia began to drop only in the 1650s. If that
were the case, it makes sense that only then, when slaves became a

profitable commodity, would laws come to be passed formally establishing their chattel status. Whatever the reasons may have been, one thing
seems clear: Slavery did not flourish markedly along with the boom of
1620.

Sometime between 1629 and 1630, the economic bubble popped.
The price of tobacco plummeted from 3 shillings to 1 penny a pound.
Virginians tried desperately to prop it up again, either by limiting production or by simple edict, but they did not succeed. Tobacco prices in
the 1630s occasionally floated as high as sixpence, but more often they
stayed at three. That meant planters still could make money, but the
chance for a quick fortune had vanished—"into smoke," as Sandys or
one of his disillusioned investors would no doubt have remarked. The
Virginia Company's experiment in social reconstruction had failed, but
the records of their investments, their wranglings, and the fortune-
hunting survived them. Not all the records survived, by any means.
Many of them were lost, many more burned with the capture of Richmond during the Civil War. But enough survived in Richmond, in
London, in the estates of English lords and gentry to piece together the
story of the early Virginians, rich and poor, and the social structure that
bound them together. It is much to the credit of historians that the
feverish world of the Chesapeake has not, like its cash crop, entirely
vanished into smoke.

Additional Reading

The works of Captain John Smith make a delightful introduction to Virginia. Smith is one of those Elizabethans whose prose struts, bounces, jars, and jounces from one page to the next. His writings are conveniently gathered in Edward Arber and A. G. Bradley, eds., *The Travels and Works of Captain John Smith,* 2 vols. (Edinburgh, 1910). Although caution is necessary in reading Smith, much within these pages provides excellent source material for learning about early encounters between Europeans and native Americans. Henry Adams's attack on the Pocahontas story can be found in Charles Francis Adams, *Chapters of Erie and Other Essays* (Boston, 1871), while the best modern defense of the captain's veracity is Philip Barbour, *The Three Worlds of Captain John Smith* (London, 1964). A recent interpretation of white-Indian contact in the New World is Francis Jennings, *The Invasion of America* (Chapel Hill, N.C., 1975), a book that is deliberately provocative yet often convincing.

Pictorial evidence provides additional information about Indian life at the time of early colonization, but such evidence has its pitfalls. We discuss some of them in Chapter 5 of this book. The best drawings available for Indians in the southern colonies were done by artist John White during earlier expeditions to Roanoke in 1584 and 1585. They are most readily available in Stefan Lorant, *The New World,* rev. ed. (New York, 1965).

The reconstruction of boom-country Virginia described in this chapter depends heavily on the research presented in Edmund S. Morgan's *American Slavery, American Freedom* (New York, 1975). Morgan's account combines a lucid and engaging prose style with the imaginative and thorough research that is a model for the discipline. His book makes an excellent starting place for those wishing to learn more about seventeenth-century Virginia. For information on Sir Edwin Sandys's reform program and its ultimate failure, see Wesley F. Craven, *The Dissolution of the Virginia Company* (New York, 1932).

Those readers wishing to explore primary source material on early Virginia will probably find that contemporary narratives like Smith's provide the best introduction. Many are available in Philip Barbour, ed., *The Jamestown Voyages Under the First Charter, 1606–1609,* 2 vols. (Cambridge, 1969) and in the older but more complete Alexander Brown, *The Genesis of the United States* (Boston, 1890). Additional details about the starving time of 1609–1610 can be found in George Percy, "A Trewe Relacyon of the Procedinges and Occurentes of Momente..." in *Tyler's Quarterly Historical and Genealogical Magazine,* II (1922),

260–282. Much rougher going than these collections are the official records of the Virginia Company and the colony. As we have seen, however, they provide vital evidence. Interested readers will most profit if they bring to their reading a definite idea of the sorts of facts and the specific questions they wish to answer. For the early years, see Alexander Brown's collection; the period from 1619–1624 is covered in Susan Kingsbury, ed., *The Records of the Virginia Company of London,* 4 vols. (Washington, D.C., 1906–1935). For the later period, surviving records can be found in H. R. McIlwaine, ed., *Minutes of the Council and General Court of Colonial Virginia* (Richmond, Va., 1924) and William W. Hening, *The Statutes at Large: Being a Collection of All the Laws of Virginia* (Richmond, Va., 1809–1823).

The question of why slavery did not develop during the first tobacco boom is discussed in Morgan's *American Slavery, American Freedom.* A more wide-ranging treatment of the slavery question is available in Winthrop Jordan's excellent *White Over Black: American Attitudes Toward the Negro, 1550–1812* (Chapel Hill, N.C., 1968). For more detailed though opposing discussions of how the institution of slavery evolved in Virginia, see Oscar and Mary F. Handlin, "Origins of the Southern Labor System," in *William and Mary Quarterly,* 3rd Series, VII (1950), 199–222; Carl N. Degler, "Slavery and the Genesis of American Race Prejudice," *Comparative Studies in Society and History,* II (1959), 49–66; and Paul C. Palmer, "Servant Into Slave: The Evolution of the Legal Status of the Negro Laborer in Colonial Virginia," *South Atlantic Quarterly,* LXV (1966), 355–370.

The Visible
and Invisible
Worlds of Salem

Historians, we have seen, are in the business of reconstruction. Seventeenth-century Virginia, with its world of slaves, indentured servants, small planters, and tobacco barons, had to be built anew, not just lifted intact from the record. It follows, then, that if historians are builders, they must decide at the outset on the scale of their projects. How much ground should be covered? A year? Fifty years? Several centuries? How will the subject matter be defined or limited? The story of slavery's arrival in Virginia might be ranked as a moderately large topic. It spans some sixty years, involves thousands of immigrants and an entire colony. Furthermore, it is large as much because of its content as its reach over time and space. The genesis of slavery surely ranks as a central strand of the American experience; to understand it adequately requires more research and discipline than, for instance, the history of American hats over a similar time span. The lure of topics both broad and significant is undeniable, and there have always been historians willing to pull on their seven-league boots, from Edward Gibbon and his *Decline and Fall of the Roman Empire,* to Ariel and Will Durant with their *Story of Civilization.*

The great equalizer of such grand plans is the twenty-four hour day. Historians have only a limited amount of time, and the hours, they sadly discover, are not expandable. Obviously, the more years that are covered, the less time there is available to research the events in each one.

Conversely, the narrower the area of research, the more it is possible to become immersed in the details of a period. Relationships and connections can be explored that would have gone unnoticed without the benefit of a microscopic focus. Of course, small-scale history continually runs the risk of becoming obscure and pedantic. But a keen mind working on a small area will yield results whose implications go beyond the subject matter's original boundaries. Small-scale history at its best is microcosmic; that is, it reflects in miniature the structure and dynamics of the larger world around it. By understanding what has taken place on a small patch of ground, the historian can begin to see more clearly the forces shaping the larger historical landscape.

Salem Village in 1692 is a microcosm familiar to most students of American history. That was the place and the time witchcraft came to New England with a vengeance, dominating the life of the village for ten months. Because the witchcraft episode exhibited well-defined boundaries in both time and space, it provides an excellent illustration of the way a traditional and oft-told story may be transformed by the intensive research techniques of small-scale history. Traditionally, the outbreak of witchcraft at Salem has been viewed as an incident divorced from the cause-and-effect sequences of everyday village life. Even to label the events as an "outbreak" suggests that they are best viewed as an epidemic, alien to the normal functions of the community. The "germs" of bewitchment break out suddenly and inexplicably—imposed, as it were, by some invading disease pool. Only a few townspeople are first afflicted; then the contagion spreads through the village and runs its destructive course before subsiding.

Recently, however, historians have studied the traumatic experiences of 1692 in greater detail. In so doing they have created a more sophisticated model of the mental world behind the Salem outbreaks. They have also suggested ways in which the witchcraft episode was integrally connected with the more mundane events of village life. The techniques of small-scale history, in other words, have provided a compelling psychological and social context for the events of 1692.

BEWITCHMENT AT SALEM VILLAGE

Most accounts of the trouble at Salem begin with the kitchen of the village's minister, Samuel Parris. There in the early months of 1692, a group of adolescent girls gathered to attempt a bit of crystal-ball reading. The girls sought to discover what sort of men their future husbands might be, a subject of natural enough attraction for young women. Lacking a crystal ball, they used the next available substitute, the white of a raw egg suspended in a glass of water. The girls were aided in their efforts by a West Indian slave then living with the Parrises, a woman named Tituba. At some point during the seances, things went sour. One of the girls thought she detected "a specter in the likeness of a coffin" in the crystal ball—hardly an auspicious omen—and soon the more susceptible among them began behaving in a strange manner.

Detailed accounts of the earliest fits are scarce, but the "strange and unusual" actions of the girls did include "getting into Holes, and creeping under Chairs and Stools, [using] sundry odd Postures and Antick Gestures, uttering foolish ridiculous Speeches, which neither they themselves nor any others could make sense of." The Reverend Parris was at a loss to understand the afflictions, but not so Tituba. She and her husband John Indian baked a "witch cake" made of rye meal and urine given them by the possessed girls. The cake was fed to a dog on the supposition that the charm would reveal whether any bewitchment was taking place (the theory confirmed, presumably, if the dog suffered torments similar to those of the afflicted girls).

The charm never had a chance to achieve its result because Samuel Parris got wind of the experiment and at last discovered what had been going on for so long in his kitchen. He and the other adults in the community had been greatly puzzled by the girls' strange behavior; now they began viewing the illnesses not as the result of disease, but of crime. For seventeenth-century New Englanders, witchcraft was conceived in criminal terms. If the children were being tormented, it was necessary to discover who was doing the tormenting. The hunt for witches began.

The afflicted girls were the keys to determining who was a witch. Although some of their behavior seemed merely eccentric (Abigail Williams came running through the house yelling "Whish! Whish! Whish!" arms apart as if she were flying), other incidents were more sinister. The girls claimed to see specters, invisible to others, who pinched, kicked, and choked them. Victims would writhe on the floor, scream piteously, or carry on arguments with their invisible tormentors. Deodat Lawson, a former minister of the village who visited Salem during the crisis, was horrified to observe Mary Walcott convulsed before him—being bitten, she claimed, by a specter. Lawson could not see the specter but noted with mounting astonishment the teethmarks that appeared on Mary Walcott's arm.

After Village leaders pressed the girls to identify the specters, they at last provided three names: Sarah Good and Sarah Osbourne, two old biddies unpopular in the village, and Tituba herself. Village officials arrested all three for examination, and during the questioning Tituba confessed. There were four women and a man, she said, who were causing the trouble. Good and Osbourne were among them. "They hurt the children," she testified. "And they lay all upon me and they tell me if I will not hurt the children, they will hurt me." The tale continued, complete with apparitions of black and red rats, a yellow dog with a head like a woman, "a thing all over hairy, all the face hairy, and a long nose," and midnight rides to witches' meetings where plans were being laid to attack Salem.

If a witch or wizard (a male witch) confessed, the matter of identification was simple enough. If he or she refused to admit guilt, as many of the accused did, magistrates had to look for corroborating proof. Physical evidence, such as voodoo dolls and pins found among the suspect's possessions, was the most convincing. There might be other signs, too. If the devil made a pact with someone, he supposedly required a physical mark of allegiance, and thus created a "witch's tit," where either he or his "familiar," a likeness in animal form, might suck.* Prisoners in the Salem trials were often examined to see if they had any abnormal marks on their bodies.

Aside from physical signs, villagers looked for evidence of a cause-and-effect relationship between a witch's act of malice and consequent suffering on the part of the victim. Sarah Gadge, for instance, testified that two years earlier she had refused Sarah Good lodging for the night. According to Gadge, Good "fell to muttering and scolding extreamly and so told said Gadge if she would not let her in she should give her something . . . and the next morning after to said Deponents best remembrance one of the said Gadges Cowes Died in a Sudden terrible and Strange unusuall maner. . . ." In an attempt to confirm the connection between malice and torment, the magistrates kept the afflicted girls in the courtroom to observe their behavior. Sure enough, when an accused witch shifted position while on the witness stand, the girls would often be afflicted in the same way, as if tormented by the action. Rebecca Nurse, another accused witch, "held her neck on one side and Eliz. Hubbard (one of the sufferers) had her neck set in that posture where-upon another patient Abigail Williams, cryed out, set up Goody Nursis head, the maid's neck will be broke. And when some set up Nurse's head Aaron Way observed that Betty Hubbards was immediately righted."**

*Hence the expression still used today, "Cold as a witch's tit." Tradition had it that the mark, formed of unnatural flesh, would be cold and lifeless.

The magistrates also considered what they called "spectral evidence," at once the most damning and dangerous kind of proof. Spectral evidence involved the visions of specters—likenesses of the witches —that victims reported seeing during their torments. The problem was that spectral evidence could not be corroborated by others; generally only the victim saw the shape of her tormentor. Furthermore, some people argued that the devil might assume the shape of an innocent person. What better way for him to spread confusion among the faithful? All the same, the magistrates were inclined to believe that Satan could not use a shape without that person's permission—not very often, at any rate—so they tended to accept spectral evidence in their pretrial examinations.

During the first seventy years of settlement in New England, few witchcraft cases had come before the courts. Those that had were despatched quickly, and calm soon returned. Salem proved different. In the first place, Tituba had described several other witches and a wizard, though she claimed she was unable to identify them personally. The villagers felt they could not rest while other witches remained at large. Furthermore, the girls continued to name names—and now not just old hags but respectable church members from the community. The new suspects joined Tituba, Sarah Gadge, and Sarah Osbourne in jail. By the end of April the hunt had led to no less a personage than the Reverend George Burroughs, a former minister of the village living in Maine. Constables marched to Maine, fetched him back, and threw him in jail.

Throughout the spring of 1692, no trials of the accused had been held, for the simple reason that Massachusetts was without legal government. In 1684 King James II had revoked the colony's original charter and set up his own arbitrary government, but in 1689, William of Orange forced James to flee England. In the years following, Massachusetts continually attempted to have its original charter restored. Until it succeeded, however, court cases had been brought to a standstill. Finally in May 1692 the new governor, Sir William Phips, arrived with a charter and promptly established a special court of Oyer and Terminer to deal with the witchcraft cases.

On June 2 the court heard its first case, that of tavernkeeper Bridget Bishop. Bishop was soon convicted and eight days later, hanged from

**"Goody" was short for "Goodwife," a term used for most married women. Husbands were addressed as Goodman. The terms *Mr.* and *Mrs.* were reserved for those of higher social standing.

a scaffold on a hill just outside Salem Town. The site came to be known as Witch's Hill—with good reason, since on June 29 the court again met and convicted five more women. One of them, Rebecca Nurse, had been found innocent, but the court's Chief Justice, William Stoughton, disapproved the verdict and convinced the jurors to change their minds. On July 19 Goody Nurse joined the other four women on the scaffold, staunch churchwoman that she was, praying for the judges' souls as well as her own. Sarah Good remained defiant to the end. "I am no more a witch than you are a wizard," she told the attending minister, "and if you take away my life, God will give you blood to drink."

Still the accusations continued; still the court sat. As the net was cast wider, more and more accused were forced to work out their response to the crisis. A few, most of them wealthy, went into hiding until the furor subsided. Giles Cory, a farmer whose wife Martha was executed as a witch, refused even to plead innocent or guilty, in effect denying the court's right to try him. The penalty for such a refusal was the *peine fort et dure,* in which the victim was placed between two boards and heavy stones placed on him until he agreed to plead. On September 19, Cory was slowly crushed to death, stubborn to the end. His last words were said to be, "More weight."

Some of the accused admitted guilt, the most satisfactory solution for the magistrates. Puritans were a remarkably forgiving people. They were not interested in punishment for its own sake. If a lawbreaker gave evidence of sincere regret for his misdeeds, Puritan courts would often reduce or suspend his sentence. So it was in the witchcraft trials, but the policy had unforeseen consequences. Those who were wrongly accused quickly realized that if they did *not* confess, they were likely to be hanged. If they did confess, they could escape death, but would have to demonstrate their sincerity by providing details of their misdeeds and names of other participants. The temptation must have been great to confess and, in so doing, to implicate other innocent people.

Given such pressures, the web of accusations continued to grow. August produced six more trials and five hangings. Elizabeth Proctor, the wife of another tavernkeeper, received a reprieve because she was pregnant, the court being unwilling to sacrifice the life of an innocent child. Her husband John was not spared. September saw another eight victims hanged with no end in sight. Over a hundred suspected witches remained in jail.

Pressure to stop the trials had been building, however. One member of the court, Nathaniel Saltonstall, resigned in protest after the first execution. More important, the ministers of the province were becoming uneasy. They had supported the trials publicly but in private had written letters cautioning the magistrates in their use of evidence. Finally in early October Increase Mather, one of the most respected divines in the province, published a sermon signed by fourteen other pastors which strongly condemned the use of spectral evidence. Mather argued that to convict on the basis of a specter, which everyone agreed was the devil's creation, in effect took Satan at his own word. That, in Mather's view, risked disaster. "It were better that ten suspected witches should escape, than that one innocent person should be condemned," he concluded.

Mather's sermon convinced Governor Phips that the trials had gone too far. He forbade any more arrests and dismissed the court of Oyer and Terminer. The following January a new court met to dispose of the remaining cases, but this time the great majority of defendants were acquitted. Phips immediately granted a reprieve to the three women who were convicted and in April released the remaining prisoners. Satan's controversy with Salem was finished.

That, in outline, is the witchcraft story as it has come down to us for so many years. Rightly or wrongly, it is a story that has become an indelible part of American history. The startling fits of possession, the drama of the court examinations, the eloquent pleas of the innocent condemned—all these make for a superb drama that casts into shadow the rest of Salem's more pedestrian history.

Indeed, the episode is unrepresentative. Witchcraft epidemics were not a serious problem in New England or in any of the other American colonies. Such persecutions were much more common in old England and Europe, where they had reached frightening proportions. The death of some 25 people at Salem is sobering, but the magnitude of the event diminishes considerably alongside the 900 witches burned in the city of Bamberg during the first half of the seventeenth century or the 5,000 over a similar period in the province of Alsace. Furthermore, it can be safely said that the witchcraft affair had no lasting effect on the political or religious history of America, or even of Massachusetts.

Now, a curious thing has resulted from this illumination of a single, isolated episode. Again and again, the story of Salem Village has been told, quite naturally, as a drama complete unto itself. The workaday history that preceded and followed the trials—the petty town bickerings, the arguments over land and ministers, the Village's economic patterns —all this has been largely passed over. Yet the disturbances at Salem did not occur in a vacuum. They may indeed have constituted an epidemic but not the sort caused by some mysterious germ pool brought into the village over the rutted roads from Boston. So the historian's first task is to take the major strands of the witchcraft affair and see how they are woven into the larger fabric of Salem society. Salem Village is small enough so that virtually every one of its residents can be identified. We can find out who owned what land, the amount of taxes each resident paid, what sermons people listened to on Sundays. In so doing, a richer, far more intriguing picture of Salem Village life begins to emerge.

THE INVISIBLE SALEM

Paradoxically, the most obvious facet of Salem life that the historian must recreate is also the most insubstantial: what ministers of the period would have called the "invisible world." Demons, familiars, and witches all shaped the world of seventeenth-century New England, just as they shaped the worlds of Britain and Europe. For Salem Villagers, Satan was a living, supernatural being who could and did appear to people, either in his own form or that of another. He could converse with mortals, bargain with them, even enter into agreements with them. The witches who submitted to such devilish compacts bargained their souls in return for special powers or favors: money and good fortune, perhaps, or the ability to revenge themselves on others.

The outlines of such beliefs are easily enough sketched, but they convey the emotions of witchcraft about as successfully as a recital of the Apostle's Creed conveys the fire of the Christian faith. The historian who does not believe in a personal, witch-covenanting devil is entering a psychological world in which he is an outsider. He may think it a simple matter to understand how a Salem Villager would behave, but people who hold beliefs foreign to our own do not often act the way that we think they should. Over the years, historians of the Salem incident have insufficiently appreciated that fact.

One of the first people to review Salem's troubles was Thomas Hutchinson, who in 1750 published a history of New England's early days. Hutchinson did not believe in witchcraft; fewer and fewer educated people did as the eighteenth century progressed. Therefore he faced an obvious historical question. If the devil was not behind the Salem witch trials, who or what was? The question centered on motivation. The girls claimed they were being afflicted by witches, as the historical record made clear. Yet, reasoned Hutchinson, if the devil never actually covenanted with anyone, how were the girls' actions to be explained? Some of Hutchinson's contemporaries argued that the bewitched were suffering from "bodily disorders which affected their imaginations." He disagreed. "A little attention must force conviction that the whole was a scene of fraud and imposture, begun by young girls, who at first perhaps thought of nothing more than being pitied and indulged, and continued by adult persons who were afraid of being accused themselves."

Charles Upham, a minister who published a two-volume study of the episode in 1867, was even harder on the young women:

> Those girls, by long practice in 'the circle' [in Parris's kitchen]. . . had acquired consummate boldness and tact. In simulation of passions, sufferings and physical affections; in sleight of hand, and in the management of voice and feature and attitude,—no necromancers have surpassed them. There has seldom been better acting in a theatre than displayed in the presence of the astonished and horror-stricken rulers.

The view that the girls were shamming has persisted well into the twentieth century. The deception is not always portrayed as being quite so calculated or mean-spirited, but the outline remains the same. The fits begin as pranks played by high-spirited girls, who are elaborating magical tales heard from Tituba. The girls are surprised when the rest of the community takes their fancies so seriously. Suddenly they find themselves at the center of attention, constantly questioned, deferred to, regarded with a mixture of fascination and awe. Having gotten in so deep, they find it increasingly difficult to admit that the whole affair is a joke. Finally, rather than shame themselves by admitting the truth, they plunge on, emboldened by their success, perhaps even intoxicated by it. Six or seven adolescent girls have the whole village standing on its hands.

The historical record does supply some evidence to substantiate the hypothesis. Several defenders of the accused witches reported that on occasion the accusers seemed to be caught in their own jesting. One girl who cried out that she saw the specter of Elizabeth Proctor was immediately challenged by several spectators. The girl replied, "She [Elizabeth Proctor] did it for sport; they must have sport." Then in April Mary Warren, another of the girls, recovered from her fits and began to claim "that the afflicted persons did but dissemble"—that is, they were shamming. For the first time, the girls began seeing Mary's specter, and the court quickly summoned her on suspicion of witchcraft. The tables had been turned.

On the witness stand, Mary again fell into a fit "that she did neither see nor hear nor speak." The examination record continues:

> Afterwards she started up, and said I will speak and cryed out, Oh! I am sorry for it, I am sorry for it, and wringed her hands, and fell a little while into a fit again and then came to speak, but immediately her teeth were

set, and then she fell into a violent fit and cryed out, oh Lord help me! Oh Good Lord Save me!

And then afterwards cryed again, I will tell I will tell and then fell into a dead fit againe.

And afterwards cryed I will tell, they did, they did they did and then fell into a violent fit again.

After a little recovery she cryed I will tell they brought me to it and then fell into a fit again which fits continueing she was ordered to be had out. . . .

The scene is tantalizing. It appears as if Mary Warren is about to confess, when pressure from the other girls forces her back to her former role as one of the afflicted. In the following months the magistrates questioned Mary repeatedly, with the result that her fits returned and she again joined in the accusations. Such evidence suggests that the girls may well have been acting.

Yet such a theory leaves certain points unexplained. If the girls were only acting, what are we to make of the many other witnesses who testified to deviltry? One nearby villager, Richard Comans, reported seeing Bridget Bishop's specter in his bedroom. Bishop lay upon his breast, he reported, and "so oppressed" him that "he could not speak nor stur, noe not so much as to awake his wife" sleeping next to him. After two nights of torment, he asked a relative, William Comans, to keep watch with him while his wife slept in an adjoining room with a neighbor. William advised Richard to keep a sword with him as protection (its shape resembled a cross) and the sword lay in his lap, the two men talking in bed, when suddenly Richard saw Bridget Bishop and two other specters. "William heer they be all come again," he said, and

was immediately strook Speechless and could not move hand or foote and Immediately they gatt hold of my sword and strued to take it from mee but I held soe fast as thay did not get itt away and I had then Liberty of speech and Called William also my wife and Sarah Phillips that lay with my wife. Who all told mee afterwards thay heard mee but had not power to speak or stur afterwards. And the first that spake was Sarah Phillips and said in the name of God Goodman Coman what is the Matter with you, soe thay all vanished away.

Comans and others who testified were not close friends of the girls; they were obviously not conspiring with each other. How does the historian explain their actions?

Even some of the afflicted girls' behavior is difficult to explain as conscious fraud. It is easy enough to imagine counterfeiting certain fits: being flown through the room crying "whish, whish;" pretending to see other specters; being struck dumb. Yet other behavior must have required the skills of a consummate dramatic artist or a professional contortionist. Being pinched, pummeled, nearly choked to death; bodies being twisted into unnatural postures for long periods of time; tongues thrust upward until they almost touched the nose; legs crossed so tightly that several men could not pull them apart for fear of breaking them; fits so violent several grown men were required to restrain the victims. Is it conceivable that all this could be counterfeited—convincingly, realistically—day after day for five or six months?

Even innocent victims of the accusations were astounded by the girls' behavior. Rebecca Nurse on the witness stand could only look in astonishment at the "lamentable fits" she was accused of causing. "Do you think these [girls] suffer voluntary or involuntary?" asked John Hathorne, one of the examining magistrates. "I cannot tell," replied Goody Nurse hesitantly. Hathorne pressed his advantage. He knew the fits looked as genuine to Nurse as they did to everyone else. "That is strange," he replied. "Everyone can judge."

> NURSE: I must be silent.
> HATHORNE: They accuse you of hurting them, and if you think it is not unwillingly but by designe, you must look upon them as murderers.
> NURSE: I cannot tell what to think of it.

Hathorne pressed others who were accused with similar results. What ails the girls, if not your torments? "I do not know." Do you think they are bewitched? "I cannot tell." What do you think *does* ail them? "There is more than ordinary. . . ."

More than ordinary. Modern historians may accept that supposition without necessarily supposing, with Hathorne, the presence of the preternatural. Psychiatric research has long established what we now take almost for granted: that people may act for reasons they themselves do not fully understand, from motives buried deep within the unconscious. Even more: that emotional problems may be the subconscious cause of apparently physical disorders. The rationalistic psychologies of Thomas Hutchinson and Charles Upham led them to reject any middle-ground explanations of motivation. The Salem girls had not really been tormented by witches, Hutchinson and Upham reasoned; therefore they must have been acting voluntarily, consciously. But if we fully appreciate the mental attitudes that accompanied the belief in devils and witches, it is possible to understand the Salem episode, not as a game of fraud gone out of control, but as a study in abnormal psychology on a community-wide scale.

To understand why, turn to the testimony taken by the magistrates in their preliminary hearings. Here are the affadavits, the warrants for arrest, the cross-examinations—all the alleged incidents of witchcraft. Significantly, the incidents are not clustered around the pivotal year of 1692; they range over a broad period of time. "About four years agoe," an affadavit will begin; or "about six or seven years past;" "about five years sence;" "about twenty fower years ago. . . ." The record book, in other words, has acted as a magnet, drawing out for the historian stories that normally would never have been included in the record. It demonstrates just how deeply superstition ran in Salem, not just in 1692, but day in, day out. People were always taking note of strange incidents, wondering at remarkable coincidences, and seeing ominous signs.

To modern eyes, the "ominous" signs often seem inconsequential. Mary Easty complains to Sam Smith that he is "rude" in his conversation and that he might "rue it here after." As Smith is going home that night he receives "a little blow on my shoulder with I know not what and the stone wall rattled very much." Easty at work, he suspects. Martha Carrier argues with Benjamin Abbott about land he has bought, telling him he "should Repent of it afore seven years come to an end." Abbott is soon after afflicted with an infected foot and running sores. His wife notes that some cattle die strangely, others "come out of the woods with their tongues hanging out of their mouthes in a strange and affrighting manner . . . which we can give noe account of the reason of, unless it should be the effects of Martha Carrier threatenings." There are the bedside visions like Richard Comans's ("sometime about eight years since") or demon dogs, black and white, chasing men along the road, then disappearing suddenly into the ground. Lights in the night. Unaccountable illnesses. The New England villager's world was filled with what he called "remarkable providences." Most of them, to be sure, were the workings of a just and almighty God, but some were accomplished at the behest of Satan.

Follow the consequences of this mental attitude a step further. If Salem villagers believed that the devil's magic really could bestow power, might not a few people try to make use of it? Such is the suggestion of historian Chadwick Hansen, who argues that some villagers in Salem did practice witchcraft. We have already seen one instance of magical practice, the witch cake. Tituba, who baked it, confessed to being a witch. Even if her dramatic tales of supernatural meetings were embellishments to please the magistrates, her habitual sessions with the girls and her acquaintance with West Indian voodoo demonstrate a definite involvement with magic. The examination records also place Bridget Bishop under suspicion. As early as 1680 she had been unsuccessfully taken to court on the charge of witchcraft. Ever since she carried that reputation. In 1692 her own husband accused her of using the black arts, and even more damning, two laborers testified that when they dismantled a basement wall in her old house they found several rag puppets with headless pins stuck in them, sure signs of a witch at work.

Other villagers appear to have toyed with witchcraft even if they did not embrace it outright. Questioning of George Burroughs, the village's former minister, revealed some unusual and disturbing facts. When pressed, Burroughs admitted that only one of his children was baptized, despite the common Puritan custom of having children baptized as soon as was practicable after birth. When asked for the date of the last time he had taken communion, Burroughs said it "was so long since he could not tell."

Burroughs was short, compact, and extremely strong for his size. So strong, in fact, that he was reputed to have hefted large barrels of molasses and held a heavy rifle at arm's length by inserting his fingers in the barrel. Since witches were said to possess preternatural strength, this was damning evidence indeed. The historian who examines the affadavits will quickly notice that virtually all of them report what Burroughs *said* he could do, not what witnesses actually saw. Yet the testimony suggests a good deal. Burroughs, being quite short, may have been sensitive about his height and used his reputation for strength to impress acquaintances. So too he may have used magic. An unsettling incident of that sort occurred once when Burroughs and his wife were out picking strawberries with his brother-in-law. According to the brother-in-law, Burroughs disappeared into the woods. The brother and sister, after hallooing for him, started home on horseback. Burroughs was on foot, but he suddenly appeared to the others near home and began scolding his wife for derogatory remarks she had made about him on the return journey. Her brother was astonished at Burrough's ability to "read minds" and hinted that even "the Devil himself did not know so far." Burroughs is said to have answered, "My God makes known your Thoughts unto me." Similarly, the minister would often startle his wife by telling her "he knew what [she and her friends] said when he was abroad."

Perhaps Burroughs was innocent of witchcraft. But he seems at least to have promoted his image as a man of uncommon strength and uncanny mental abilities. In a world where people readily believed such claims, boasting was a dangerous business. It apparently cost Burroughs his life.

If the climate of superstition encouraged some villagers to take up witchcraft, it affected the supposed victims of bewitchment in equally palpable ways. The fear that gripped susceptible subjects certainly must have been extraordinary. Imagine a villager's feelings once he discovered that an acquaintance or even a stranger had determined to kill him. More than that, imagine being convinced that it was impossible to escape that person—that locked doors were no protection. One begins to sense the magnitude of the terror.

Historians, of course, must do more than imagine. One way of gauging the potential strength of such fear is to look for other examples with which to compare the Salem incidents. Anthropologists who have examined witchcraft in entirely different contexts provide useful cross-cultural comparisons. Their studies reveal that bewitchment can be traumatic enough to lead to death. An Australian aboriginee who discovers himself bewitched will

> stand aghast. . . . His cheeks blanch and his eyes become glassy. . . . He attempts to shriek but usually the sound chokes in his throat, and all that one might see is froth at his mouth. His body begins to tremble and the muscles twist involuntarily. He sways backwards and falls to the ground, and after a short time appears to be in a swoon; but soon after he writhes as if in mortal agony, and, covering his face with his hands, begins to moan.

Afterwards the victim refuses to eat, loses all interest in life, and dies. As might be expected, psychological attitude plays a paramount role in the bewitchment. One physician found that he could save similar victims of sorcery in Hawaii by giving them methylene blue tablets. The tablets colored the victims' urine and thus convinced them that a successful counter-charm had been administered. Although there are no well-documented cases of bewitchment death in Salem,* the anthropological studies indicate the remarkable depth of reaction possible in a community that believes in its own magic.

*The records hint that such deaths may have occurred, however. Daniel Wilkins apparently believed that John Willard was a witch and meant him no good. Wilkins sickened and some of the afflicted girls were summoned to his bedside where they claimed that they saw Willard's specter afflicting him. The doctor would not touch the case, claiming it "preternatural." Shortly after, Wilkins died.

It is even more enlightening to compare the behavior of the bewitched with the neurotic syndrome psychologists refer to as conversion hysteria. A neurosis is a disorder of behavior that functions to
avoid or deflect intolerable anxiety. Normally, an anxious person deals
with his or her emotion through conscious action or thought. If the
ordinary means of coping fail, however, the unconscious takes over.
Hysterical patients will convert their mental worries into physical
symptoms such as blindness, paralysis of various parts of the body,
choking, fainting, or attacks of pain. These symptoms, it should be
stressed, cannot be traced to organic causes. There is nothing wrong
with the nervous system during an attack of paralysis, or with the optic
nerve in a case of blindness. Physical disabilities are mentally induced.
Such hysterical attacks often occur in patterns that bear striking resemblance to some of the Salem afflictions.

Pierre Janet, the French physician who wrote the classic *Major Symptoms of Hysteria* (1907), reported that a characteristic hysterical fit begins
with a pain or strange sensation in some part of the body, often the lower
abdomen. From there, he explained, it

> seems to ascend and to spread to other organs. For instance, it often
> spreads to the epigastrium [the region lying over the stomach], to the
> breasts, then to the throat. There it assumes rather an interesting form,
> which was for a very long time considered as quite characteristic of hyste-
> ria. The patient has the sensation of too big an object as it were, a ball
> rising in her throat and choking her.

Most of us have probably experienced a mild form of the last symptom
—a proverbial "lump in the throat" that comes in times of stress. The
hysteric's lump, or *globus hystericus,* is more extreme, as are the accompa-
nying convulsions: "the head is agitated in one direction or another, the
eyes closed, or open with an expression of terror, the mouth distorted."
Often the patient will form what was known as the *arc de cercle,* head
thrown back, abdomen raised up, body arched in a backward arc.

Compare those symptoms with the ones manifested by the witching
victims. Samuel Willard, a Boston minister, described with particular
care the fit of Elizabeth Knapp, a girl who had come under his care in
1671:

> In the evening, a little before she went to bed, sitting by the fire she cried
> out, "Oh! My legs!" and clapped her hand on them; immediately, "Oh!
> My breast!" and removed her hands thither; and forthwith, "Oh! I am
> strangled!" and put her hands on her throat.

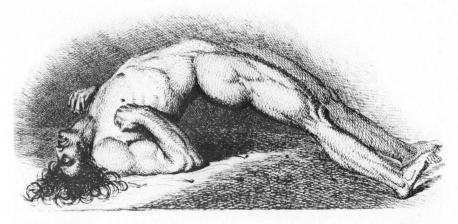

A nineteenth-century drawing of a classical hysterical symptom, the *arc de cercle.*

The fits continued, Willard wrote, "violent in body motions, leapings, strainings and strange agitations, scarce to be held in bound by the strength of three or four." During the Salem trials Elizabeth Brown's fit was described in similar fashion:

> When [the witch's specter] did come it was as birds pecking her legs or pricking her with the motion of thayr wings and then it would rize up into her stamak with pricking pain as nayls and pins of which she did bitterly complayn and cry out like a woman in travail and after that it would rise to her throat in a bunch like a pullets egg and then she would tern back her head and say witch you shant choak me.

Similar symptoms are reported throughout the trial records. Choking is unusually common; there are cases of *arc de cercle;* and the hysteric's ability to induce bruises or welts on the skin may well explain some of the "teeth" marks and other signs of tormentors that so astonished the Salem authorities.

The diagnosis of hysteria goes a long way toward resolving the historical debate over the afflicted girls' motivation. Adolescents, especially in the presence of Tituba, might very well have succumbed to the suggestion of bewitchment. The fits they experienced were very likely genuine, born of anxiety over a magic that threatened to overpower them. The diagnosis also explains many of the adult fits experienced by those who were convinced that their neighbors were conjuring against them. This

A hysterical convulsive attack of one of the patients in Salpêtrière Hospital during the nineteenth century. J. M. Charcot, the physician in charge of the clinic, spent much of his time studying the disorder. Note the crossed legs, similar to some of the Salem girls' fits.

is not to say that there was no acting at all; indeed, hysterics are notably suggestible, and no doubt the girls shaped their performances, at least instinctively, to the expectations of the community. "Differences between malingerers and hysterics are not absolute," notes one modern psychiatry text, "and we often find many hysterical traits in malingerers and some near-conscious play acting in the hysterical patient." We will probably never know for sure how much of the girls' behavior was play acting, but it seems clear that in a world where witches were reputed to possess the powers of life and death and where preternatural occurrences were an everyday affair, Abigail Williams, Mary Warren, and the other girls suffered torments that were very real indeed.

THE VISIBLE SALEM

So far, our reconstruction has dealt with only one aspect of the microcosm that was Salem in 1692—its invisible world. The area is a natural one to examine because it helps answer the central question of why the actors in the drama behaved the way they did. It would be tempting, having made the diagnosis of conversion hysteria, to suppose that we had pretty well explained the Salem trials. There is the natural satisfaction of placing the symptoms of the twentieth-century hysteric next to those of the seventeenth-century bewitched and seeing them match. Further correlations obtained from the primary sources make the explanation a convincing one. Yet it takes only a moment's reflection to see that, by narrowing the inquiry to the girls' motivations, we have left many other facets of the Salem episode unexplored.

In the first place, hysteria as a cause deals with the Salem trials on a personal rather than a social level. Hysteria is, after all, a disorder that affects individuals. In Salem it spread far enough to be labelled mass hysteria, but even that is less a social explanation than a personal one writ large. Granting for the moment that the afflicted really did make their accusations out of hysterical delusion, there are the accused themselves to consider—some 150 of them all told. Why were those particular people singled out? A few may have been practicing witchcraft, but the majority were innocent. Is there any common bond among the 150 that would explain why they, and not others, were accused? Only after we have examined their social identities can we answer that question.

Another indication that we need to examine the social context of Salem Village is the nature of hysteria itself. Hysterics are notably suggestible: sensitive to the influence of their environment. Nineteenth-century patients who were kept in insane asylums along with epileptics, for example, began having seizures that mimicked those suffered by the epileptics. If hysterics, then, are especially influenced by the expectations and behavior of those around them, it seems logical to assume that the afflicted girls at Salem might have been influenced by the expectations of the adult community. Scattered testimony in the court record suggests that sometimes when the girls saw specters whom they could not identify, adults suggested names. "Was it Goody Cloyse? Was it Rebecca Nurse?" If such conditions were operating, they confirm the need to move beyond strictly personal motivations to the social setting of the community.

In doing so, a logical first step would be to look for correlations: characteristics common to groups that might explain their behavior. Are the accusers all church members and the accused non-church members? Are the accusers wealthy and respectable while the accused are poor and disreputable? The historian assembles the data, patiently shuffles them around, and looks for match-ups.

Take the two social characteristics already mentioned, church membership and wealth. Historians can compile lists from the trial records of both the accusers and the accused. With those lists in hand, they can begin checking the church records to discover which people on each list were church members. Or they will search tax records to see whose tax rates were highest and thus which villagers were wealthiest. Records of land transactions are recorded, indicating which villagers owned the most land. Inventories of personal property are made when a member of the community dies, so at least historians have some record of an individual's assets at his death, if not in 1692. Other records may mention a trade or occupation, which will give a clue to relative wealth or social status.

If you make such calculations for the Salem region, you will quickly find yourself at a dead end, a spot altogether too familiar to practicing historians. True, the first few accused witches were not church members, but soon enough the faithful found themselves in jail along with non-church members. A similar case holds for wealth: although Tituba, Sarah Good, and Sarah Osbourne were relatively poor, merchants and wealthy farmers were accused as the epidemic spread. The correlations fail to check.

This was roughly the point that had been reached by two historians, Paul Boyer and Stephen Nissenbaum, when they were inspired, in effect, to take literally the advice about going back to the drawing board. More than a hundred years earlier Charles Upham had made a detailed map of Salem for his own study of the witchcraft episode. Upham examined the old town records, paced the actual sites of old houses, and established to the best of his knowledge the residences of a large majority of Salem Villagers. Boyer and Nissenbaum took their list of accuser and accused and noted the location of each Village resident on the map.* The results were striking, as can be seen from the map, on the next page.

*Since many of the so-called witches and their accusers came from surrounding towns, only those from the Village and from the area close by were included in the calculations. A few villagers' residences were also unknown.

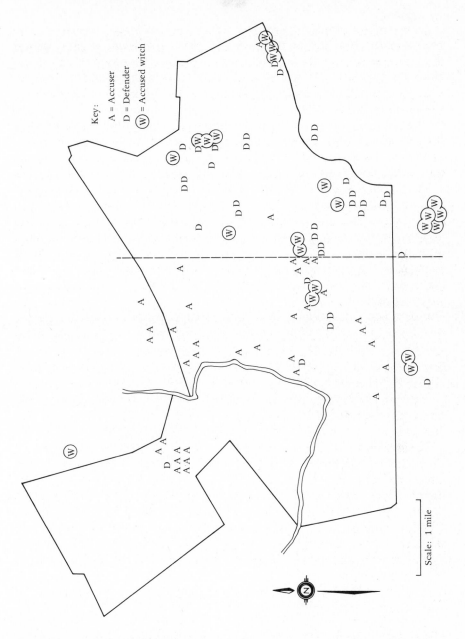

"The Geography of Witchcraft," after Boyer and Nissenbaum, *Salem Possessed* (Harvard University Press, 1974).

Of the fourteen accused witches living in the Village, twelve lived in the eastern section. Of the thirty-two adult Villagers who testified against the accused, thirty lived in the western section. "In other words," concluded Boyer and Nissenbaum, "the alleged witches and those who accused them resided on opposite sides of the Village." Furthermore, of twenty-nine residents who publicly defended the accused in some way (marked by a "D" on the map), twenty-four lived in the eastern half of the village. Often they were close neighbors of the accused. It is moments like these that make the historian want to behave, were it not for the staid air of research libraries, like Archimedes in his fabled bathtub.

The discovery is only the beginning of the task. The geographic chart tells us more about what the trials were *not* than what they were. We can see, at least, that the controversy did not arise out of neighborhood quarrels in the narrow sense of the word—people thinking their next-door neighbors were witches and accusing them. What seems to be at work is a larger division. What that division is, other than a general "east–west" split, the map does not say. But it does provide a clue about where to begin.

Boyer and Nissenbaum began to explore the history of the village itself, expanding their microcosm of 1692 backward in time. They investigated a condition that historians had long recognized but had never associated with the Salem witch trials. That was Salem Village's anomalous relation to its social parent, Salem Town.

Salem Town's settlement followed the pattern of most coastal New England towns. Original settlers usually set up houses around a central location and carved their farmlands out of the surrounding countryside. As a settlement prospered, the land in its immediate vicinity came to be completely taken up. In many cases, a group of settlers would then move out and start a new settlement, like bees hiving off for a new home. Other times, the process was less deliberate. Houses were erected farther and farther away from the central meeting house. When enough outlying residents found it inconvenient to come to church or attend to other civic duties, they sought recognition as a separate village, with their own church, their own taxes, and their own elected officials.

Here the trouble started. The settlers who lived toward the center of town were reluctant to let their outlying neighbors break away. Everyone paid taxes to support a minister for the town church, to maintain the roads, and to care for the poor. If a chunk of the village split off, revenue would be lost. Furthermore, outlying settlers would no longer share the common burdens, such as guarding the town at night. So the centrally located settlers usually resisted any movement for autonomy by their

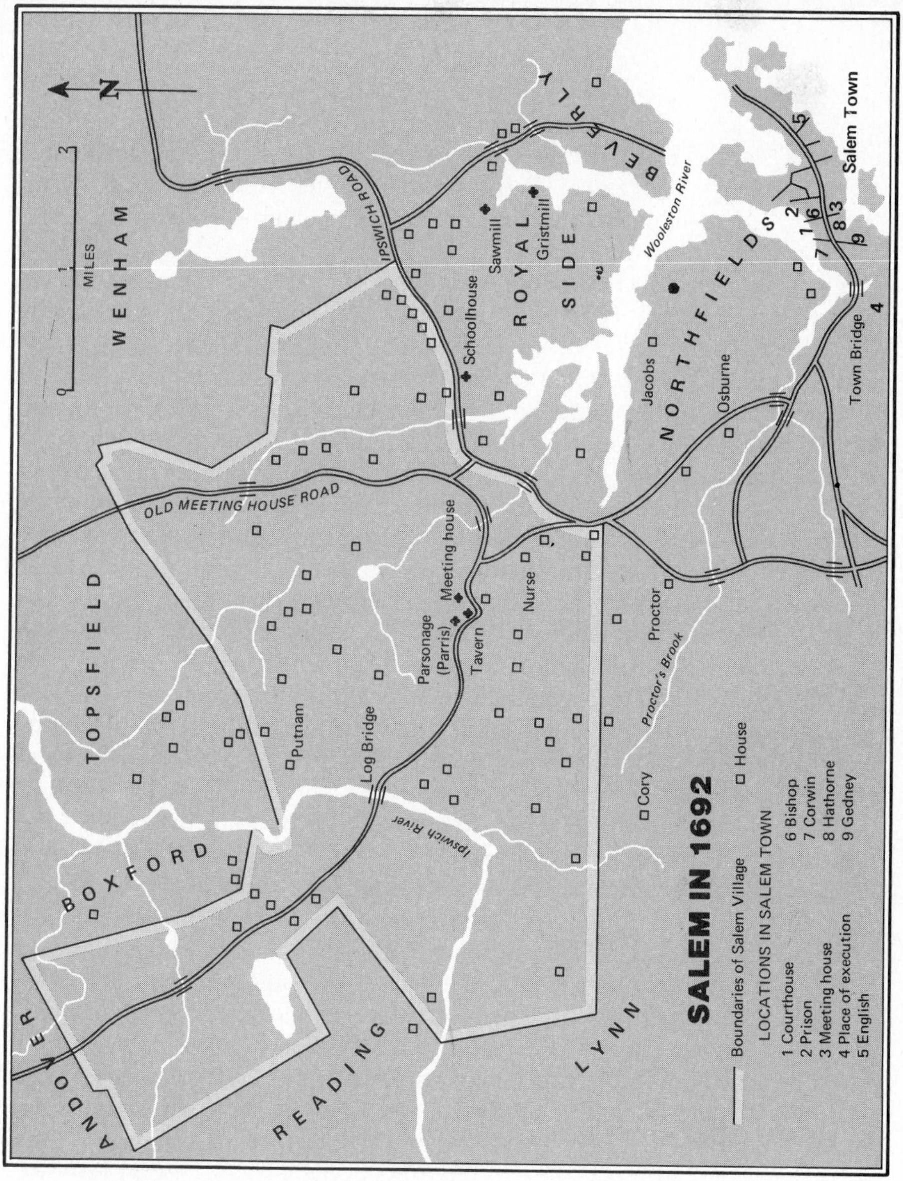
SALEM IN 1692
Boundaries of Salem Village
House
LOCATIONS IN SALEM TOWN
1 Courthouse
2 Prison
3 Meeting house
4 Place of execution
5 English
6 Bishop
7 Corwin
8 Hathorne
9 Gedney
MILES
0
1
2
N
WENHAM
TOPSFIELD
BOXFORD
ANDOVER
READING
LYNN
BEVERLY
ROYAL SIDE
NORTHFIELDS
Salem Town
Town Bridge
IPSWICH ROAD
OLD MEETING HOUSE ROAD
Ipswich River
Wooleston River
Proctor's Brook
Schoolhouse
Sawmill
Gristmill
Meeting house
Parsonage (Parris)
Tavern
Nurse
Proctor
Cory
Putnam
Log Bridge
Jacobs
Osburne

"Salem in 1692," from *Freedom and Crisis* by R. Jackson Wilson and Allen Weinstein (Random House, 1974), p. 83.

more distant neighbors. Such disputes were a regular feature of New England life.

Salem Town had followed this pattern. Its first settlers located on a peninsula extending into Massachusetts Bay, where they might ply a prosperous colonial trade. By 1668 four outlying areas (Wenham, Manchester, Marblehead, and Beverly) had already become separate towns. Now the "Salem Farmers," living directly to the west, were petitioning for a similar settlement, and the "Townsmen" were resisting. In 1672 the General Court of Massachusetts, the colony's legislature, allowed Salem Village to build its own meeting house instead of forcing residents to worship in Salem Town. In other matters, however, the Court kept the Village dependent. Salem Town still collected Village taxes, chose Village constables, arranged for Village roads, established the prices at which certain grains could be sold, and continued to oversee Village land grants. The General Court records include petition after petition from Villagers, submitted to no avail, complaining about tax rates, patrol duties, boundary rulings. Admittedly, the Village's semi-autonomous status was unusual. In most town disputes the General Court either allowed a new settlement to separate or it didn't. But for whatever unknown reasons, the Court granted autonomy only in 1752, sixty years after the witchcraft episode.

Here, then, is one definite "east–west" split. But it is important to remember that thus far, we have described a division between the Village and the Town. The line so graphically drawn on Boyer and Nissenbaum's map is within the Village itself. What cause would the Village have for division?

Many causes, the records indicate; chief among them the choice of a minister. Not long after the Village received the right to build its own meeting house, it settled down to arguing over who ought to preach from its pulpit. Matters began well enough in 1673 with the selection of James Bayley, but then complaints began to be heard. Bayley didn't attend regularly to his private prayers. Church members had not been fully consulted before his selection. After a flurry of petitions and counter-petitions, Bayley left in 1680, and George Burroughs was hired. Three years later Burroughs left in another dispute. He was succeeded by Deodat Lawson, who lasted through four more years of quarrels. Finally Samuel Parris occupied the pulpit after 1688. His term was equally stormy, and in 1696 his opponents finally succeeded in starving him out of the job by refusing to collect taxes to pay his salary.

The maneuverings that went on during the years of bickering were intricate enough to discourage most historians from bothering with them. But Boyer and Nissenbaum recognized that the church records, the petitions and counter-petitions, the minutes of the Village Committee provided an invaluable key to local divisions. At bottom, it was not the piety of the ministers alone that was in dispute. Equally crucial was who had power in the Village—power over piety or anything else. When the lists from the different quarrels were compared, Boyer and Nissenbaum found that the same names were being grouped together. The people who supported James Bayley usually supported George Burroughs and then opposed the second two ministers. Conversely, the supporters of Deodat Lawson and Samuel Parris had been the people who complained about Bayley and Burroughs. And—here is the connecting link—the two lists from those disputes coincide closely with the divisions in 1692 between accusers and accused.

Suddenly the Salem witch trials take on an entirely new appearance. Instead of being a dramatic disruption that appears out of nowhere in a village kitchen and then disappears as equally suddenly at the end of ten months, it becomes an elaboration of a quarrel that has gone on for nearly twenty years!

What lay behind the divisions? One reading of the evidence suggests that the larger split between Salem Town and Salem Village was reflected in the Village itself, with the Villagers on the east retaining enough of a common bond with the Town to continue their affiliation and the westerners favoring complete separation. Boyer and Nissenbaum argue that the division also went beyond the simple geographical one to a difference in outlook and lifestyle. Salem Town was entering into its own as one of the two major commercial centers of New England. It had a growing merchant class whose wealth would soon support the building of fine mansions and an opulent living style. By contrast the farmers in the western portion of Salem Village were tied more closely to traditional agrarian life: subsistence farming, spartan daily lives, a suspicion of the commercial habits of credit extension and speculative investment. What was worse, the Salem Farmers found themselves increasingly hard-pressed economically. The land available in the Village was dwindling. What land there was proved less fertile than the broad plains on the eastern side of the Village and along the northern flats of Salem Town.

Once again, the statistics of the social historian substantiate this portrait. Draw a map of Salem Village indicating land holdings, and you will find the eastern faction's property tending to enclose the Village on all but its western borders. Study the wills of Salem Townsmen, and you will find that from 1660 to 1681, the richest 10 percent of its citizens held 62 percent of its wealth, approximately three times as much as the richest 10 percent had controlled a generation earlier. Make a list of the farmers and merchants who were elected Town selectmen, and you will find that before 1665, twice as many farmers as merchants were chosen, but from

1665 to 1700 the ratio was six to one in favor of the merchants. If you look at the Village tax rolls to see who was paying the highest taxes, and therefore who was the wealthiest, you will find that although some moderately prosperous farmers were included among the accusers, in general the eastern faction, with its good land and connections to the town, held more property, paid more taxes, had a greater influence, and defended the accused.

Look, too, at the occupations of the accused witches and their defenders. Many of them lived along the Ipswich Road, a route that passed by the Village rather than through it, a main thoroughfare for travellers and for commerce. The tradesmen who had set up shop there included a carpenter, sawmill operator, shoemaker, miller. And of course there were the taverns, mainstays of travellers, yet always slightly suspect to Puritans. The people along the Ipswich Road were not rich, most of them, but their commercial links were with Salem Town and with outsiders; they were small-scale entrepreneurs rather than farmers. Out of twenty-one Villagers who lived along or near the road, only two signed petitions linking them with the western faction; thirteen signed petitions linking them with the eastern faction. Two tavernkeepers, John Proctor and Bridget Bishop, were hung as witches; Elizabeth Proctor barely escaped with her life; and Joshua Rea, another tavernkeeper on the road, signed a petition defending Goody Nurse.

Given this emerging portrait of the Village's factions (and only its broadest outlines have been sketched here), we can begin to suggest an alternate way of looking at the Salem trials. Traditional accounts place Samuel Parris, the examining magistrates, and their supporters as the protagonists, terrorizing innocent Villagers and controlling the trials as undisputed leaders of the Village. Certainly Parris's supporters had their day in 1692, but from the longer perspective they appear to have been fighting a losing battle. The Salem trials can be seen as an indirect yet anguished protest of a group of villagers whose agrarian way of life was being threatened by the rising commercialism of Salem Town. Similar conflicts were to be repeated, in different forms, throughout American history. Thomas Jefferson in his own day would contrast the corrupting influence of cities and manufacturers with the virtuous life of the independent yeoman farmer; western Populists a century later would arraign the "Money Power" of the East for its commercial sins. Salem's uniqueness lay, if Boyer and Nissenbaum's reconstruction proves correct, in the indirect means by which the conflict was expressed. Their reconstruction suggests that the Salem body politic was experiencing its own social analogue of conversion hysteria. When the political and religious institutions of town and village government were unable to resolve divisions on a conscious level, the conflict was converted into the camouflaged symptoms of an entirely different sort—a plague from the invisible world.

To admit that the factions of Salem Village and the rising commercial ethic of Salem Town played significant roles in shaping the witchcraft trials does not mean we must necessarily discard our earlier theories about the personal motivations of the accusers or the Villagers' sincere belief in witches. The controversy may well have started innocently enough in the kitchen of Samuel Parris. Tituba, Bridget Bishop, and others may well have been practicing magic. Certainly an agrarian faction in the Village did not consciously "get up" the trials to punish their commercial neighbors. But as the girls were led to accuse more and more people and as the controversy grew to engulf the town, it was only natural that the longstanding animosities and suspicions were inexorably drawn into the issue. The interconnections between a people's religious beliefs, their habits of commerce, their political institutions, even their dream and fantasy lives, are intricate and fine, entangled one with another like the delicate root system of a growing plant. Only historians who limit their examination to a small area of time and space are able to untangle, through gentle, persistent probing, the many strands of emotions, motivations, and social structures that provided the context for those slow processions to the gallows on Witch's Hill.

Additional Reading

Marion Starkey's *The Devil in Massachusetts* (New York, 1949) is the book most often cited as the best "lively" account of the Salem episode. It probably is, although to our way of thinking it idealizes both the accused and the Salem world in general. Giles Corey, George Burroughs, and Bridget Bishop may have been martyrs, but they were also a lot stranger and more interesting than Starkey makes them out to be. A helpful corrective is Chadwick Hansen's *Witchcraft at Salem* (New York, 1969), which catches the temper of Salem's invisible world much more accurately. For a detailed reconstruction of the seventeenth-century heritage of magic and superstition, see Keith Thomas, *Religion and the Decline of Magic* (London, 1971).

On the subject of hysteria, Pierre Janet's *Major Symptoms of Hysteria* (New York, 1907) provides instructive case histories, though it should be supplemented by a modern psychiatry text such as F. C. Redlich and D. X. Freedman, *Theory and Practice of Psychiatry* (New York, 1966). Ilza Veith, *Hysteria: The History of a Disease* (Chicago, 1965) provides background on how the disorder has been interpreted and treated over the centuries.

Paul Boyer and Stephen Nissenbaum apply the techniques of social history with unusual lucidity and grace in *Salem Possessed: The Social Origins of Witchcraft* (Cambridge, Mass., 1974). Their thesis, sketched only in outline here, is elaborated there in full. For purposes of comparison, there is Alan Macfarlane's social history of witchcraft in Essex County, England, *Witchcraft in Tudor and Stuart England* (New York, 1970).

The most fascinating primary sources are the records of pretrial examinations made by the Salem magistrates. They contribute as much to a portrait of the seventeenth-century mind as they do to a history of the Salem outbreak. W. Elliott Woodward published them originally in 1864 as the *Records of Salem Witchcraft Copied from the Original Documents;* they were reprinted in 1969. More accurate and complete transcripts of the records are available in typescript at the Essex Institute, Salem. George Lincoln Burr, ed., *Narratives of the Witchcraft Cases, 1648–1706* (New York, 1914; reissued 1968) is a convenient compendium of some of the contemporary accounts. Boyer and Nissenbaum have collected their own anthology of primary documents in *Witchcraft at Salem Village* (Belmont, Calif., 1972). The collection includes Upham's map and many church records, deeds, wills, and petitions that can be used to reconstruct the social portrait of the town. With this book, Burr's collection, and Woodward's

Records, the lay reader can make a good start at an investigation without having to trek to a major library.

Studies to date have by no means exhausted serious avenues of inquiry. Our social portrait in this chapter has done nothing with the fact that a significant majority of the accused witches at Salem were women, that witches generally were much more common than wizards, and that hysteria was primarily, though by no means exclusively, a woman's disease. John Demos's article, "Underlying Themes in the Witchcraft of Seventeenth-Century New England," *American Historical Review* (1970), 1311–1326, is one preliminary assessment of some of these themes. Readers may find it interesting to compare the Salem mass hysteria to a modern outbreak described in James A. McKnight et al., "Epidemic Hysteria: A Field Study," *American Journal of Public Health,* 55 (1965), 858–865. This case occurred in 1962 in a southern Louisiana high school where some twenty-two students, all but one female, experienced hysterical fits over a period of six months. Some interesting parallels can be drawn. In the area of social reconstruction, Boyer and Nissenbaum's study deals only with the relationships between accused and accusers in Salem Village itself. Many of the accused came from Andover and other surrounding areas; thus far no historian has tied these towns' factional disputes to the witchcraft cases. Can correlations between agrarian and commercial orientations be made elsewhere? If not, how and why does the witchcraft epidemic spread to the surrounding towns? There is plenty of digging left to be done here.

THREE

Declaring Independence

Good historians share with magicians a talent for elegant sleight of hand. In both professions, the manner of execution conceals much of the work that makes the performance possible. Like the magician's trapdoors, mirrors, and other hidden props, historians' primary sources are essential to their task. But the better historians are at their craft, the more likely they will focus their readers' attention on the historical scene itself and not on the supporting documents. The more polished the historical narrative, the less the audience will be aware of how much labor has gone into the reconstruction.

Contrary to prevailing etiquette, we have gone out of our way to call attention to the preliminary questions that historians ask, the problems of evidence to be solved before a historical narrative is presented in its final, polished form. As yet, however, we have not examined in detail the many operations a historian must perform on a single document, from the first encounter with it to its final use in a narrative. What at first seems a relatively simple job of collecting, examining, and cataloguing may become remarkably complex, especially when the document in question is of major importance.

So let us narrow our focus even more than in the previous two chapters, by concentrating not on a region (Virginia) or a town (Salem), but on one document. The document in question admittedly carries more import than most that historians encounter in their daily work. Yet it remains brief enough to be read in several minutes. It also has the merit of being one of the few primary sources which virtually every reader of this book already will have encountered: the Declaration of Independence.

The Declaration, of course, is one of the most celebrated documents in the nation's history. Drafted by Thomas Jefferson, adopted by the Second Continental Congress, published for the benefit of the world, memorialized throughout the nineteenth century in patriotic speeches, it is today respectfully hawked on authentic simulated parchment, emblazoned on restaurant placemats, and given the place of honor on basement recreation-room walls. Every schoolchild knows that Congress declared the colonies' independence by issuing the document on July 4, 1776; nearly everyone has seen the painting by John Trumbull which depicts members of Congress receiving the parchment for signing on that day.

So the starting place is familiar enough. Yet there is a good deal to establish when unpacking the facts about such a basic document. Under what circumstances did Jefferson write the Declaration? What people, events, or other documents influenced him? If changes were made in Jefferson's original draft, when were they made and why? Only when such questions are answered in more detail does it become clear that quite a few of the "facts" enumerated in the previous paragraph are either misleading or incorrect. And the confusion begins in trying to answer the most elementary questions about the Declaration.

A CONTEXT FOR INDEPENDENCE

In May 1776 Thomas Jefferson travelled to Philadelphia, as befit a proper gentleman, in a coach and four with two attending slaves. He promptly took his place on the Virginia delegation to the Second Continental Congress. This was not Jefferson's first appearance; he had represented Virginia on and off since the first Congress met in May 1775. After twelve months of fighting, he found Congress still debating whether the break with England was irreparable. Sentiment for independence ran high in many areas but by no means everywhere. The greatest reluctance lay in the middle colonies, particularly in Pennsylvania. Many of the Pennsylvania delegation, including the distinguished John Dickinson, still hoped to patch up the quarrel with England.

Such cautious sentiments infuriated the more radical members of Congress, especially John and Samuel Adams. The two Adamses had worked for independence from the opening days of Congress, but found the going slow. America, complained John, was "a great, unwieldy body. It is like a large fleet sailing under convoy. The fleetest sailers must wait for the dullest and the slowest." And so the radicals continued their patient, persistent efforts. "We have been obliged to keep ourselves out of sight," Adams wrote in a letter home, "and to feel pulses, and to sound the depths; to insinuate our sentiments, designs and desires by means of other persons."

Jefferson also favored independence, but he lacked the Adamses' taste for political infighting. While the men from Massachusetts pulled their strings in Congress, Jefferson only listened attentively and took notes. Thirty-three years old, he was one of the youngest delegates, and no doubt this contributed to his diffidence. Privately, he conversed more easily with friends, sprawling casually in a chair with one shoulder cocked high, the other low, and his long legs akimbo. He got along well with the other delegates, and performed his committee assignments dutifully.

In May of 1776, however, Jefferson hoped only to leave Philadelphia as quickly as possible and return to the convention meeting at Williamsburg, Virginia. There, in his opinion, lay the most challenging theater of action. Congress would putter interminably over the question of independence while his "country," Virginia, took the bold step of drawing a new frame of government. Jefferson had definite ideas about what ought to be incorporated in the Virginia constitution; he wanted to be on hand when it was drafted.

But it was last-minute news from Virginia that brought affairs to a head in Philadelphia. In late May, delegate Richard Henry Lee arrived from Williamsburg under instructions to force Congress to act. On Friday, June 7, Lee rose in Congress and offered the following resolutions:

> That these United Colonies are, and of right ought to be, free and independent States, that they are absolved from all allegiance to the British crown, and that all political connection between them and the state of Great Britain is, and ought to be, totally dissolved.
>
> That it is expedient forthwith to take the most effectual measures for forming foreign alliances.
>
> That a plan of confederation be prepared and transmitted to the respective colonies for their consideration and approbation.

On Saturday and again on Monday, moderates and radicals earnestly debated the propositions. They knew that a declaration of independence would make the breach with England final. The Secretary of the Congress, Charles Thomson, cautiously recorded in his minutes only that "certain resolutions" were "moved and discussed"—the certain resolutions, of course, treasonous in the extreme.

Still, sentiment appeared to be running with the radicals. Delegate James Wilson of Pennsylvania surprised the Congress by announcing that he felt ready to vote for independence. He asked only that action on the resolutions be postponed three weeks, until the Pennsylvania legislature had an opportunity to get firmly behind the movement. The radicals grudgingly agreed, but not without setting the wheels for independence in motion by appointing a five-member committee "to prepare a Declaration to the effect of the said first resolution."

The events that followed can be traced, in bare outline at least, in a modern edition of Secretary Thomson's minutes, edited by Worthington Ford. Using the Ford edition, we learn that on June 11, 1776 Congress constituted Jefferson, John Adams, Benjamin Franklin, Roger Sherman, and Robert Livingston as a Committee of Five responsible for drafting the declaration. Then, for over two weeks, Thomson's *Journal* remains silent on the subject. Only on Friday, June 28 does it note that the committee "brought in a draught" of an independence declaration.

On Monday, July first, Congress resolved itself into a Committee of the Whole "to take into consideration the resolution respecting independency." Since Thomson's official minutes did not record the activities of committees, Congress could freely debate the sensitive question of independence as a "Committee of the Whole" without leaving any record of debate or disagreement in the official minutes. On July second, the Committee of the Whole went through the motions of "reporting back" to Congress (that is, to itself). The minutes note only that Richard Lee's resolution, then "being read" in formal session, "was agreed to as follows"—printing the original resolves of June 7.

Thus the official Journal makes it clear that Congress voted for independence on July second, not the fourth. And the adopted resolution was not the five-member committee's declaration but Richard Henry Lee's original proposal of June 7. When John Adams wrote home on July third to his wife Abigail, he exulted in the actions of Congress, predicting that July second would be remembered as "the most memorable Epoca in the History of America. I am apt to believe that it will be celebrated, by succeeding Generations, as the great anniversary Festival. . . . It ought to be solemnized with Pomp and Parade, with Shews, Games, Sports, Guns, Bells, Bonfires and Illuminations from one End of this Continent to the other from this Time forward forever more."

As it turned out, Adams picked the wrong date for the fireworks. Although Congress had officially broken the colonies' ties with England, the declaration *explaining* the action to the rest of the world had not yet been approved. On July third and fourth Congress again met as a Committee of the Whole. Only then was the formal declaration reported back, accepted, and sent to the printer. Ford's edition of the *Journal* notes, "The foregoing declaration was, by order of Congress, engrossed, and signed by the following members. . . ." Here is the enactment familiar to everyone: the "engrossed" parchment (one written in large, neat letters) beginning with its bold, "IN CONGRESS, JULY 4, 1776" and concluding with the president of the Continental Congress's signature, so flourishing that we still speak of putting our John Hancock to paper. Below that, the signatures of fifty-five other delegates appear more modestly inscribed.

If mention of the Declaration in Thomson's minutes concluded with the entry on the fourth, schoolchildren might emerge with their memories reasonably intact. But it continues, confusingly. For July 19: *"Resolved,* that the Declaration passed on the 4th, be fairly engrossed in parchment, with the title and stile of 'The unanimous declaration of the thirteen United States of America,' and that the same, when engrossed, be signed by every member of Congress." This is a surprise. Hasn't the Declaration been engrossed and signed already—on the fourth? The entry of August second compounds the problem: "The declaration of independence being engrossed and compared at the table was signed by the members."

Thus the *Journal* appears to record *two* signings of the Declaration— one the fourth of July, one the second of August. Yet there is only one engrossed copy. What is the explanation?

A check of the introduction to Ford's edition reveals that, in fact, there was more than one *Journal* of Congress. Secretary Thomson made his original entries in the "rough" Journal. From these minutes Thomson and his assistants then prepared a "corrected" version, which formed the basis of the text as Congress later printed it. Ford's edition indicates that the entry which has the Declaration being "engrossed and signed" on July fourth appeared only in the corrected journal. In the rough journal, Thomson did not copy the Declaration or insert an engrossed copy; he only left a space and then pasted in a copy of the version Congress had ordered printed. This version does not include the phrase, "The unanimous declaration of the thirteen United States of America" (as the engrossed copy does), nor does it include the fifty-six signatures—only the printed names of Hancock (the president) and Thomson (the secretary).

In all likelihood, then, the Declaration was not signed on the fourth after all, but on the second of August. To muddy the waters even further, it appears that not all those who signed the Declaration did so on August second. In 1906 historian John Hazelton established that not all the signers were even in Philadelphia on August second. Some of them could not have signed the document until October or November.

So the upshot of the historian's preliminary investigation is that (1) Congress declared independence on the second of July, not the fourth; (2) most members officially signed the engrossed parchment only on the second of August; and (3) all the signers of the Declaration never met together in the same room at one time, John Trumbull's famous painting notwithstanding. In the matter of establishing the most basic facts surrounding a document, historians are all too ready to agree with John Adams's bewildered search of his recollections: "What are we to think of history? When in less than 40 years, such diversities appear in the memories of living men who were witnesses."

In this painting by the artist John Trumbull, *The Declaration of Independence,* the Committee of Five—Adams, Sherman, Livingston, Jefferson, and Franklin— present the document to John Hancock, president of the Continental Congress. When Hancock finally put his elaborate signature to the engrossed copy, he is reported to have said, "There! John Bull can read my name without spectacles, and may now double his reward of £500 for my head."

THE TRANSFORMATION OF A TEXT

Although the details of the Declaration's signing are at first confusing, historians can, with patience, sort them out. And they have available an authentic text—the engrossed parchment signed on August second. Yet the official document does not answer many questions about the writing of the Declaration. Although Jefferson drafted it, what did the Committee of Five contribute? What happened during the congressional debate on July third and fourth? If the delegates made changes in Jefferson's version, for what purpose? A historian will want to know which parts of the completed document were most controversial; even more, whether certain passages were so controversial, Congress eliminated them altogether. Surviving copies of earlier drafts could shed valuable light on these questions.

The search for an accurate version of the Declaration's drafting began even while the protagonists were still living. Some forty years after the signing, both Jefferson and John Adams tried to set down the sequence of events. Adams recalled the affable and diplomatic Jefferson suggesting that Adams write the first draft. "I will not," replied Adams.

"You shall do it," persisted Jefferson.

"Oh no!"

"Why will you not do it? You ought to do it."

"I will not."

"Reasons enough."

"What can be your reasons?"

Adams ticked them off. "Reason 1st. You are a Virginian and a Virginian ought to be at the head of this business. Reason 2nd. I am obnoxious, suspected and unpopular; you are very much otherwise. Reason 3rd. You can write ten times better than I can."

"Well," said Jefferson, "if you are decided, I will do as well as I can."

Jefferson, for his part, did not remember this bit of diplomatic shuttlecock. In a letter to James Madison in 1823 he asserted that

The Commitee of 5 met. . . [and] they unanimously pressed on myself alone to undertake the draught. I consented; I drew it; but before I reported it to the committee I communicated it separately to Dr. Franklin and Mr. Adams requesting their corrections; . . . and you have seen the original paper now in my hands, with the corrections of Dr. Franklin and Mr. Adams interlined in their own handwriting. Their alterations were two or three only, and merely verbal [that is, changes of phrasing, not substance]. I then wrote a fair copy, reported it to the committee, and from them, unaltered to the Congress.

So far so good. Jefferson's "original paper"—which he endorsed on the document itself as the "original Rough draught"—is preserved in the Library of Congress. But what exactly is this "original" draft? Take a look at the two reproductions on this page and the next. One of them is a section of the "original Rough draught," the other a fragment of a different copy, discovered in 1947 by Julian Boyd. Which of the two was written first?

Comparing the documents phrase by phrase, it becomes clear that Jefferson's "original" rough draft actually had a predecessor. Both documents read, "at this very time, too, they are permitting their chief magistrate to send over not only soldiers of our common blood but Scotch & foreign mercenaries. . . ." But when Jefferson wrote the fragmentary draft, he first used "at this time are permitting," before correcting it to read "at this very time too, they are permitting." Similarly he changed "our own blood" to "our common blood" and "foreign mercenaries" to "Scotch & foreign mercenaries." The "rough" draft has incorporated all these changes into its version smoothly, which indicates that it was a later copy. The rough draft also makes further changes that are *not* present on the earlier draft: mercenaries who "deluge us in blood" is replaced with the simpler "destroy us."

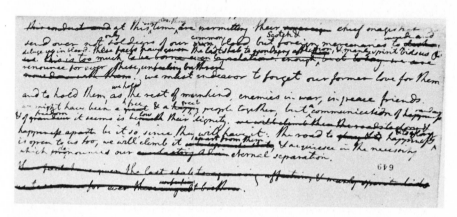

Fragment of a draft of the Declaration of Independence, discovered in 1947.

have by their free election re-established them in power. at this very time too they are permitting their chief magistrate to send over not only soldiers of our common blood, but Scotch & foreign mercenaries to invade & destroy us. these facts ... the last stab to agonizing affection, and manly ... ... renounce ; ... these unfeeling brethren. we must endeavor to forget our former love for them, and to hold them as we hold the rest of mankind, enemies in war, in peace friends. we might have been a free & a great people together; but a communication of grandeur & of freedom it seems is below their dignity. be it so, since they will have it; the road to glory & to happiness, is open to us too; we will ... it ... apart from them, and acquiesce in the necessity which denounces our ... ... separation!

The same section of the Declaration in Jefferson's "Rough draught."

For these and other reasons, Julian Boyd has argued that this fragmentary draft is part of Jefferson's earliest attempt to compose the Declaration. The later "original Rough draught" appears to be the first smooth copy of his efforts. Obviously the fragmentary draft, with all its corrections, made for difficult reading. Jefferson would have wanted to put it into more legible form before showing it to Franklin and Adams.

Yet even the rough draft, as it now stands, is not a smooth copy. As historian Carl Becker pointed out,

> the inquiring student, coming to it for the first time, would be astonished, perhaps disappointed, if he expected to find in it nothing more than the 'original paper . . . with the corrections of Dr. Franklin and Mr. Adams interlined in their own handwriting.' He would find, for example, on the first page alone nineteen corrections, additions or erasures besides those in the handwriting of Adams and Franklin. It would probably seem to him at first sight a bewildering document, with many phrases crossed out, numerous interlineations, and whole paragraphs enclosed in brackets.

This makes the rough draft more difficult to read, but in the end also more rewarding. For the fact is, Jefferson continued to record on this copy successive alterations of the Declaration, not only by Adams and Franklin, but by Congress in its debates of July third and fourth. In addition, Jefferson allowed copies to be made of his rough draft at different times during those weeks.

Thus by careful comparison and reconstruction, we can accurately establish the sequence of changes made in one crucial document, from the time it was first drafted on several pieces of paper, through corrections in committee, to debate and further amendment in Congress, and finally on to the engrossed parchment familiar to history. The changes were not slight. In the end, Congress removed about one-quarter of Jefferson's original language. Eighty-six alterations were made by one person or another, including Jefferson.

To these alterations the original author behaved as might be expected of any creator proud of his work: he squirmed. As Congress debated the document, Jefferson followed his usual custom and remained silent, but the pain must have been evident on his face. Benjamin Franklin noticed, and leaned over with a few consoling words. "I have made it a rule," he said,

> whenever in my power, to avoid becoming the draughtsman of papers to be reviewed by a public body. I took my lesson from an incident which I will relate to you. When I was a journeyman printer, one of my companions, an apprentice Hatter, having served out his time, was about to open shop for himself. His first concern was to have a handsome signboard, with a proper inscription. He composed it in these words: 'John Thompson, Hatter, makes and sells hats for ready money,' with the figure of a hat subjoined. But he thought he would submit it to his friends for their amendments. The first he shewed it to thought the word 'hatter' tautologous, because followed by the words 'makes hats' which shew he was a hatter. It was struck out. The next observed that the word 'makes' might as well be omitted, because his customers would not care who made the hats. If good and to their mind, they would buy, by whomsoever made. He struck it out. A third said he thought the words 'for ready money' were useless as it was not the custom of the place to sell on credit. Every one who purchased expected to pay. They were parted with, and the inscription now stood 'John Thompson sells hats.' '*Sells* hats' says his next friend? Why nobody will expect you to give them away. What then is the use of that word? It was stricken out, and 'hats' followed it, the rather, as there was one painted on the board. So his inscription was reduced ultimately to 'John Thompson' with the figure of a hat subjoined.

Most historians agree that the majority of changes made by Congress weakened the Declaration rather than hindered it. They are grateful, however, that Jefferson retained enough pride in his creation to preserve the original drafts that now make it possible to chart the course of the document over those fateful three weeks of 1776.

THE TACTICS OF INTERPRETATION

So far, our analysis has been confined to laying groundwork: establishing the actual text of the Declaration and sketching the circumstances of its origin. Having done that, the historian must attempt the more complicated task of interpreting the document.

Here, historians' paths are most likely to diverge—and understandably so. To determine the historical significance of a document requires placing it within the larger context of events. Because that context is so varied and complex, historians quite easily find many different combinations of significant facts. There is no single proper method for approaching and analyzing a document; if there were, the historical profession would be a good deal simpler, if not a great deal duller.

The situation is not so chaotic as it appears, however. While historians consistently interpret documents differently, they do share certain common analytical tactics—general approaches that have consistently yielded profitable results. Historians will not employ all of these tactics each time they confront a document, but they will usually employ more than one, in order to approach their subject from several perspectives. Each new approach requires the historian to read the document afresh, subjecting it to different questions, searching it for previously unnoticed relationships.

What follows, then, is one set of tactical approaches to the Declaration of Independence. These are by no means the only ways of making sense of the document. But they do suggest some range of the interpretive options that historians normally call upon.

The document is read, first, to understand its surface content. This step may appear too obvious to bear mentioning, but not so. The fact is, most historians examine a document for specific reasons, from a particular and potentially limiting viewpoint. A diplomatic historian, for instance, may approach the Declaration with an eye to the role it played in cementing a formal alliance with France. A historian concerned with political theory would more likely focus on the theoretical justifications of independence. Both perspectives are legitimate, but by beginning with such specific interests, historians risk prejudging the document. They are likely to notice only the kinds of evidence they are seeking.

So it makes sense to begin by temporarily putting aside any specific questions and approaching the Declaration as a willing, even uncritical listener. Ask only the most basic questions. How is the document organized? What are its major points, briefly summarized?

THE UNANIMOUS DECLARATION OF THE THIRTEEN UNITED STATES OF AMERICA.

When in the Course of human events, it becomes necessary for one people to dissolve the political bands, which have connected them with another, and to assume among the powers of the earth, the separate and equal station to which the Laws of Nature and of Nature's God entitle them, a decent respect to the opinions of mankind requires that they should declare the causes which impel them to the separation.—We hold these truths to be self-evident, that all men are created equal, that they are endowed by their Creator with certain unalienable Rights, that among these are Life, Liberty and the pursuit of Happiness.—That to secure these rights, Governments are instituted among Men, deriving their just powers from the consent of the governed,—That whenever any Form of Government becomes destructive of these ends, it is the Right of the People to alter or to abolish it, and to institute new Government, laying its foundation on such principles and organizing its powers in such form, as to them shall seem most likely to effect their Safety and Happiness. Prudence, indeed, will dictate that Governments long established should not be changed for light and transient causes; and accordingly all experience hath shewn, that mankind are more disposed to suffer, while evils are sufferable, than to right themselves by abolishing the forms to which they are accustomed. But when a long train of abuses and usurpations, pursuing invariably the same Object evinces a design to reduce them under absolute Despotism, it is their right, it is their duty, to throw off such Government, and to provide new Guards for their future security.—Such has been the patient sufferance of these Colonies; and such is now the necessity which constrains them to alter their former Systems of Government. The history of the present King of Great Britain is a history of repeated injuries and usurpations, all having in direct object the establishment of an absolute Tyranny over these States. To prove this, let Facts be submitted to a candid world.—He has refused his Assent to Laws, the most wholesome and necessary for the public good.—He has forbidden his Governors to pass Laws of immediate and pressing importance, unless suspended in their operation till his Assent should be obtained; and when so suspended, he has utterly neglected to attend to them.—He has refused to pass other Laws for the accomodation of large districts of people, unless those people would relinquish the right of Representation in the Legislature, a right inestimable to them and formidable to tyrants only.—He has called together legislative bodies at places unusual, uncomfortable, and distant from the depository of their public Records, for the sole purpose of fatiguing them into compliance with his measures.—He has dissolved

Representative Houses repeatedly, for opposing with manly firmness his invasions on the rights of the people.—He has refused for a long time, after such dissolutions, to cause others to be elected; whereby the Legislative powers, incapable of Annihilation, have returned to the People at large for their exercise; the State remaining in the meantime exposed to all the dangers of invasion from without, and convulsions within.—He has endeavoured to prevent the population of these States; for that purpose obstructing the Laws for Naturalization of Foreigners; refusing to pass others to encourage their migrations hither, and raising the conditions of new Appropriations of Lands.—He has obstructed the Administration of Justice, by refusing his Assent to Laws for establishing Judiciary powers. —He has made Judges dependent on his Will alone, for the tenure of their offices, and the amount and payment of their salaries.—He has erected a multitude of New Offices, and sent hither swarms of Officers to harrass our people, and eat out their substance.—He has kept among us, in times of peace, Standing Armies without the Consent of our legislatures.—He has affected to render the Military independent of and superior to the Civil power.—He has combined with others to subject us to a jurisdiction foreign to our constitution, and unacknowledged by our laws; giving his Assent to their Acts of pretended Legislation.—For quartering large bodies of armed troops among us:—For protecting them, by a mock Trial, from punishment for any Murders which they should commit on the Inhabitants of these States:—For cutting off our Trade with all parts of the world:—For imposing Taxes on us without our Consent:—For depriving us in many cases, of the benefits of Trial by Jury:—For transporting us beyond Seas to be tried for pretended offenses:—For abolishing the free System of English Laws in a neighboring Province, establishing therein an Arbitrary government, and enlarging its Boundaries so as to render it at once an example and fit instrument for introducing the same absolute rule into these Colonies:—For taking away our Charters, abolishing our most valuable Laws, and altering fundamentally the Forms of our Governments: —For suspending our own Legislatures, and declaring themselves invested with power to legislate for us in all cases whatsoever.—He has abdicated Government here, by declaring us out of his Protection and waging War against us.—He has plundered our seas, ravaged our Coasts, burnt our towns, and destroyed the lives of our people.—He is at this time transporting large Armies of foreign Mercenaries to compleat the works of death, desolation and tyranny, already begun with circumstances of Cruelty & perfidy scarcely parallelled in the most barbarous ages, and totally unworthy the Head of a civilized nation.—He has constrained our fellow Citizens taken Captive on the high Seas to bear Arms against their

Country, to become the executioners of their friends and Brethren, or to fall themselves by their Hands.—He has excited domestic insurrections amongst us, and has endeavoured to bring on the inhabitants of our frontiers, the merciless Indian Savages, whose known rule of warfare, is an undistinguished destruction of all ages, sexes and conditions. In every state of these Oppressions We have Petitioned for Redress in the most humble terms: Our repeated Petitions have been answered only by repeated injury. A Prince whose character is thus marked by every act which may define a Tyrant, is unfit to be the ruler of a free people. Nor have We been wanting in attentions to our Brittish brethren. We have warned them from time to time of attempts by their legislature to extend an unwarrantable jurisdiction over us. We have reminded them of the circumstances of our emigration and settlement here. We have appealed to their native justice and magnanimity, and we have conjured them by the ties of our common kindred to disavow these usurpations, which would inevitably interrupt our connections and correspondence. They too have been deaf to the voice of justice and of consanguinity. We must, therefore, acquiesce in the necessity, which denounces our Separation, and hold them, as we hold the rest of mankind, Enemies in War, in Peace Friends.—

We, therefore, the Representatives of the united States of America, in General Congress, Assembled, appealing to the Supreme Judge of the world for the rectitude of our intentions do, in the Name, and by Authority of the good People of these Colonies, solemnly publish and declare, That these United Colonies are, and of Right ought to be Free and Independent States; that they are Absolved from all Allegiance to the British Crown, and that all political connection between them and the State of Great Britain, is and ought to be totally dissolved: and that as Free and Independent States, they have full Power to levy War, conclude Peace, contract Alliances, establish Commerce, and to do all other Acts and Things which Independent States may of right do.—And for the support of this Declaration, with a firm reliance on the protection of divine Providence, we mutually pledge to each other our Lives, our Fortunes and our sacred Honor.

As befits a reasoned and lucid public document, the Declaration can be separated fairly easily into its component parts. The first sentence begins by informing the reader of the document's purpose. The colonies, having declared their independence from England, intend to announce "the causes which impel them to the separation."

The causes which follow, however, are not all of a piece. They break

naturally into two sections: the first, a theoretical and general justification
of revolution, and the second, a list of the specific grievances that justify
this particular revolution. Because the first section deals in general,
"self-evident" truths, it is the one most often remembered and quoted.
"All men are created equal," "unalienable rights," "life, liberty and the
pursuit of happiness," "consent of the governed"—these principles have
relevance far beyond the circumstances of America in the summer of
1776.

But the Declaration devotes far greater space to a list of British actions
which Congress labelled "a long train of abuses and usurpations" designed to "reduce [Americans] under absolute despotism." Since the
Declaration concedes that revolution should never be undertaken
lightly, the document proceeds to demonstrate that English rule has been
not merely unwieldy and inconvenient, but so full of "repeated injuries"
that "absolute tyranny" is the result. What threatens Americans most,
the Declaration proclaims, is not the individual measures, however inju-
rious, but the existence of a deliberate plot by the king to deprive a "free
people" of their liberties. So Congress would have the candid world
believe.

The final section of the Declaration turns to the colonial response.
Here the Declaration incorporates Richard Lee's resolution passed on
July second and ends with the signers solemnly pledging their lives,
fortunes, and sacred honor to support the new government.

Having begun with this straightforward reading, the historian is less
likely to wrench out of context a particular passage, magnifying its importance at the expense of the rest of the document. Yet taken by itself,
the reading of 'surface content' may distort a document's import. Significance, after all, depends upon the circumstances under which a statement
is made as much as upon the statement itself. Thus the historian must
approach a document from several perspectives in order to establish its
historical context.

*The context of a document may be established, in part, by asking what the
document might have said but did not.* When Jefferson retired to his second-
floor lodgings on the outskirts of Philadelphia, placed a portable writing
desk on his lap, and put pen to paper, he had many options. The Declaration in its final form was hardly a foregone conclusion. Yet the modern
reader, seeing only the end result, is tempted to view the document as
the logical, even inevitable result of Jefferson's deliberations. Perhaps it
was, but the historian needs to ask how it might have been otherwise.
What might Jefferson and the Congress have declared but did not? As

Jefferson himself remarked, "The sentiments of men are known not only by what they receive but by what they reject also." Only by identifying the range of alternatives in any historical situation can we appreciate why one path was chosen over another.

One way of reconstructing the might-have-been's in the Declaration is to locate them in earlier drafts. Here are the paths Jefferson wished to take, which Congress ultimately rejected. Perhaps most interesting is his discussion of slavery, originally included among the grievances against the king:

> He has waged cruel war against human nature itself, violating it's most sacred rights of life and liberty in the persons of a distant people who never offended him, captivating & carrying them into slavery in another hemisphere or to incur miserable death in their transportation thither. This piratical warfare, the opprobrium of *infidel* powers, is the warfare of the *Christian* king of Great Britain. Determined to keep open a market where *Men* should be bought & sold, he has prostituted his negative [used his veto power] for suppressing every legislative attempt to prohibit or to restrain this execrable commerce. And that this assemblage of horrors might want no fact of distinguishing die, he is now exciting those very people to rise in arms among us, and to purchase that liberty of which he has deprived them, by murdering the people on whom he also obtruded them: thus paying off former crimes committed against the *Liberties* of one people, with crimes which he urges them to commit against the *lives* of another.

Blaming the king for slavery in America certainly was tortuous logic. Jefferson based his charge on the fact that several times during the eighteenth century, Virginia's legislature passed a tariff designed to restrict the importation of slaves. It did so not so much out of humanitarian motives, although these were occasionally mentioned, but because the slave population in Virginia was expanding rapidly. Importing too many slaves would lower the price of domestic slaves whom Virginia planters wanted to sell. It would also create an unfavorable balance of trade, drawing out of the colony funds used to pay for imported slaves. The British administration, however, consistently disallowed such laws —and thus the king had "prostituted his negative for suppressing every legislative attempt to prohibit or to restrain this execrable commerce." In part, the laws were disallowed because many Americans wished the slave trade to continue—Virginian landowners who would have benefitted from the lower prices, as well as Georgians and South Carolinians who (as Jefferson himself admitted) "had never attempted to restrain the importation of slaves, and who on the contrary still wished to continue it."

To accuse the king of enslaving colonial blacks was ridiculous enough, but Jefferson's indictment appeared even more absurd because it then turned around and hotly accused the king of *freeing* colonial blacks. In November 1775 the loyal Governor Dunmore of Virginia proclaimed that any slave who deserted his master to fight for the king would be freed. Hence Jefferson, after condemning the awful practice of slavery, called King George to account for the vile "crime" of freeing slaves who remained loyal. Congress wisely dropped the long passage and only accused the king more generally of encouraging "domestic insurrections."

Jefferson's rough draft reveals those issues he raised which Congress rejected, but it necessarily provides no clue to the alternatives which *neither* Jefferson nor Congress included in the Declaration. That there had been other alternatives can be seen by looking at a declaration made some ten years earlier by another intercolonial gathering, the Stamp Act Congress. This declaration, like Jefferson's, began by outlining general principles before proceeding to list specific grievances. In reading the first three resolves, note the difference between their premises and those of the Declaration.

> I. That his Majesty's Subjects in these Colonies, owe the same Allegiance to the Crown of *Great-Britain,* that is owing from his Subjects born within the Realm, and all due Subordination to that August Body the Parliament of *Great-Britain.*

> II. That his Majesty's Liege Subjects in these Colonies, are entitled to all the inherent Rights and Liberties of his Natural born Subjects, within the Kingdom of *Great-Britain.*

> III. That it is inseparably essential to the Freedom of a People, and the undoubted Right of *Englishmen,* that no Taxes be imposed on them, but with their own Consent, given personally, or by their Representatives.

Significantly, the rights emphasized by the Stamp Act Congress in 1765 differ from those emphasized in 1776. According to the Stamp Act resolutions, the colonists are entitled to "all the inherent Rights and Liberties" of "Subjects, within the Kingdom of *Great-Britain.*" They possess "the undoubted Right of *Englishmen.*" Nowhere in Jefferson's

Declaration are the "rights of Englishmen" once mentioned as justification for protesting the king's conduct. Instead, the Declaration magnifies what the Stamp Act only mentions in passing—natural rights inherent in the "Freedom of a People," whether they be English subjects or not.

The shift from English rights to natural rights resulted from a change in the political situation in the colonies. In the years following 1765, Americans attempted to redress their grievances within the British imperial system. Quite logically, they cited rights they felt due them as British subjects. But in 1776, the Declaration was renouncing all ties with the mother country. If the colonies were no longer a part of Great Britain, what good would it do to cite their rights as Englishmen? Thus the natural rights "endowed" all persons "by their Creator" took on paramount importance.

The Declaration makes another striking omission. Nowhere in the long list of grievances does it use that word in the first resolve of the Stamp Act Congress—"Parliament." The omission is all the more surprising because the Revolutionary quarrel had its roots in the dispute over Parliament's right to tax and regulate the colonies. The Sugar Act, the Stamp Act, the Townshend duties, the Tea Act, the Coercive Acts, the Quebec Act—Parliament is at the center of the dispute. The Declaration alludes to those legislative measures but always in the context of the king's actions, not Parliament's. Doing so admittedly required a bit of circumlocution: when Jefferson introduced the Parliamentary grievances, he wrote that the king had "combined with others [namely Parliament] to subject us to a jurisdiction foreign to our constitution and unacknowledged by our laws, giving his Assent to their Acts of pretended Legislation." Only once again did he allude to Parliament, when castigating the British people for wrongly allowing "their legislature" to extend its jurisdiction over the colonies.

Obviously, the omission came about for much the same reason that Jefferson excluded all mention of the "rights of Englishmen." At the Stamp Act Congress of 1765, virtually all Americans were willing to grant Parliament some jurisidiction over the colonies. Not the right to lay taxes without American representation, certainly, but at least the right to regulate colonial trade. Robert Livingston, who was on the committee to draft the Declaration in 1776, had also been at the Stamp Act Congress. "All agreed that we ought to obey all acts of trade [passed by Parliament] and that they should regulate our Trade," he recalled, "but many were not for making an explicit declaration of and an acknowledgment of such a Power." In the end the Congress compromised, noting only in Resolution I that Parliament deserved "all due Subordination." What exactly that meant, they left their readers to imagine; but at least they granted Parliament some sovereignty.

By 1775 the more radical colonists would not grant Parliament any authority over the colonies. They had come to recognize what an early pamphleteer had noted, that Americans could be "as effectually ruined by the powers of legislation as by those of taxation." The Boston Port Bill, which closed Boston harbor, was not a tax, nor did it violate any traditional right. Yet the radicals argued, quite correctly, that Parliament could take away Americans' freedoms by such legislation.

Although many colonists had totally rejected all Parliamentary authority in 1775, most had not yet advocated independence. How, then, were the colonies related to England if not through Parliament? The only link, radicals argued, was through the king. The colonies possessed their own sovereign legislatures, but they shared with all British subjects one monarch. It was to the king that all grievances should be addressed. Thus, when the final break with England came, the Declaration carefully laid all blame at the king's feet. Even to recognize Parliament would be tacitly to admit that it had some legitimate connection with the colonies.

What the Declaration does *not* say, then, proves to be as important as what it did say. Historians can recognize the importance of such unstated premises by continually remembering that the actors in any drama possess more alternatives than the ones they finally choose.

A document may be understood by seeking to reconstruct the intellectual worlds behind its words. We have already seen, in the cases of Virginia and Salem, how much history involves the task of reconstructing whole societies from fragmentary records. The same process applies to the intellectual worlds that lie behind the words of an individual document.

The need to perform this reconstruction is often hidden, however, because the English language has changed over the past two hundred years, while the words themselves remain the same. As a result, we may find ourselves reading an eighteenth-century sentence whose meaning appears perfectly clear, when in fact it had an entirely different sense for its author.

The importance of change over time in a language can be demonstrated more forcibly if we imagine how Jefferson or some other eighteenth-century American would try to make sense out of twentieth-century prose. Below are three passages taken from twentieth-century writers:

The age of widescreen began in September 1952 with the release of *This Is Cinerama.* . . . Employing stereophonic sound, Cinerama, the invention of Fred Waller, used three cameras and three projectors to cover a huge, curved screen.

The newspaper feature, the magazine article, the radio program, do not attain the dignity of being ends in themselves; they are rather means to an end: that end, of course, is to catch the reader's attention so that he will then read the advertisement or hear the commercial.

Middle-class life came to power and wealth by breaking ancient restraints; and the more successful middle classes fear new restraints upon their sometimes quite inordinate powers and privileges.*

Most likely, an eighteenth-century reader would find the first excerpt most difficult to comprehend and the third excerpt the easiest. The passage on "Cinerama," "widescreen," and "stereophonic sound" would of course be indecipherable to Jefferson. It describes a totally unfamiliar world, using a strange and unknown vocabulary. The second excerpt appears more promising, although still puzzling. Jefferson would be familiar with "newspaper" and "feature," but would not know what a "newspaper feature" was, except perhaps to guess that it might be some distinguishing mark or detail—the meaning of "feature" in his day. "Commercial" he would be accustomed to reading as an adjective, not a noun; he would be at a loss to imagine what in the world it meant to "hear" a commercial. Yet Jefferson could probably deduce the general meaning of the passage—that articles in a newspaper served only as a vehicle to get subscribers to read the advertisements.

The final passage Jefferson would comprehend easily. The general subject is political power, an area familiar to him. "Middle class" might seem a bit infelicitous on his tongue; colonists more often referred to "the middling class of people" or "the middling sort." But the meaning of the passage would appear quite clear.

Appearances, however, can be deceiving. Jefferson would surely misinterpret the last two passages, simply because he was unaware of

*The excerpts are from James Monaco, *How to Read a Film* (New York, 1977), p. 88; David Potter, *People of Plenty* (Chicago, 1954), pp. 181–182; and Reinhold Niebuhr, *The Irony of American History* (New York, 1962), p. 106.

the changed context behind the words. He would likely think foolish, for example, the idea that newspapers were printed for the benefit of advertisers rather than readers. The advertising of his day played a minor cultural role in comparison with today's multi-billion-dollar industry. Similarly, Jefferson might have spoken of a "middling class of people," but the writings of Karl Marx have made it impossible today to use the word "class" without implying a whole range of meanings beyond the loose definition of the eighteenth century. To take another example, Jefferson would recognize terms such as "repression" and "unconscious," but without a knowledge of Freudian psychology, he would find their associations as shown in twentieth-century prose entirely foreign.

By the same token, eighteenth-century documents may appear deceptively lucid to twentieth-century readers. When Jefferson wrote that all men were "endowed by their Creator with certain unalienable Rights," including "Life, Liberty and the pursuit of happiness," the meaning seems reasonably clear. But is it? Does "pursuit of happiness," for example, have the same commonsense meaning that we attribute to it today?

Essayist and historian Garry Wills has offered his own reconstruction of the intellectual worlds behind the Declaration. Jefferson's "pursuit of happiness," he argues, should not be interpreted merely as a vague and idealistic sentiment. Jefferson stood in the great eighteenth-century tradition of the Enlightenment; as one who had read widely in the works of European philosophes, he shared with them the belief that the study of human affairs should be conducted as precisely as study of the natural world had come to be.

During the seventeenth century, natural philosophers had increasingly relied upon mathematical equations and formulae to predict the motions of the planets, explain the principles of optics, and formulate the law of gravity. In particular, the prodigious syntheses of Isaac Newton stood as a monument to scientific progress. Alexander Pope expressed the adulation of the eighteenth century in his couplet, "Nature and Nature's laws lay hid in night: / God said, Let Newton be! and all was light." The philosophes of Pope's day hoped to extend the precision of the natural sciences to the study of man, including his psychology and his motivations.

The results of such endeavors may seem quaint today, but the philosophes took their work seriously. In 1725 Francis Hutcheson, a leader of the Scottish Enlightenment and a philosopher well known to Jefferson, attempted to quantify such elusive concepts as morality. The result was a string of equations where qualities were abbreviated by letters (B =

Benevolence, A = Ability, S = Self-love, I = Interest) and placed in their proper relations: "M = (B + S) × A = BA + SA; and therefore BA = M − SA = M − I, and B = $\frac{M - I}{A}$."

Jefferson possessed a similar passion for precision and quantification. He repeatedly praised the American astronomer David Rittenhouse and his orrery, a mechanical model of the solar system whose gears replicated the relative motions of the earth, moon, and planets. Jefferson also applied classification and observation as a gentleman planter. If it were possible to discover the many relationships within the natural order, he reasoned, farmers might better plant and harvest to those rhythms. For years Jefferson kept detailed notes indicating when the first dogwood blossomed, when the first whippoorwill was heard, when the first fireflies appeared, when the first asparagus came to table, when the first peaches were ripe, when the first shad arrived. Even in the White House, Jefferson kept his eye on the Washington markets and recorded the seasons' first arrivals of thirty-seven different vegetables.

Wills argues that Jefferson conceived the "pursuit of happiness" in equally precise terms. Francis Hutcheson had suggested that a person's actions be judged by how much happiness they brought to other people. "Virtue," he argued, "is in a compound ratio of the quantity of good and number of enjoyers. . . . that action is best which accomplishes the greatest happiness for the greatest number." Such conceptions led the English deist William Wollaston to envision a balance-scale of pleasure and pain where the two opposites could be totted up metaphorically. "For nine degrees of pleasure, less by nine degrees of pain, are equal to nothing; but nine degrees of one, less by three degrees of the other, give six of the former net and true."

According to Enlightenment science, then, pleasure was a quality embedded in human nature itself, the pursuit of which governed a person's actions as surely as the laws of gravity governed walking. Further, since happiness could be quantified, a government's actions could be weighed in the balance scales to discover whether they measurably impeded a citizen's right to pursue happiness as he saw fit. When rightly apprehended, the science of government, like the science of agriculture or celestial mechanics, would take its place in the advancing progress of humankind.

Garry Wills's reconstruction of Jefferson's intellectual world, brilliant as it is, proves more speculative and uncertain than it first seems. Granted, Francis Hutcheson developed a calculus of "benevolence"; his ideas were in the air in 1776. But any number of ideas can be said to be "in the air" at a particular time. It is one thing to point out their existence, another to prove they actually influenced another person. How do we know Jefferson drew upon Hutcheson when composing the Declaration? Jefferson certainly knew of the Scottish philosopher, but had he read his works or taken them to heart? Wills has been forced to rely on circumstantial evidence, such as the presence of Hutcheson's works in Jefferson's library and Jefferson's love of precision in other fields of knowledge.

Whether or not Wills's specific case stands up to examination, his method of research is one which historians commonly employ. By understanding the intellectual world from which a document arose—by tracing, in effect, its genealogy—we understand better the document itself.

Lastly, a document may be interpreted according to the way it functions within a specific social situation. This approach relates a piece of evidence to its contemporary context rather than its genealogical past. The Declaration, after all, was written to explain and justify the circumstances of 1776. As a public document, it was addressed to a particular audience—or audiences. Who were they? What messages were being sent to those audiences and how was the Declaration designed to send them? Historians recognize that every document functions as a tool, fashioned to accomplish certain purposes within its own social situation. By studying the shape of the tool, historians can appreciate what goals the Declaration hoped to achieve and what audiences it expected to reach.

If the Declaration is to be conceived as a tool, it would be well to imagine something on the order of a fat, multibladed Swiss army knife. For the Declaration attempts to accomplish many goals and speak to several sorts of readers. True, its stated audience is a general one—the "candid world" addressed out of "a decent respect to the opinions of mankind." On the face of it, Congress seems to be appealing to a vague court of world opinion. And certainly the Declaration's preamble, grounded as it is upon the common denominator of natural rights, speaks to this general audience. It does not descend to tortuous specifics; it only outlines the general right of a people to revolt when a government becomes repressive and tyrannical. International readers need not be familiar with technical precedents of English constitutionalism to understand such arguments.

But other sections of the Declaration seem designed for specific audiences abroad. The most obvious audience is the king, his ministry, and (indirectly) Parliament, who as we have already seen, find a detailed listing of grievances laid at their door. The midsection of the Declaration reads very much like a lawyer's brief (indeed, many of the delegates were lawyers). The grievances have not been redressed, Congress concludes; therefore, it cites them one last time as the legal justification for revolution.

A second audience across the Atlantic is the British people. Once Congress disposes of the specific grievances, it looks beyond king and Parliament to the ultimate source of political power, the people. In his original rough draft, Jefferson bitterly reproached his "Brittish brethren" for permitting their elected representatives to tyrannize the colonists. Congress, aware that their English audience included those still sympathetic to the American cause, tempered Jefferson's attack, much to his displeasure. "The pusillanimous idea that we had friends in England worth keeping terms with," he complained, "still haunted the minds of many. For this reason those passages which conveyed censures on the people of England were struck out, lest they should give them offense."*

The Declaration addressed an entirely different foreign audience, but an equally crucial one, when it declared that the "United Colonies" had "full Power to levy War, conclude Peace, contract Alliances, establish Commerce, and to do all other Acts and Things which Independent States may of right do." The prime audience for this passage was France, for in July 1776 Congress wanted nothing more than to conclude a beneficial alliance. We have already followed Silas Deane, as he energetically sought aid in Paris during the summer of 1776; Congress clearly recognized that Deane would not succeed so long as France viewed America's quarrel as an internal affair of the British empire. As one delegate noted during the debate over independence, "A declaration of Independance alone could render it consistent with European delicacy for European powers to treat with us." Another influential Virginian concluded, "I am clearly of opinion that unless we declare openly for independency there is no chance for foreign aid." Thus, one of Richard Lee's June 7 resolutions directed Congress "to take the most effectual measures for forming alliances."

Although the Declaration proclaimed that its audience was the world at large, it directed its message equally to colonists at home. American sentiment for independence was by no means unanimous. Congress knew that in making the final break with England, it had moved ahead of many citizens it claimed to represent. Thus the detailed list of griev-

---

*Those censures included the rough draft passage examined earlier, condemning the British people for allowing the king to send over "Scotch and foreign mercenaries to invade and destroy us."

ances also served to remind wavering Americans of the evils wrought by king and Parliament: that the threat of tyranny was real and the patriot cause just.

In particular, some grievances appear to have been included as war propaganda designed to mobilize public opinion. The Declaration raised the spectre of the Quebec Act, which had incorporated the French territory into the British empire without providing its citizens representative government. Britain, the Declaration warned, might soon introduce "the same absolute rule into these colonies." Jefferson also called attention to alleged atrocities of war: foreign mercenaries with their "works of death, desolation and tyranny;" slaves arising against their masters; savage Indians incited to wage war against "all ages, sexes and conditions." In short, the king and his minions had "plundered our seas, ravaged our Coast, burnt our towns, and destroyed the lives of our people."

The "candid world" addressed by the Declaration was thus hardly one and indivisible. Different parts of the document addressed different audiences in order to accomplish specific goals. By analyzing the Declaration as a rhetorical tool, historians are able to delineate more clearly the ways that it functioned in the complex situation of 1776.

When the time came, on August second, to sign the document that had undergone so many revisions, alterations, and amendments, the delegates in Philadelphia perhaps came to recognize the Declaration's final audience: themselves. As president of the Congress, John Hancock was the first delegate to sign the engrossed copy. Taking pen in hand he reportedly remarked, "We must be unanimous; there must be no pulling different ways; we must all hang together." To which Ben Franklin replied, "Yes, we must indeed all hang together, or most assuredly we shall all hang separately." The conversation may only be a bit of folklore, added later to embellish the momentous occasion. Apocryphal or not, the exchange reinforces the import of Jefferson's concluding lines. "For the support of this Declaration," he wrote, "we mutually pledge to each other our Lives, our Fortunes and our sacred Honor." Many delegates took that final step only with great reluctance; even radicals like the Adamses recognized that the war was far from being won. The Declaration forced delegates to commit themselves publicly and symbolically to the Revolution, whether or not it finally succeeded. For the brief instant that each member stood in front of the table and signed, the Declaration had an audience of one. The rest of the candid world would come later.

Additional Reading

The Declaration of Independence, surely one of the most scrutinized documents in American history, stands at the center of the American Revolution, surely one of the most scrutinized events in that history. Consequently, the interested reader has plenty of material upon which to draw.

For background on the American Revolution, Edmund S. Morgan's *Birth of the Republic,* rev. ed. (Chicago, 1977) is a lively, brief, and lucid account with an up-to-date bibliography. For additional detail see John R. Alden, *A History of the American Revolution* (New York, 1969). David F. Hawke provides an engaging yet scholarly discussion of the drafting of the Declaration in *A Transaction of Free Men* (New York, 1964).

For more detailed analyses of the Declaration see Herbert Friedenwald's *The Declaration of Independence: An Interpretation and an Analysis* (New York, 1904). John H. Hazelton, *The Declaration of Independence: Its History* (New York, 1906) has much detailed material, including the investigation of who signed the Declaration and when. Perhaps the most elegant as well as most often-cited work is Carl Becker's *The Declaration of Independence: A Study in the History of Political Ideas* (New York, 1942). This volume is the best introduction both for an account of the drafting process and for the natural rights doctrines that Jefferson drew upon in summarizing the radicals' philosophy of revolution. More recently Garry Wills has provided a wide-ranging contextual analysis of the Declaration in *Inventing America: Jefferson's Declaration of Independence* (New York, 1978). Wills argues that Jefferson depended less on the ideas of John Locke (contrary to what Carl Becker had argued) and more on the philosophers of the Scottish Enlightenment. Undeniably Wills overstates his case, and he has been called to task by Ronald Hamowy in a classic cut-and-thrust maneuver entitled "Jefferson and the Scottish Enlightenment: A Critique of Garry Wills's *Inventing America,*" *William and Mary Quarterly,* third Ser., XXXVI, no. 4 (October 1979), 503–523. Devastating as Hamowy's criticisms are, they do not invalidate all of Wills's arguments. *Inventing America* is still very much worth reading.

Readers wishing to do some of their own textual analysis will find Julian P. Boyd's *The Declaration of Independence: The Evolution of the Text* (Princeton, N.J., 1945) a good starting place. Boyd's text provides facsimiles of Jefferson's "Rough Draught" of the Declaration, plus other copies Jefferson sent to friends, and Adams's copy transcribed while the document was still in committee. Until his death Boyd also edited the definitive *Papers of Thomas Jefferson*

(Princeton, N.J., 1950–); Volume I contains a facsimile of the earliest fragment of the Declaration, as well as excellent discussions by Boyd of textual matters. All in all, it is a textbook case on editing texts.

As a starting point for the role of the Continental Congress, see Worthington C. Ford, ed., *Journals of the Continental Congress: 1774–1789* (Washington, D.C., 1904–1937). The reader will soon find, however, that Charles Thomson's minutes are tantalizingly brief and only hint at the issues on the delegates' minds. To supplement this, Edmund C. Burnett published a collection of the *Letters of Members of the Continental Congress* (Washington, D.C., 1921–1936), which provides much more material. Since Burnett's collection was by no means complete, however, the Library of Congress has sponsored a new edition of letters as a bicentennial project, Paul H. Smith, ed., *Letters of Delegates to Congress, 1774–1789* (Washington, D.C., 1976–). At this writing, only the first two volumes, covering the period through the end of 1775, are available, but they provide much fuller coverage than Burnett (some 1,250 pages versus about 290 pages for a comparable period in Burnett).

In addition to Garry Wills's study of Jefferson's intellectual world, earlier useful works include Adrienne Koch, *The Philosophy of Thomas Jefferson* (New York, 1943) and Daniel Boorstin, *The Lost World of Thomas Jefferson* (New York, 1948), as well as Dumas Malone's biography, *Jefferson and His Time,* 6 vols. (Boston, 1948–1981). Perhaps the most indispensible aid to tracing the change of a word's meaning over time is the *Oxford English Dictionary.* This thirteen-volume work provides short natural histories of words, complete with examples taken from published works to demonstrate usage changes over time. Once again, Wills's *Inventing America* supplies abundant examples of this sort of word detective-work.

Finally, readers interested in further exercises in establishing the context of a document may wish to consult Philip S. Foner's collection of subsequent declarations of independence, *We, the Other People* (New York, 1976). The excerpts range from the "Workingman's Declaration of Independence" issued in 1829 to one put out by the "People's Bicentennial Commission" in 1975.

CHAPTER

FOUR

❖

Jackson's Frontier– and Turner's

Ceremony, merriment, and ballyhoo came to Chicago in the summer of 1893, and predictably, the crowds swelled the fairgrounds to get a taste of it. Buffalo Bill's Wild West Show went through its usual bronco-busting, war-whooping routines. Visitors gawked at a giant map of the United States, fashioned entirely from pickles. Also on display were a huge telescope, destined for Yerkes Observatory; a long-distance telephone, connected with New York City; and oil paintings and porcelains by the thousands. A splendid time was guaranteed for all.

The excuse for the fuss was Chicago's "World's Columbian Exposition," held ostensibly to salute the four-hundredth anniversary of the discovery of America. More plausibly, the fair allowed proud Chicagoans to prove that they were more than hog-butchers to the world and that they could out-exposition any metropolis on the globe. Given the total attendance of 27 million people over six months, the city made its case.

As an adjunct to the fair, and to add further glory and respectability, the exposition convened several scholarly congresses, including a World's Congress of Historians and Historical Students. And so on July 12, the curious tourist had the opportunity (or misfortune) of straying away from the booming cannibal drums of the Midway Plaisance and into the Art Institute, where five eager historians waited to present the fruits of their labors.

Now, historical conferences are not the sort of events to be entered upon lightly under any circumstances, but the audience on this hot evening had to endure a particularly heavy bombardment from the podium. Five papers were read back-to-back without respite, ranging from a discussion of "English Popular Uprisings in the Middle Ages," to "Early Lead Mining in Illinois and Wisconsin." The hardy souls who weathered the first four presentations saw a young man in starched collar rise to present yet another set of conclusions, this time on "The Significance of the Frontier in American History."

The young man was Frederick Jackson Turner, a historian from the University of Wisconsin. Although none in the audience could have suspected it, his essay on the frontier eventually sparked four generations of scholarship and historical debate. The novelty of Turner's essay resulted not from his discovery of any previously unknown facts, but because he proposed a new theory, one that took old facts and placed them in an entirely different light. Known popularly as Turner's "frontier hypothesis," it is a theory that even today attracts staunch defenders.

THE SIGNIFICANCE OF THEORY

Turner's hypothesis is only one of many theoretical concepts that historians have advanced in order to unify and make sense of the chaotic past. Yet thus far, this book has avoided a direct discussion of the term *theory*. It has done so partly because many historians work with theory more intuitively than explicitly. Even those practitioners who attempt a certain theoretical consistency, such as Marxist or Freudian theorists, often argue among themselves over who is most accurately following in the master's footsteps. Yet despite theory's generally low profile and nebulous character, it remains an essential, inseparable part of the discipline.

At one level, theory can be defined simply as hypothesis. In this sense, it is the analysis that explains a relationship between two or more facts. During the Salem witch trials, "afflicted" townspeople acted in certain violent but consistent ways. Before historians can conclude that these acts constituted symptoms of neurotic behavior, they must have accepted the concept of conversion hysteria as a valid theoretical explanation. Note that the Salem records do not provide this interpretation; theory is indispensable to the explanation.

In a broader sense, theory can be defined as a body of theorems presenting a systematic view of an entire subject. We use the term this way when speaking of the "theory of wave mechanics" or a "germ theory of disease." Often, small-scale theoretical constructs are a part of a larger theoretical framework. Conversion hysteria is only one of many behavioral syndromes classified as neuroses; in turn, the concept of neurosis is only one part of the larger body of theory accepted by modern psychology. Physicists, chemists, and other natural scientists often use mathematic formulae to summarize their general theories, but among social scientists and humanists, theorems become less mathematic and more elastic. Even so, when historians discuss a "theory of democracy" or a "theory of economic growth," they are applying a set of coherent principles to the study of a particular situation.

Because historians study an event or period in its entirety, historical narrative usually incorporates many theories rather than just one. The historian of early Virginia will draw on theories of economic behavior (the development of joint stock companies as a means of capital formation), sociology (the rise of slavery as an institution of color), psychology (the causes of friction between white and black laboring classes), and so on. In this broadest sense historical theory encompasses the entire range of a historian's training, from competence in statistics to opinions on politics and philosophies of human nature. It is derived from formal education, reading, even from informal discussions with academic colleagues and friends.

It follows that theory in this wider sense—"grand theory," as it might be called—plays a crucial role in historical reconstruction. While small-scale theory is called on to explain specific puzzles (why didn't slavery become entrenched in Virginia before 1660?), grand theory is usually part of a historian's mental baggage *before* he immerses himself in a particular topic. It encourages historians to ask certain questions, and not to ask others; it tends to single out particular areas of investigation as worthy of testing, and to dismiss other areas of inquiry as either irrelevant or uninteresting. Thus anyone who ventures into the field of history —the lay reader as well as the professional researcher—needs to be aware of how grand theory exerts its pervasive influence. Nowhere in American history is this influence better illustrated than in Frederick Jackson Turner's venerable frontier hypothesis.

Turner began his Chicago lecture with a simple yet startling fact he had culled from the 1890 census. "Up to and including 1880, the country had a frontier of settlement," the census reported, "but at present the unsettled area has been so broken into by isolated bodies of settlement that there can hardly be said to be a frontier line." Turner seized upon this "event"—the passing of the frontier—as a "great historic moment." The reason for its importance seemed clear: "Up to our own day, American history has been in a large degree the history of the colonization of the Great West. The existence of an area of free land, its continuous recession, and the advance of American settlement westward, explain American development."

Turner's broad assertion—a manifesto, really—challenged on several counts the prevailing historical wisdom. Scholars of Turner's day had approached their subject with an Atlantic-coast bias. They viewed the East, and especially New England, as the true bearer of American culture; developments in the mid- and far-west were either ignored or treated sketchily. Turner, who had grown up in the rural setting of Portage, Wisconsin and taken his undergraduate degree at the University of Wisconsin, resented that attitude.

In addition, the reigning scholarship focused almost exclusively on political and constitutional developments. "History is past Politics and Politics present History" ran the slogan on the wall of the Johns Hopkins

Frederick Jackson Turner in 1893, the year he presented his thesis at Chicago's Columbian World Exposition; and the Johns Hopkins University seminar room for history students. At the head of the table is Professor Herbert Baxter Adams, who argued that American democratic institutions could be traced to British and European roots. "It is just as improbable that free local institutions should spring up without a germ along American shores as that English wheat should have grown there without planting," he wrote. Turner, for his part, resented the lack of interest in the West which he encountered at Hopkins. "Not a man I know here," he commented, "is either studying, or is hardly aware of the country behind the Alleghenies." (left, Collection of the University of Wisconsin-Madison Library; right, The Huntington Library, San Marino, California)

seminar room where Turner had taken his Ph.D. In contrast, young Turner strongly believed that this narrow political perspective neglected the broader contours of social, cultural, and economic history. Historians who took the trouble to examine those areas, he felt, would discover that the unique physical and cultural conditions of the frontier, and not eastern cities, had shaped American character.

The frontier's effect on American character had been recognized in a casual way by earlier observers, but Turner attempted a more systematic analysis. In doing so, he drew upon the scientific "grand theory" most prominent in his own day, Charles Darwin's theory of evolution. Where Darwin had proposed an explanation for evolution in the natural world, Turner suggested that America was an ideal laboratory for the study of cultural evolution. The American frontier, he argued, returned man to a primitive state of nature. With the trappings of civilization stripped away, the upward process of evolution was re-enacted. Dramatically, Turner recreated the sequence for his audience:

> The wilderness masters the colonist. It finds him a European in dress, industries, tools, modes of travel, and thought. It takes him from the railroad car and puts him in the birch canoe. It strips off the garments of civilization and arrays him in the hunting shirt and the moccasin. It puts him in the log cabin of the Cherokee and Iroquois and runs an Indian palisade around him. Before long he has gone to planting Indian corn and plowing with a sharp stick; he shouts the war cry and takes the scalp in orthodox Indian fashion. In short, at the frontier the environment is at first too strong for the man. He must accept the conditions which it furnishes, or perish, and so he fits himself into the Indian clearings and follows the Indian trails. Little by little he transforms the wilderness, but the outcome is not the old Europe. . . . The fact is that here is a new product that is American.

Turner suggested that the evolution from frontier primitive to civilized townsman occurred not just once but time and time again, as the frontier moved west. Each time, settlers shed a bit more of their European ways, each time a more distinctively American culture emerged. That was why the perspective of Eastern historians was so warped: they stubbornly traced American roots to English political institutions, or even worse, the medieval organization of the Germanic town. "The true point of view in the history of this nation is not the Atlantic coast," Turner insisted, "it is the Great West."

From this general formulation of the frontier's effects, Turner deduced several specific traits that the recurring evolutionary process produced. Chief among them were nationalism, independence, and democracy.

Nationalism, Turner argued, arose as the frontier broke down the geographic and cultural identities of the Atlantic coast: New England with its Yankees and the tidewater South with its aristocratic planters. The mixing and amalgamation of sections was most clearly demonstrated in the middle states, where both Yankees and Southerners migrated over the mountains, where Germans and other northern Europeans joined Englishmen in seeking free land. There a new culture developed, possessing "a solidarity of its own with national tendencies. . . . Interstate migration went steadily on—a process of cross-fertilization of ideas and institutions."*

The frontier also promoted independence, according to Turner. The first English settlements had depended on the mother country for their material goods, but as settlers pressed farther west, England found it difficult to supply the backcountry. Frontier towns became self-sufficient, and Eastern merchants increasingly provided westerners with American rather than English products. The economic system became more American, more independent.

Most important, suggested Turner, the individualism of the frontier promoted democracy and democratic institutions. "Complex society is precipitated by the wilderness into a kind of primitive organization based on the family," Turner argued. "The tendency is anti-social. It produces antipathy to control, and particularly to any direct control." Thus Westerners resented being taxed without being represented, whether by England and Parliament or by the Carolina coastal planters whom the backcountry Regulators fought. The frontier also broke down social distinctions that were so much a part of the East and Europe. Given the fluid society of the frontier, poor farmers or traders could and did become rich almost overnight. Social distinctions disappeared when placed against the greater necessity of simple survival.

Turner even argued that the West, with its vast supply of free land, encouraged democracy in the East. The frontier acted as a safety valve, he suggested, draining off potential sources of discontent before they disrupted society. "Whenever social conditions tended to crystallize in the East, whenever capital tended to press upon labor or political restraints to impede the freedom of the mass, there was this gate of escape

*Once again, note the Darwinian metaphor.

to the free conditions of the frontier. . . . Men would not accept inferior wages and a permanent position of social subordination when this promised land of freedom and equality was theirs for the taking."

The upshot of this levelling process was nothing less than a new American character. Turner waxed eloquent in his description of frontier traits:

> That coarseness and strength combined with acuteness and inquisitiveness; that practical, inventive turn of mind, quick to find expedients; that masterful grasp of material things, lacking in the artistic but powerful to effect great ends; that restless, nervous energy; that dominant individualism, working for good and for evil, and withal that buoyancy and exuberance which comes with freedom—these are the traits of the frontier, or traits called out elsewhere because of the existence of the frontier.

This was what Turner offered his Chicago listeners—not only "the American, this new man," as Hector St. John de Crevecoeur had called him in 1778—but also a systematic explanation of *how* the new American had come to be.

It would be proper etiquette here to scold Turner's Chicago audience for failing to recognize a masterpiece when they were read one. But in some ways it is easier to explain his listeners' inattention than account for the phenomenal acceptance of the frontier thesis by later historians. Undeniably, Turner's synthesis was fresh and creative. But as he himself admitted, the essay was a hypothesis in need of research and testing. Of this, Turner proved constitutionally incapable. Although he loved to burrow in the archives for days on end, he found writing an unbearable chore, especially when attempting a book-length effort.

Consequently, Turner published only magazine articles in the influential *Atlantic Monthly* and other journals; for the most part, they merely reiterated his thesis. The articles, along with numerous lectures and a flock of enthusiastic students, proved sufficient to make Turner's reputation, but they also made trouble. Publishers flocked to Wisconsin seeking books by the celebrated historian. Turner, with hopelessly misplaced optimism, signed contracts with four publishers to produce eight separate manuscripts. None ever saw the light of day. The single full-length book he completed appeared only through the frantic efforts of yet another editor, Albert Bushnell Hart, who was driven to wheedling, cajoling, and threatening in order to obtain the desired results. "It ought to be carved on my tombstone," Hart later remarked, "that I was the only man in the world that secured what might be classed an adequate volume from Turner."*

Why Turner's remarkable success? Certainly not because of his detailed research, which remained unpublished. Success was due to the attraction of his grand theory. Later critics have taken Turner to task for imprecision and vagueness, but these defects are compensated by an eloquence and magnificence of scale. "The United States lies like a huge page in the history of society," Turner would declaim, and then proceed to lay out history with a continental sweep. The lure of his hypothesis for historians was much like the lure of a unified field theory for natural scientists—a set of equations, as physicist Freeman Dyson has remarked, that would "account for everything that happens in nature. . . . a unifying principle that would either explain everything or explain nothing." In similar (though less galactic) fashion, Turner's theory captured historians' imaginations. "The existence of an area of free land, its continuous recession, and the advance of American settlement westward, explain American development." That is about as all-encompassing a proposal as a historian could desire!

The theory seemed encompassing, too, in its methods. Using the techniques of social science in historical research is so familiar today, we forget the novelty and brilliance of Turner's insistence on "unifying" the tools of research. Go beyond politics, he argued; relate geography, climate, economics, and social factors to the political story. Not only did he propose this, Turner also provided a key focus—the frontier—as the laboratory in which these variables could be studied. The fresh breeze of Turner's theory succeeded in overturning the traditional approaches of Eastern historians.

By the time Turner died in 1932, a tide of reaction had set in. Some critics pointed out that the frontier thesis severely minimized the democratic and cultural contributions of the English heritage. Others attacked Turner's vague definition of the "frontier." (Was it a geographical place? A type of population, such as trappers, herders, and pioneers? Or a process, wherein European traits were stripped off and American ones formed?) Other critics disputed the notion of the frontier as a "safety valve" for the East. Few European immigrants actually settled on the frontier; if anything, population statistics showed more farmers moving to the cities.

*Turner also reprinted some of his essays in *The Frontier in American History* (New York, 1920). The book Hart edited was *The Rise of the New West,* which appeared in 1906.

For our own purposes, however, it would be misleading to focus on these battles. Whether or not Turner was right, his theory dramatically influenced the investigations of other historians. To understand how, we need to take Turner's general propositions and see how he and others applied them to a specific topic.

An ideal subject for this task is the man whose name Turner himself shared—Andrew Jackson.* Jackson is one of those figures in history who, like Captain John Smith, seems always to be strutting about the stage just a bit larger than life. Furthermore, Jackson's wanderings took him straight into the most central themes of American history. "Old Hickory" led land-hungry pioneers into the southeastern United States, displacing Native Americans from their lands east of the Mississippi, expelling the Spanish from Florida, and repelling the English from New Orleans. As President, he launched the war against the "monster" Bank of the United States, placing himself at the center of the perennial American debate over the role of economic power in a democracy. Above all, he came to be seen as the political champion of the common people, his backwoods origins and forceful personality epitomizing the style of the new American democracy. Here is a man whose career makes it impossible to avoid dealing with the large questions grand theory will suggest.

How, then, did Turner's frontier hypothesis shape historians' perception of Jackson? What features of his career did it encourage them to examine?

JACKSON: A FRONTIER DEMOCRAT (TARNISHED)

For Frederick Turner, Andrew Jackson was not merely "one of the favorites of the west," he was "the west itself." Turner meant by that rhetorical proclamation that Jackson not only spoke for the West, his whole life followed precisely that pattern of frontier evolution wherein eastern culture was stripped bare and replaced by the "contentious, nationalistic democracy of the interior."

Jackson's Scotch-Irish parents had joined the stream of eighteenth-century immigrants who landed in Pennsylvania, pushed westward until they bumped up against the Appalachians, and then filtered southwest

---

*The bond of names is more than coincidental. Frederick Jackson Turner's father, Andrew Jackson Turner, was born in 1832 and named in honor of the President re-elected that year.

into the Carolina backcountry. This was the process of "mixing and amalgamation" that Turner outlined in his essay. Turner had also shown how the frontier stripped away higher social organizations, leaving only the family as a sustaining bond. Andrew Jackson was denied even that society. His father died before Jackson's birth, his only two brothers and his mother died during the Revolution. At the age of seventeen, Andrew left Waxhaw, his boyhood home, never to return again. In effect, he was a man without a family—but not, as Turner saw it, a man without a backcountry.

Jackson first moved to the town of Salisbury, North Carolina, reading law by day and, with the help of similarly high-spirited young friends, raising hell by night. Brawling in barrooms, sporting with young ladies, moving outhouses in the hours well past midnight—such activities gave Jackson a reputation as "the most roaring, game-cocking, horse-racing, card-playing, mischievous fellow that ever lived in Salisbury," according to one resident.

In 1768 the footloose Jackson grabbed the opportunity to become public prosecutor for the Western district of North Carolina, a region that then stretched all the way to the Mississippi. There, in the frontier lands that now comprise Tennessee, Jackson hoped to make his reputation. It was still primitive land. Two hundred miles of wilderness separated eastern Tennessee settlements around Jonesborough from the western Cumberland Valley and Nashville. Travel between the two areas invited clashes with Indians. Into this life Jackson plunged with ambitious enthusiasm. Once settled in Nashville, he handled between a quarter and a half of all court cases in his home county during the first few years of his arrival. On top of that, he made the hazardous journey to Jonesborough three times a year to pursue cases there.

Jackson dispensed justice with the kind of "coarseness and strength" Turner associated with the frontier personality. When one enraged defendant stepped on prosecutor Jackson's toe to indicate his displeasure, Jackson calmly cold-cocked the offender with a stick of wood. On another occasion, when Jackson had been appointed superior court judge in the newly created state of Tennessee, he stalked off the bench to summon a defendant before the court when no one else dared, including the sheriff and posse. The man in question, one Russell Bean, had threatened to shoot the "first skunk that came within ten feet," but when Jackson came roaring out of the courthouse, Bean pulled in his horns. "I looked him in the eye, and I saw shoot," said Bean, "and there wasn't shoot in nary other eye in the crowd; and so I says to myself, says I, hoss, it's about time to sing small, and so I did."

Jackson the frontiersman: Russell Bean surrenders to Justice Jackson, as depicted in an 1817 biography. Wrote Turner, "If Henry Clay was one of the favorites of the west, Andrew Jackson was the west itself. . . . the very personification of the contentious, nationalistic democracy of the interior. . . . In 1788, with a caravan of emigrants, Jackson crossed the Alleghenies to Nashville, Tennessee, then an outpost of settlement still exposed to the incursions of Indians. During the first seven or eight years of his residence he was public prosecutor—an office that called for nerve and decision, rather than legal acumen, in that turbulent country."

All in all, Jackson seemed a perfect fit for frontier democrat—a man who indeed "was the west itself." Turner described in characteristic terms Jackson's election to the House of Representatives in 1796:

The appearance of this frontiersman on the floor of Congress was an omen full of significance. He reached Philadelphia at the close of Washington's administration, having ridden on horseback nearly eight hundred miles to his destination. Gallatin (himself a western Pennsylvanian) afterwards graphically described Jackson, as he entered the halls of Congress, as "a tall, lank, uncouth-looking personage, with long locks of hair hanging over his face, and a cue down his back tied in an eel-skin; his dress singular, his manners and deportment those of a rough backwoodsman." Jefferson

afterwards testified to Webster: "His passions are terrible. When I was
President of the Senate, he was a Senator, and he could never speak, on
account of the rashness of his feelings. I have seen him attempt it repeatedly, and as often choke with rage." At length the frontier, in the person
of its leader, had found a place in the government. This six-foot backwoodsman, angular, lantern-jawed, and thin, with blue eyes that blazed on
occasion; this choleric, impetuous, Scotch-Irish leader of men; this expert
duellist and ready fighter; this embodiment of the contentious, vehement,
personal west, was in politics to stay.

This was Turner at his rhetorical best, marshalling all the striking personal details that supported his theory. But he was not writing a full-
length biography and so confined his discussion of Jackson either to a few
paragraphs of detail or to the traditional rousing generalities.

One of Turner's graduate students went further. Thomas Perkins
Abernethy studied at Harvard during the period when the university
had lured Turner east from his home ground at the University of Wisconsin. Abernethy believed that to test the frontier hypothesis adequately, it ought to be examined on a local level, in more detail. In this
respect, he felt, previous historians had not been scientific enough. "Science is studied by the examination of specimens, and general truths are
discovered through the investigations of typical forms," he asserted. In
contrast, "history has been studied mainly by national units, and the field
is too broad to allow of minute examination." But Tennessee provided
a perfect "specimen" of the western state. It broke away from its parent,
North Carolina, during its frontier days; it was the first area of the nation
to undergo territorial status; and from its backwoods settlements came
Andrew Jackson himself, the embodiment of western democracy. Why
not trace the leavening effects of the frontier within this narrower com-
pass? Abernethy set out to do just that in his book, *From Frontier to
Plantation in Tennessee.*

Obviously, he had learned his mentor's techniques well. Turner encouraged students to trace the effects of geography and environment on
politics. Abernethy perceived that Tennessee's geography divided it into
three distinct agricultural regions, providing a "rare opportunity to
study the political effects of these several types of agricultural economy."
Turner emphasized the role of free land as a crucial factor in the west.
Abernethy agreed that land was "the chief form of wealth in the United
States in its early years" and paid particular attention to the political
controversies over Tennessee's vast tracts of land. Always, he was determined to look beyond the surface of the political arena to the underlying
economic and geographic considerations.

These were Turner's techniques, all right, but the results produced anything but Turner's conclusions. *From Frontier to Plantation* is dedicated to Frederick Jackson Turner, but the book directly refutes Turner's optimistic version of western history.

As Abernethy began unravelling the tangled web of Carolina-Tennessee politics, he discovered that Americans interested in western free land included more than pioneer squatters and yeoman farmers of the "interior democracy." Prosperous speculators who preferred the comforts of the civilized east perceived equally well that land which stood forested and uncultivated would skyrocket in value once settlers poured over the Appalachians in search of homesteads.

The scramble for land revealed itself in the strange and contradictory doings of the North Carolina legislature. During the Revolutionary War, inflation had plagued the state, largely because the legislature had continuously issued its own paper money when short of funds. The value of this paper money plummeted to a fraction of its original face value. After the war, the legislature retrenched by proclaiming that all debtors would have to repay their debts in specie (i.e., gold or silver coins) or its equivalent in paper. If a person owed £10 and the going rate set £400 in paper notes as equal to £1 in actual silver, debtors who repaid using paper money would owe £4000. In effect, the legislature was repudiating its paper currency and saying that only specie would be an acceptable medium of exchange.

This made sense if the legislature was trying to put the state's finances on a stable footing. But Abernethy noticed that in the same session, the legislature turned around and issued a *new* run of paper money—printing up a hundred thousand dollars. Why issue more paper money when you've just done your best to get rid of the older stuff?

Abernethy also noticed that during the same legislative session, land offices were opened up to sell some of North Carolina's western lands. The state sold these lands only under certain conditions. The claimant had to go out into the woods and mark the preliminary boundaries of his claim. Then he had to come back and enter the claim at a designated land office. Finally, a government surveyor would survey the lot, submit his report to the Secretary of State for the governor's authentication, and enter it in the county register.

And how were these lands to be paid for? Well, gold or silver was permissible, of course, but so was *the state's paper money*—at rates specified by the legislature.

The situation hardly confirmed Turner's conception of the frontier, Abernethy concluded. First, who ended up being able to buy the new land? Not the squatter or yeoman farmer, certainly—few of them could fulfill the requirements of marking out land, returning east to register it, having it officially surveyed, and entering it. Instead, land speculators in the east, including state legislators, stepped in to make a killing. The career of William Blount, one of the most successful of speculators, illustrated the process at work. As a state legislator, Blount had led in passing the land legislation; at the same time, he paid James Robertson, a Tennessee pioneer, to go west and mark out vast tracts of land. Blount, for his part, registered the claim and paid for the land.

Sometimes the money that paid for the land was the old paper currency, bought up for a fraction of its original price from poorer folk who had no means of claiming their own land. The new paper money could also be used at face value to pay for the lands. Was it coincidence only that Blount had been the legislator proposing the new issue of paper money? Abernethy thought not.

Instead of confirming Turner's version of a hardy democracy, then, Abernethy painted a picture of "free" Tennessee lands providing fortunes for already-powerful men. Blount used "the entire Southwest [as] his hunting ground and he stuffed his pockets with the profits of his speculations in land. In the maw of his incredible ambition—or greed— there originated land grabs involving thousands of choice acres." And Blount was only one of many across the country. "In those days," Abernethy concluded, "America was run largely by speculators in real estate."

It was into this free-for-all country that Andrew Jackson marched in 1788, but Abernethy's new frame of reference placed his career in a different light. Compare Turner's description of Jackson's "pioneer" ride to Philadelphia with Abernethy's version of Jackson's horseback arrival in Tennessee. "Tradition has it," reported Abernethy, that Jackson

> arrived at Jonesboro . . . riding a fine horse and leading another mount, with saddle-bags, gun, pistols, and fox-hounds. This was elaborate equipment for a struggling young lawyer, and within the year he increased it by the purchase of a slave girl. . . . Jackson still found time to engage in his favorite sport of horse-racing, and he fought a bloodless duel with Waightstill Avery, then the most famous lawyer in western North Carolina. All this makes it clear that the young man had set himself up in the world as a "gentleman." Frontiersmen normally fought with their fists rather than with pistols, and prided themselves more upon physical prowess, than upon manners. Though commonly looked upon as a typical Westerner, Jackson was ever an aristocrat at heart.

Jackson the gentleman: Thomas Abernethy argued that the history of Jackson's Tennessee demonstrated how "the wealthy rose to the top of affairs even on the frontier, and combined through their influence and common interests to control economic legislation. From time to time they found it necessary to make some obvious concession to democracy, such as broadening the suffrage or lowering the qualifications for office. But, while throwing out such sops with one hand, they managed to keep well in the other the more obscure field of economic legislation." The portrait of Jackson is by Thomas Sully.

Jackson cemented his ties with the upper layers of society in more substantial ways. Turner had noted Jackson's practice as a "public prosecutor—an office that called for nerve and decision, rather than legal acumen, in that turbulent country." What frontier lawyering also called for, which Turner neglected to mention, was a knack for collecting debts, since Jackson most often represented creditors intent on recovering loans. During his first month of legal practice, he issued some seventy writs to delinquent debtors. This energetic career soon came to the notice of none other than William Blount, who had by this time gotten himself appointed governor of the newly created Tennessee territory. He and Jackson became close political allies.

Jackson too had an eye for speculating, and it almost ruined him. Like Blount, he had cashed in on Tennessee's lands, buying 50,000 acres on the site of the future city of Memphis. In 1795 Jackson took his first horseback ride to Philadelphia, a year before the one Turner eloquently described, in order to sell the Memphis land at a profit. Few Philadelphians wanted to buy, but Jackson finally closed a deal with David Allison, another of Blount's cronies. Allison couldn't pay in cash, so he gave Jackson promissory notes. Jackson, in turn, used the notes to pay for goods to stock a trading post he wanted to open in Tennessee.

Scant months after Jackson returned home, he learned that David Allison had gone bankrupt. Even worse, since Jackson had signed Allison's promissory notes, Allison's creditors were now after Jackson. "We take this early opportunity to make known to you that *we* have little or no expectations of getting paid from him," they wrote, "and that we shall have to get our money from you." Suddenly Jackson found himself in the middle of a financial nightmare. He was, he admitted, "placed in the Dam'st situation ever a man was placed in."

To get himself out, he was forced to speculate even more heavily. Buy a parcel of land here, sell it there. Cash in his trading post, make a small profit, invest it in more land. Exchange the new land for another buyer's promissory note. And so on. Not until 1824 did he settle the final claims in the tangle. Abernethy sketched these financial transactions in a chapter entitled "Andrew Jackson as a Land Speculator." Clearly, he believed that Jackson's horseback rides on behalf of real estate deserved more emphasis than any romantic notions of a galloping frontier democrat.

Despite such a devastating attack on the frontier thesis, Abernethy's admiration for Turner was genuine, no doubt because he recognized how much the thesis had guided his research. It is easy to conclude that the value of a theory rests solely on its truth. Yet even if Turner's hypothesis erred on many points, it provided a focus that prodded Abernethy to investigate important historical questions—the implications of western land policy, the effect of environment on character, the social and geographical foundations of democracy. All these topics had been slighted by historians.

Theory, in other words, is often as important for the questions it raises as for the answers it provides. In this sense it performs the same function in the natural sciences. Thomas Kuhn, a historian of science, has demonstrated just how indispensable an older scientific theory is in pointing the way to the theory that replaces it. As the old theory is tested, attention is naturally focused on problem areas—places where the results are not what the old theory predicts. The new theory emerges, Kuhn pointed out, "only for the man who, knowing *with precision* what he should expect, is able to recognize that something has gone wrong." Abernethy was able to discern that something had "gone wrong" in Tennessee politics, but only because Turner's hypothesis had shown him what questions needed to be asked and where to look for answers.

JACKSON: WORKINGMAN'S FRIEND

Theory, then, can actually sharpen a historian's vision by limiting it—aiding the process of selection by zeroing in on important issues and data. It stands to reason, however, that trade-offs are made in this game. If a theory focuses attention on certain questions, it necessarily also causes a historian to ignore other facts, trends, or themes. Theory can limit in a negative as well as a positive sense.

Abernethy's disagreement with Turner illustrates this problem. Although the two historians reached diametrically opposed conclusions about Andrew Jackson, they carried on the whole debate within the framework of Turner's thesis. Did Jackson embody the democratic, individualistic West? Yes, argued Turner. No, countered Abernethy. Yet both men accepted the premise suggested by Turner's thesis, that the influence of the West was the crucial issue to examine.

That might serve well enough for a study limited to Tennessee politics, but Jackson went on to achieve national fame at New Orleans and was elected to the Presidency in 1828. He triumphed in all the southern coastal states, in Pennsylvania, and also received a majority of New York's electoral votes. In New York too he cemented an alliance with Martin Van Buren, the sophisticated eastern leader of the "Albany Regency" political faction.

Such facts call attention to something that Turner's frame of reference overlooked. As a national president, Jackson made friends in the East as well as the West, in cities as well as in the country. Historian Arthur Schlesinger, Jr., believing that Abernethy as well as Turner overemphasized the importance of Jackson's western roots, determined to examine the eastern sources of Jackson's democratic coalition. "A judgment on the character of Jackson's democracy must be founded on an examination of what Jackson did as President," he argued, "and on nothing else; certainly not on an extrapolation made on the basis of his career before he became President." The result of Schlesinger's research was *The Age of Jackson* (1945), a sweeping study that highlighted the influence of eastern, urban laboring classes on Jacksonian democracy.

In part, Schlesinger's theoretical approach had been the natural consequence of his upbringing. He spent his childhood within the civilized environs of Cambridge, Massachusetts, where his father, Arthur Meier Schlesinger, Sr., held a chair in history at Harvard. Like Turner, Schlesinger Sr. preferred the wider horizons of social and cultural history over traditional political history. Unlike Turner, he emphasized the role of urban society and culture in American life. His article, "The City in American History," sparked a generation of scholarship on peculiarly urban problems such as industrial labor and immigration. The article, Schlesinger later suggested generously, "did not seek to destroy the frontier theory but to substitute a balanced view: an appreciation of both country and city in the rise of American civilization." Nevertheless, Schlesinger Sr.'s interest clearly lay with the cities.

The younger Schlesinger admired his father—so much so that at the age of fifteen he changed his name from Arthur Bancroft Schlesinger to Arthur Meier Schlesinger, Jr. More significant, the son shared the same scholarly dispositions. After schooling at the prestigious Phillips Exeter Academy, Arthur completed a brilliant undergraduate and graduate career at Harvard.* It was out of this intellectual training that Schlesinger wrote his book.

The Age of Jackson also reflected a set of attitudes and emphases popular in the 1930s that distanced Schlesinger from the Progressive outlook Turner had shared at the turn of the century. The thirties saw the country plunged into a depression so severe that it shook many Americans' faith

*Like many midwesterners, Schlesinger Sr. believed wholeheartedly in the virtues of public education. But he felt compelled to send Arthur Jr. to Exeter after discovering that his tenth-grade public school teacher taught that "the inhabitants of Albania were called Albinos because of their white hair and pink eyes."

in the traditional economic system. Theories of class struggle, of conflict between capital and labor, became popular in scholarly circles. As an avid supporter of Franklin Roosevelt, Schlesinger by no means accepted the doctrines of the communist left, but he did believe that class conflict played a greater role in American history than the sectional disputes that Turner had emphasized. Significantly, Schlesinger used a quotation from George Bancroft, a radical Jacksonian from New England, as the super-scription for his book. It affirmed the importance of class struggle but still embraced the liberal's hope for a nonviolent resolution of conflict:

> The feud between the capitalist and laborer, the house of Have and the house of Want, is as old as social union, and can never be entirely quieted; but he who will act with moderation, prefer fact to theory, and remember that every thing in this world is relative and not absolute, will see that the violence of the contest may be stilled.

Given Schlesinger's background and temperament, his research focused on substantially different aspects of Jackson's career. It portrayed Old Hickory as a natural leader who, though he came from the West, championed the cause of laborers in all walks of life—city "mechanicks" as well as yeoman farmers. Jackson's chief political task, argued Schlesinger, was "to control the power of the capitalist groups, mainly Eastern, for the benefit of the noncapitalist groups, farmers and laboring men, East, West, and South." Schlesinger made his opposition to Turner abundantly clear:

> The basic Jacksonian ideas came naturally enough from the East, which best understood the nature of business power and reacted most sharply against it. The legend that Jacksonian democracy was the explosion of the frontier, lifting into the government some violent men filled with rustic prejudices against big business does not explain the facts, which were somewhat more complex. Jacksonian democracy was rather a second American phase of that enduring struggle between the business commu-nity and the rest of society which is the guarantee of freedom in a liberal capitalist state.

Consequently, much of *The Age of Jackson* is devoted to people the Turner school neglected entirely: the leaders of workingmen's parties, the broader labor movement, and the efforts of Democratic politicians to bring them within the orbit of Jackson's party. Abernethy's treatment of Jackson as land speculator is replaced by attention to Jackson's vigor-

Jackson, champion of the working people: "The specific problem was to control the power of the capitalistic groups, mainly Eastern, for the benefit of the noncapitalist groups, farmers and laboring men, East, West and South," wrote Arthur Schlesinger, Jr. "The basic Jacksonian ideas came naturally enough from the East, which best understood the nature of business power and reacted most sharply against it. The legend that Jacksonian democracy was the explosion of the frontier, lifting into the government some violent men filled with rustic prejudices against big business, does not explain the facts. . . ." Here, 'King Mob' goes to work on a giant cheese at one of Jackson's public receptions. The strong odor of the cheese lingered in the White House for months.

ous war on the Second Bank of the United States, where Democratic leaders are shown forging an alliance with labor. "During the Bank War," Schlesinger concluded, "laboring men began slowly to turn to Jackson as their leader, and his party as their party."

Like Turner, Schlesinger came under critical fire. Other historians have argued that much of Jackson's so-called labor support was actually

middle- or even upper-class leaders who hoped to channel worker sentiments for their own purposes. At the same time, many in the real laboring classes refused to support Jackson. But again—what is important for
our present purposes is to notice how Schlesinger's general concerns
shaped his research. It is not coincidental that Jackson's celebrated
kitchen cabinet, in Schlesinger's retelling, bears a marked resemblance
to Franklin Roosevelt's "brain trusters." It is not coincidental that Jackson attacks the "monster Bank" for wreaking economic havoc much the
way that FDR inveighed against the "economic royalists" of the Depression era. Nor is it coincidental that *The Age of Jackson* was followed, in
1957, by *The Age of Roosevelt.* Schlesinger may have displayed his political
and economic philosophy more conspicuously than most historians, but
no scholar can escape bringing some theoretical framework to his or her
research. One way or another, theory inevitably limits and focuses the
historian's perspective.

JACKSON: THE GREAT WHITE FATHER

Schlesinger's urban orientation encouraged him to shift focus away from
the "old facts" that Turner's theory emphasized, instead dealing with an
entirely different area of research. But theory can produce new results
simply by providing a means of viewing the "old facts" in a new light.
Historian Michael Rogin's biography of Andrew Jackson, *Fathers and
Children,* illustrates this process at work. Rogin's research covered
ground already well-examined by Turner and other historians. In fact,
Fathers and Children reiterated some of Turner's major assumptions and
metaphors. It acknowledged that the conditions of the frontier gave
American culture its unique stamp. "The new American world undermined the authority provided by history, tradition, family connection,
and the other ties of old European existence," Rogin agreed. He also
accepted Turner's metaphor of evolutionary development, that "America was continually beginning again on the frontier." Such assertions, he
pointed out, were commonplace even during the period of westward
expansion.

Yet Rogin drew radically different conclusions from Turner's postu-
lates, primarily because his own theoretical training was so much at
variance with Turner's progressive philosophy. For one, Rogin did his
research during the late 1960s and early 1970s, when American society
had become increasingly conscious of minority groups and cross-cultural
conflict. Turner's original frontier thesis largely ignored Native Ameri-

can cultures, by implicitly denying that any significant "culture" existed. For Turner, Indian society was no society, the bottom rung on the cultural ladder, where the frontiersman at first found himself pitched. ("Before long . . . he shouts the war cry and takes the scalp in orthodox Indian fashion. . . .")

This lack of interest in the Indian led to a curious result, Rogin noted. Undeniably, the growth of the United States from thirteen Atlantic colonies to a continental empire constituted a major theme in American history. Yet historians largely ignored the policies of Indian removal needed to accomplish that goal—policies which Andrew Jackson supported and vigorously executed. Historians, he argued, "have failed to place Indians at the center of Jackson's life. They have interpreted the Age of Jackson from every perspective but Indian destruction, the one from which it actually developed historically."

Rogin wished not only to tell the story of Indian removal but also to probe the psychological motives that impelled Americans to destroy Indian culture so thoroughly. To do so, he relied on Freudian psychological theory, a second theoretical perspective that distanced him from Turner. Rogin admitted that many readers would consider Freudian analysis unnecessary. "The sources of white expansion onto Indian land . . . seem straightforward," he granted. "Surely land hunger and the building of a national empire provided the thrust." But Rogin argued that the psychological dimensions of Indian removal were too significant to be ignored.

Indeed, the language with which nineteenth-century Americans described Indians and white–Indian relationships has remarkable psychological overtones. Paternal and familial metaphors were used often. Treaty negotiators constantly urged Indians to make peace with their "white father," the President of the United States. If friendly tribes did not conclude treaties, Jackson once warned, "We may then be under the necessity of raising the hatchet against our own friends and brothers. Your father the President wishes to avoid this unnatural state of things."* White American leaders were seen as the "fathers" of civilization, Indians as "untutored children of the forest." Remarked editor Horace Greeley, "The Indians are children. . . . Any band of schoolboys from ten to fifteen years of age, are quite as capable of ruling their appetites. . . ." Historian Francis Parkman, who journeyed westward along the Oregon Trail in 1846, referred to the Indian as an "irreclaima-

*At the time, in 1818, Jackson was negotiating the cession of land from the Choctaw Indians on behalf of the Monroe administration.

ble son of the wilderness, the child who will not be weaned from the breast of his rugged mother."

Why had historians remained "systematically deaf" to such familial rhetoric, with its imagery of children "weaned from the breast" and talk of an "unnatural state of things" among white–Indian "family" relations? Rogin believed that such deafness resulted from a theoretical block. "Lacking a theory which sensitized them to such a vocabulary and helped them interpret it, they could not hear what was being said. Let us, to begin with, take seriously the words of those who made our Indian policy."

Because Jackson was so prominent in shaping Indian policy, and because he embodied "in extreme form the central cultural tensions of his time," Rogin began with a close examination of Andrew's childhood development. Like Turner, he made much of the independence forced on the young boy by his early loss of family. But Rogin doubted whether the loss fostered a genuine psychological maturity. Psychoanalytic theory has stressed the rage and resentment an infant feels when being separated from his mother and from the comfort and security of suckling at her breast. Later childhood or even adult shocks, it suggests, may sometimes revive the fears and rages arising from maternal separation. Although no clinical evidence survived to connect Jackson's mature temperamental outbursts with his childhood experiences, Rogin noted certain suggestive facts: "Jackson was a posthumous child; did his father's death affect his mother during his infancy? Problems in infancy, involving feeding, weaning, or holding the child, often intensify infantile rage and accentuate later difficulties in the struggle of the child to break securely free of the mother." Like Turner, Rogin quoted Jefferson's description of Jackson "choking with rage" on the Senate floor, and noted that according to eyewitnesses, Jackson often slobbered and spoke incoherently when excited or angry. "Jackson's slobbering," argued Rogin, "suggests early problems with speech, mouth, and aggression. Speech difficulties often indicate a problematic oral relationship."

Even if Jackson's adult rages reflected the resentment felt by his childhood separation experiences, he certainly did not allow childhood fantasies to dominate his adult life. Indeed, Jackson's political success came from mastering his rages and using them for his own political purposes. He successfully "externalized inner enemies, and battled them in the world." In doing so, Rogin argued, Jackson reflected American culture of the period. For Jackson's "externalized" enemies were also the enemies of other Americans of the backcountry: the native "untutored children of the forest."

Indian society and behavior contrasted strikingly with "civilized" life-styles, as Americans repeatedly perceived. To European-Americans, Rogin argued, Indians appeared playful, violent, improvident, wild, and in harmony with nature. American society exalted contrasting virtues: discipline, work, the acquisition of private property. Such ascetic values "generated a forbidden nostalgia for childhood," Rogin believed, "—for the nurturing, blissful, primitively violent connection to nature that white Americans had to leave behind." The result was envy and rage; envy that Indian "children" were so apparently free to indulge every childish whim; and rage, in an attempt to prove white independence from childhood by mastering and destroying any evidence of such infantile behavior. Thus white Americans were impelled to break the Indian's tie with nature, "literally by uprooting him, figuratively by civilizing him, finally by killing him."

For Rogin, Jackson's career demonstrated that such conflicting feelings were resolved by developing a paternalistic attitude toward "childlike" adversaries. He argued that since Jackson had grown up without a father, he compensated in adult life by stressing his own role as "father" to Indians. Perhaps equally significant, Jackson was denied the pleasure of becoming a natural father in adult life; he and his wife Rachael had no children. Here too, the couple compensated, raising a dozen infants, most of them orphaned relatives of the Jacksons' families.

Among the adopted children was a three-year-old Indian boy, Lincoya, encountered during the Creek war. The boy had been found "pressed to the bosom of its lifeless mother," explained one of Jackson's friends, and because the rest of the baby's family were dead, the Creek women meant to kill Lincoya. But Jackson intervened, in part because he recognized the similarity to his own childhood: "he[,] as to his relations—is so much like myself I feel an unusual sympathy to him. . . ." Both fatherless and childless, then, Jackson adopted a particularly strong paternal outlook. By demanding that Indian "children" obey their "white fathers" in their own best interests, he and similarly minded Americans "indulged primitive longings to wield total power," concluded Rogin. "They sought to regain the primal infant–mother connection from a position of domination instead of dependence."

For Jackson, this paternalism extended beyond Indians. Rogin argued that as president, Jackson applied the same emotional relationship to his conception of democracy. "Jackson had successfully asserted paternity . . . over Indians. Might not fatherhood now also extend its protecting arm to the generality of poor, weak, and virtuous? Might it not reform the civilian world?" Jackson approached the presidency acutely aware of the burden imposed on him by political paternity—the heritage of the Founding Fathers. He recognized that his generation lived in the shadow, to use his own words, "of the illustrious actions of their fathers in the war of the revolution." The younger generation had to demonstrate that they were not "a degenerate race . . . unworthy of the blessings which the blood of so many thousand heroes has purchased for them." Thus Jackson strove to identify himself with the "Fathers"— indeed, adopted them as his own—while identifying nearly everyone else as his children. He became champion of the downtrodden because his primary relation to the electorate was as a father to his sons.

Jackson, the "effectionate parent": "Pressed with mutiny and sedition of the volunteer infantry—To suppress it, having been compelled to arrange my artillery, against them, whom I once loved like a father loves his children. . . . I felt the pangs of an effectionate parent, compelled from duty to chastise his child —to prevent him from destruction & disgrace and it being his duty he Shrunk not from it—even when he knew death might ensue." So Jackson wrote to his wife, describing how he singlehandedly quelled a mutiny of Tennessee troops during his campaign against the Creek nation.

Viewed through Rogin's theoretical framework, many of Jackson's well-known actions as President took on new significance. When South Carolina attempted to nullify the tariff law passed by Congress, Jackson demanded obedience—just as a stern father might command his unruly children. In a draft of his nullification speech, he addressed South Carolinians in distinctly paternal tones: "Seduced as you have been my fellow Countrymen by the delusive theories and misrepresentation of ambitious, deluded and designing men, I call upon you, in the language of truth and with the feelings of a father to retrace your steps."

Similarly, when making war on the Bank of the United States, Jackson viewed himself paternally. "It is the natural instinct of wealth and power to reach after new acquisitions," he lectured his Cabinet. "It was to arrest them that our Fathers perilled their lives." As heir to "the Fathers," Jackson clearly implied, he too might peril his life. "The bank, Mr. Van Buren, is trying to kill me," he once told his ally, *"but I will kill it."* As one of his contemporaries acutely observed, Old Hickory was much like George Washington: "Providence denied him children, that he might be the father of his country."

Rogin freely admitted that for many readers his psychoanalytical approach to Jackson, Indian removal, and the new Democracy "must seem bizarre." Indeed, many professional historians, let alone lay readers, find the use of such analytical concepts as "infant rage" and "problematic oral relationships" inappropriate or even ludicrous. The use of psychiatric theory by historians certainly deserves closer scrutiny, and we will return to the topic in a later chapter. For the present, however, the merits of the case concern us less than the undeniable effect theory has had in shaping historical research. Rogin's sensitivity to familial language and his interest in the psychological dynamics of childhood have led him to evaluate old evidence in a new light. However debatable his conclusions, he has rightly perceived that once sensitized to familial language, inquiring historians will find in nineteenth-century sources far more references than they expected to "white fathers," Revolutionary "fathers," Indian "sons," the "mother country" England—even "Mother Bank," as one pro-Jacksonian cartoon noted. Once again, theory has helped to focus on a previously unperceived problem.

After such a procession of grand historical theories, what may be said of the "real" Andrew Jackson? Skeptics may be tempted to conclude that there was not one, but four Old Hickories roaming the landscape of Jacksonian America—Jackson the frontier democrat; Jackson the aristocratic planter and speculator; Jackson, friend of labor; and Jackson, paternal ruler of both Indians and common folk. The use of historical theory seems to have led the reader into a kind of boggy historical relativism, where there is no real Jackson, only men conjured up to fit the formula of particular historical theories.

But that viewpoint is overly pessimistic. It arises from the necessary emphasis of this chapter, where our concern has been to point out the general effects of grand theory rather than to evaluate the merits of each case. Theory, we have stressed, provides a vantage point which directs a researcher's attention to significant areas of inquiry. But the initial theorizing is only the beginning. Theories can be and are continually tested. Sometimes old theories are thrown out, replaced by new ones. In such fashion did Copernicus replace Ptolemy. But some theories stand up to testing, or are merely refined to fit the facts more closely. In yet other instances, old theories are incorporated into more-encompassing frameworks. Newtonian mechanics are still as valid as ever for the everyday world, but they have been found to be only a special case of the broader theories of relativity proposed by Einstein. And of course, Einstein continued to search for ways to incorporate his special theories of relativity into a more general, unified field theory.

Similarly we may argue that, far from having four different Jacksons roaming the historical landscape, we are seeing various aspects of Jackson's personality and career which need to be incorporated into a more comprehensive framework. It is the old tale of the blind men describing the different parts of an elephant: the elephant is real enough, but the descriptions are partial and fragmentary. Frederick Jackson Turner was writing about a nebulous Jacksonian style—indeed, one may as well come out with it—"democracy" and "individualism" were, for Turner, little more than styles. Abernethy, on the other hand, was looking at the concrete material interests and class alliances that Jackson developed during his Tennessee career, with almost no attention to the presidential years. Schlesinger did precisely the opposite: picked up Jackson's story only after 1824, and in the end was more concerned with the Jacksonian movement than with its nominal leader. Finally, enter Rogin, who examined Jackson's career from childhood to old age, in Tennessee and in Washington, but whose real subject was the peculiar psychological intensity, even ferocity, that Jackson brought to his experience.

Would it be possible to incorporate these various viewpoints within a larger framework? One can imagine the outlines of such a general construct. Fatherless, poor boys in a highly mobile frontier setting are driven by the potential "democracy" and "individualism" inherent in such settings to identify themselves as much as possible with elites—to set themselves apart from the common masses. But given the pervasive rhetoric of equality and democracy, they do so in a way that is uneasy, and always vulnerable to some sudden exposure of their rootless, lower-class origins. Their attitudes toward wealth and authority are ambivalent. They will seek both. But they will need constantly to have their status and power ratified by the common consent of all—their neighbors, at first, but if their careers take a political shape, by every possible constituency: farmers, soldiers, eastern workingmen—even those "children of the forest," Indians.

A unified field theory for Jacksonian America? Perhaps the outlines are there, but the task must be left to some future Turner of the discipline. What remains clear is that, however much particular theories will continue to be revised or rejected, theory itself will accompany historians always. Without it, researchers cannot begin to select from among an infinite number of facts; they cannot separate the important from the incidental; they cannot focus on a manageable problem. Albert Einstein put the proposition succinctly. "It is the theory," he concluded, "which decides what we can observe."

Additional Reading

The reader who doubts our assertion that the theories of Turner, Schlesinger, and others have been evaluated and analyzed, need only spend an afternoon in the card catalog of any major library. A recent bibliographical essay on Jacksonian America, listing only the "more important" books and articles, ran to over 700 entries.

Andrew Jackson himself may be most easily approached through several of many biographies (most of which are rather unimaginatively titled, *The Life of Andrew Jackson*). Earliest is John Reid and John Henry Eaton, *The Life of Andrew Jackson* (Philadelphia, 1817; reissued, 1974). The volume has much authentic material for Jackson's early years, but beware later "campaign" editions of 1824 and 1828, to which chunks of political puffery were added. One of the more critical biographies was done by James Parton, *The Life of Andrew Jackson,* 3 vols. (Boston, 1866); it includes the recollections of Jackson's boyhood neighbors, whom Parton interviewed many years later. Marquis James, *The Life of Andrew Jackson,* 2 vols. (Indianapolis, Ind., 1938) is a modern and extremely flattering portrait. Robert Remini's *Andrew Jackson and the Course of American Empire: 1767–1821* (New York, 1977) incorporates the most recent scholarship yet remains eminently readable. Its sympathetic but by no means uncritical account of Jackson's early career will be followed by a second volume, currently in preparation, on the presidential years.

Primary sources are less conveniently available. John Spencer Bassett has edited the *Correspondence of Andrew Jackson,* 6 vols. (Washington, D.C., 1926–1933). Many of Jackson's papers are in the Library of Congress and are also available on microfilm in some university libraries. Jackson's backwoods spelling and punctuation can be slow going.

To understand the role of theory, in both science and history, readers will profit from Thomas Kuhn, *The Structure of Scientific Revolutions* (Chicago, 1962). The revised edition (1970) contains a few remarks by Kuhn on the applicability of his theory to social science disciplines. Further background on the major interpretations of Jackson and Jacksonian America is available in Charles G. Sellers, "Andrew Jackson Versus the Historians," *Mississippi Valley Historical Review* (currently issued as the *Journal of American History*), XLIV (March, 1958), 615–634 and Edward Pessen, *Jacksonian America,* rev. ed., (Homewood, Ill., 1978).

Frederick Jackson Turner's major works are *The Frontier in American History*

(New York, 1920), *The Rise of the New West* (New York, 1906), and *The Significance of Sections in American History* (New York, 1932). The best accounts of Turner's life and work are by Ray Billington, who probably set to print more words on Turner than Turner himself ever got to press on American history. *Frederick Jackson Turner: Historian, Scholar, Teacher* (New York, 1973) is a full and entertaining biography, while *The Genesis of the Frontier Thesis* (San Marino, Calif., 1971) describes just that. A contrasting view may be found in Richard Hofstadter, *The Progressive Historians: Turner, Beard, Parrington* (New York, 1968). David Potter, *People of Plenty* (Chicago, 1954) has an excellent discussion of Turner and the concept of national character.

In addition to Thomas Abernethy's *From Frontier to Plantation in Tennessee* (Chapel Hill, N.C., 1932), see his views in "Andrew Jackson and the Rise of Southwestern Democracy," *American Historical Review*, XXXIII (October, 1927), 64–77 and his biography of Andrew Jackson in the *Dictionary of American Biography*. A few remarks on Abernethy's career may be found in Darett Rutman, ed., *The Old Dominion: Essays for Thomas Perkins Abernethy* (Charlottesville, Va., 1964). Arthur Schlesinger, Jr.'s *Age of Jackson* (Boston, 1945) has generated much discussion among historians, summarized well in Edward Pessen's bibliographical essay, cited above. Information on Schlesinger's career may be gained from his father's autobiography, *In Retrospect* (New York, 1963) and from the essay on Schlesinger, Jr., in Marcus Cunliffe and Robin Winks, eds., *Pastmasters: Some Essays on American Historians* (New York, 1969).

Michael Rogin's *Fathers and Children: Andrew Jackson and the Subjugation of the American Indian* (New York, 1975) has appeared too recently to have attracted much systematic examination. Remini's biography, cited above, carries on a polite but firm running war in the footnotes. Of the major reviews by historians, the most interesting includes one by Lewis Parry in *History and Theory*, XVI, no. 2 (1977), 174–195 which, among other things, points out that Jackson's drooling in adult life might have been caused by mercury poisoning that Jackson sustained from medication that he often took—a potion of gin, sugar of lead, and calomel. Elizabeth Fox Genovese bitterly attacks Rogin's grand theorizing in *Reviews in American History*, III (December, 1975), 407–417. Genovese is a Marxist and she accuses Rogin of mating a fraudulent Marxism with an improperly conceived Freudianism. The result, she claims, is a mule of dubious pedigree. Readers will quickly discover that Andrew Jackson and his generation are not the only ones who argue over their legitimate paternity.

FIVE

The 'Noble Savage' and the Artist's Canvas

April 10, 1833 was a mild spring day in St. Louis and even if the guns hadn't been fired in salute, the crowd had reason enough to turn out and see the *Yellowstone* off. A few miles north, the Missouri River completed its long, 2,500-mile course through the interior; St. Louis was the trade nexus between the Missouri's hinterlands and the populous East. The largest firm that plied Missouri waters was John Jacob Astor's American Fur Company, which had sent its large steamer, the *Yellowstone,* on an annual trip upriver since 1831. For the townspeople who owed their livelihood to the trade, its departure supplied legitimate enough excuse for sociability and celebration.

As the crowd waved the steamer off, three passengers on deck undoubtedly stood out from the ship's fur company employees. Most impressive in his own eccentric way was a Prussian, Alexander Philipp Maximillian, Prince of Wied-Neuwied. If Maximillian's name and title sounded aristocratic, the man himself cut a less orthodox figure. At age fifty, he was still energetic and healthy, though pretty much without teeth. A pipe habitually filled that vacancy. The prince most often travelled in a white slouch hat, old black velvet coat, and—according to one company official—"probably the greasiest pair of trousers that ever encased princely legs."

That Prince Maximillian was standing on the banks of the Mississippi at all, rather than on his home ground next to the Rhine, resulted from an accident of birth. As the eighth child of the family, Max was an unlikely heir to the leadership of his house. Consequently he had become a naturalist and anthropologist. In 1833, along with his faithful aide-de-camp David Dreidoppel, the prince was bound for the upper Missouri, bent on recording the habits of the Plains Indians of North America.

During an earlier expedition to Brazil, Maximillian had supplemented his field notes with sketches of the people and places he visited. Apparently, family members were less than fully impressed with Max's artistic abilities. They had persuaded him to engage a young Swiss artist named Karl Bodmer for his new expedition. Twenty-four years old, Bodmer was hale and hearty, young, talented, ready to travel. Together, Maximillian, Bodmer, and Dreidoppel made a congenial trio.

As the *Yellowstone* picked its way up the often-treacherous Missouri, Bodmer began sketching. Sometimes he would record the magnificent landscapes the steamer passed; other times, the herds of bison or other wildlife. Most often he painted the Indians encountered in and around the forts, from the tribes of the Missouris, Otos, and Poncas in the south, to the Assiniboin, Cree, and Blackfoot who traded at Fort Union and Fort McKenzie on the upper Missouri. There were young braves dressed in full regalia; old men bare-chested in mourning; wives in meticulously beaded skin dresses; youngsters with vermillion-smeared faces, specially decorated for the occasion by a proud father.

Indian reaction to Bodmer's sketches varied. Always an audience of eager onlookers gathered, but some tribesmen professed alarm at Bodmer's uncanny ability to capture a likeness. One brave refused to be painted, arguing that if his image were put to paper, "he must then infallibly die." Other subjects were willing, but found it difficult to stand still for the day-long sessions. Bodmer provided tobacco as an inducement, as well as whatever other entertainment he thought would stave off boredom. One tall warrior "preserved a most inflexible gravity of countenance," noted Max, "till Mr. Bodmer set his musical snuff box agoing, on which he began to laugh." Invariably, the Indians were pleased with the finished sketches; even when their language lacked an equivalent for the English 'to draw,' they noted with stolid satisfaction that "Bodmer could write very correctly."

Bodmer did indeed "write very correctly." His portfolio of watercolors makes a spectacular complement to Maximillian's thorough record of the voyage. More than that, the pictures afford a valuable look at Native American cultures that were being transformed by the pressures of American expansion and the policies of Indian removal. Although

Indian cultures east of the Mississippi had absorbed the brunt of earlier European settlement, even the Plains culture had been changed, most notably by the introduction of the horse from Spanish settlements.

The horse provided many plains tribes with prosperity and a greater mobility. Buffalo herds could be hunted at greater distances; trading with more remote tribes increased. Thus, through indirect exchange, manufactured trade goods from Americans in the East might reach Indians years before the American traders themselves. When Astor and other traders established their posts on the Missouri, contact and commerce increased.

Three years after Maximillian's voyage, the American Fur Company's annual steamboat brought a more deadly visitor—smallpox. The disease spread rapidly from tribe to tribe, killing an estimated 17,000 natives. As disease combined with two other debilitating influences of white culture, alcohol and gunpowder, tribal life around the Missouri changed drastically. Never again would the opportunity present itself to record Plains life as it did to Bodmer and a handful of other artists (the American, George Catlin, foremost among them).

Bodmer's watercolors are an example of the pictorial material available to the historian for virtually any period or subject. Yet it is probably safe to say that historians, by and large, do not make use of such material as much as they might. Certain factors, some sociological, some technical, may explain the comparative neglect. By training and out of simple necessity, historians rely on printed and manuscript sources. Paintings, prints, and photographs, by themselves, can never supply the narrative line that is so central to the historian's task.* Consequently, historians tend to treat pictorial material as a supplement: the ruffles and flourishes that will enhance their finished research.

This approach is further encouraged by the technical requirements of publishing. Illustrations increase the cost of a book not only for the publisher but also for the author, who is often expected to pay for the rights of publication. Convenience and economy dictate the selection of ten or twelve illustrations, often culled after completion of the manuscript and placed in a separate section. Since these are not integrated into the text, the reader is discouraged from referring to them, even when particular examples are cited by the authors.

All the same, if pictorial evidence cannot supply the backbone of a

---

*An exception, of course, occurs when the pictures themselves are the subject of the narrative, as in art history. Even there, however, printed sources play a significant role in establishing context.

narrative, it may still provide more than ruffles and flourishes, so long as historians employ the same aggressiveness used in examining written evidence. Pictorial sources cannot be viewed in a vacuum, considered in and of themselves simply as works of art. They must be studied closely, examined for their peculiar perspectives, correllated, compared, and supplemented by written sources. Only then will the material surrender its full measure of information.

To say all this is, in one sense, merely to say that we should apply to pictorial evidence the same procedures and methods already outlined for printed sources. Yet most historians are not used to cross-examining a picture of Niagara Falls quite the way they would a legislative record or narrative of Silas Deane's death. Because pictorial evidence imparts information through a different medium, it requires that historians adjust their methods of examination.

The adjustment is most easily made if we first recall some of the basic ways in which written sources are approached. As we have seen, a document is read first for its evident narrative content. It supplies the historian with essential who/what/where kinds of information. This first approach is almost immediately qualified by a second: the awareness that such basic facts have been recorded by an observer who may have transformed the facts in subtle ways. Thirdly, researchers recognize that recorders of events may reveal as much about themselves as they do about the subjects they describe. Thus a historian may be interested in reading a document more to learn about its author than its subject.

Although all three of these approaches may be applied to a single picture, the principles involved in using them are most clearly demonstrated by examining each approach separately. And it makes sense to begin with the most basic element, a picture's narrative content.

PICTORIAL NARRATIVE

A great many pictures—perhaps the majority—tell a story. Some of them exist almost entirely to fulfill this function: John Trumbull's *Signing of the Declaration of Independence,* for instance, or Norman Rockwell's nostalgic scenes. Yet even simpler artistic subjects, like portraits, impart a great deal of basic information: the who, what, and where of historical narrative.

Such information, although intrinsic to a picture, can be easily overlooked. Most of us have been encouraged, quite rightly, to view paint-

ings in terms of their aesthetic qualities. We admire an artist's draftsman-
ship, or his or her ability to use texture, space, or color to good effect.
It is difficult to approach the works of someone as talented as Karl
Bodmer without lingering to admire their beauty. The historian, however, must risk being thought a terrible boor and do his best to ignore
these aesthetic qualities, at least temporarily. Bodmer, after all, is drawing Indians—and drawing them with remarkable accuracy. What sort of
narrative evidence can be gotten from his magnificent portraits?

While visiting Fort McKenzie on the upper Missouri, Bodmer painted
the likeness of an Indian named Homach-Ksachkum (the Great Earth)
and his son, Makuie-Poka (the Wolf Calf), as seen on pages 118–119.
Bodmer soon learned that the mother and father of Makuie-Poka came
from different tribes, one located in the vicinity of the Missouri River's
headwaters, the other farther north and west of the headwaters.

Look at the two portraits for a moment and consider the information
that may be gained from them. Even without any specialized training in
anthropology, it is possible to determine which parent lived in which
location. Before reading further, you may wish to deduce the answer
yourself.

The key lies in the different dress of the father and son. The two men
are so differently clothed that the only visible fashion they share is a
braided choker about the neck. Homach-Ksachkum wears a leather
fringed shirt (elkskin, as it happens) and also a buffalo robe draped
around his waist and over the left shoulder. (The darker, fur side faces
inward except where it can be seen rolled back off Homach-Ksachkum's
shoulder.) Makuie-Poka is much more elaborately dressed. A striped
blanket replaces the buffalo robe. To the choker is added a bear-claw
necklace. Decorative bead-work hangs on his chest; he carries an eagle-
wing fan. Further decoration is evident in the hair ornaments and the
finger rings (twenty-seven all told!). If dress is any indication, it would
appear that Makuie-Poka has adopted the ways of his mother's tribe
rather than his father's.*

*Astute observers will be quick to point out that this deduction is hardly airtight.
Might not Makuie-Poka be wearing the ceremonial dress of his father's tribe, while
Homach-Ksachkum wears the everyday garb? Or might the differing styles not indicate a generation gap—the younger members of the tribe dressing as differently from
their elders as modern American youth does? Both questions are excellent ones to
ask. For the purposes of the present example, we may assume that the question of
ceremonial versus everyday dress is not relevant. The question of a generation gap
may indeed have relevance, as we will shortly see.

Homach-Ksachkum. Watercolor by Karl Bodmer. (InterNorth Art Foundation; Joslyn Art Museum, Omaha, Nebraska)

Assume, then, that the son is dressed in the fashion of the mother's tribe. Further reflection indicates that not only the amount of Makuie-Poka's decoration is significant, but also the source. Of the articles previously enumerated, the blanket, rings, and glass beads are definitely of white origin. As a cultural portrait, Makuie-Poka reflects significantly greater contact with Euro-American trade. Thus it is logical to assume,

Makuie-Poka. Watercolor by Karl Bodmer. (InterNorth Art
Foundation, Joslyn Art Museum, Omaha, Nebraska)

given the Missouri River's central role in Indian–white trading patterns,
that the mother's tribe lives closer to the headwaters and the traders than
does the father's tribe. And in fact that was the case. Makuie-Poka's
mother was a Blackfoot; her people inhabited the area north and west
of Fort McKenzie. Maximillian indicates that, although the young man
dressed like a Blackfoot, some of his ornaments were worn after the

fashion of the Hidatsa and Mandan tribes, located even farther down-stream. (Perhaps this is an indication of the younger generation's willing-ness to adopt new habits.) Homach-Ksachkum, the father, belonged to the Kutenai tribe, which lived farther north and west of the Missouri than the Blackfeet, in country much more effectively isolated from white trade.

This much information is evident from the decorative elements in the drawing, even to the amateur eye. When pictorial evidence is further supplemented by research in fur company archives, as well as in an-thropological literature, the decorations of Makuie-Poka become even more revealing.

Note, for example, that the beads hanging from the youth's hair are interspersed by white tubelike decorations four or five inches long. Trading records indicate that these ornaments were known as hair pipes, made from the lip of a West Indian conch shell. Such shells were regu-larly loaded as ballast on ships returning to New York from the West Indies. In New York they were bought up by merchants from Bergen County, New Jersey, where the shells were taken and chipped into their general tubular shape. A hole was drilled at each end, the two meeting in the center, and then the tube polished, first by a grindstone and then with Rockaway sand and water. The American Fur Company bought the hair pipes and shipped them up the Missouri, although not without an occasional sour blast when it discovered the New Jersey drillers had supplied pipes "not bored entirely through," which the Indians were quick to reject.

Makuie-Poka also made effective use of the popular glass trading beads, both on the chest decorations as well as in the two hair bows that hang on either temple. Merchants found that during the 1830s Plains Indians most often preferred the colors blue and white. As with the hair pipes, Indians accepted only the high quality beads, which finally forced Astor's company to go directly to the most reliable source, Alessandre Bartolla of Venice, Italy.

Intertribal trade patterns also contributed to the wardrobe. Crow Indians to the south supplied both the eagle-wing fan and the bear-claw necklace. The blanket might have come, through the trade of intermedi-aries, from the Pueblo Indians or the Spanish. Other braves elaborated on the basic hair bow decoration by hanging dentalium shells from it; such shells were obtained in trade from the Pacific Coast Indians around Nootka, near Vancouver.

Thus the simple portrait of Makuie-Poka reveals in shorthand a com-plex global trading pattern that extended from Venice, Italy and the

West Indies to New York, New Jersey, and St. Louis; from the Spanish Southwest north through the Utes and the Crow; and from the Northwest Pacific coast through the intermediary Kutenai. The portrait of a young Indian dandy contains much more narrative information than a first glance would suggest.

COPYING AND TRANSFORMATION

Bodmer's watercolors are valuable not only because he could record detail accurately but also because he made his observations firsthand. That fact may seem too obvious to be worth noting, but with pictorial evidence, just as with written materials, the circumstances of the observer/recorder will determine the accuracy of the evidence. When artists cannot work from actual models, as happens all too often, they rely on someone else's pictures, on secondary accounts—even on their own imaginations. Artists borrow every bit as much as historians. It follows, then, that researchers using secondary pictorial evidence must observe the same kind of caution employed when dealing with printed sources. In a derivative work, the original material may have been transformed, even if only subtly. Being transformed, it will be yet another step removed from reality.

A simple illustration of such transformation can be seen in the work of the nineteenth-century illustrator, Felix O. C. Darley. Darley, like Bodmer, was an excellent draftsman, though much better known to the public through his illustrations of popular books like James Fennimore Cooper's *Leatherstocking Tales,* Francis Parkman's *Oregon Trail,* and Henry Wadsworth Longfellow's *Hiawatha.* Darley's work kept him busy enough so that apparently, he never felt the need to travel west of the Alleghenies. Neither river nor mountain range, however, confined Darley's imagination.

In 1842 he sketched the buffalo-hunting scene pictured on page 122. Darley's skill appears evident in both the drafting and in the composition. The viewer's eye is drawn immediately to the Indian's face, not only because it is at the center of the picture but also because it is at the apex of the triangle formed by the lines running upward from the horse's right foreleg and from the buffalo's face along the line of the arrow. The latter line reinforces the drama of the conflict: Indian and buffalo are eye to eye. In addition Darley imparts a sense of tension and wild motion to the flying mane of the horse as well as to the Indian's own hair and garments. Even the waving grass of the Plains embellishes the effect.

Hunting Buffalo (1842). Pen and ink drawing by Felix O. C. Darley.

Yet there is one puzzling feature in the drawing's narrative: the look of terror on the Indian's mount. If the terror is caused by the nearby buffalo, the horse is looking the wrong way! True, a few other bison sport in the left background, but they hardly seem worth the notice, given the excitement closer at hand. Possibly Darley averted the horse's gaze for reasons of composition. To have the mount looking to the right would have partially blocked the audience's view of the Indian. Still, why put terror on the horse's face at all?

The puzzle becomes more comprehensible when one realizes that Darley had at hand an engraving of a similar subject by George Catlin, who had travelled throughout the West and published a narrative of his journeys in 1841. Catlin's version of the buffalo hunt can be seen on the next page.

What Catlin's picture lacks in composition and technical ability, it gains in comprehensibility. The horse still displays a wild excitement, but no longer is it looking the wrong way. It has good reason for dismay,

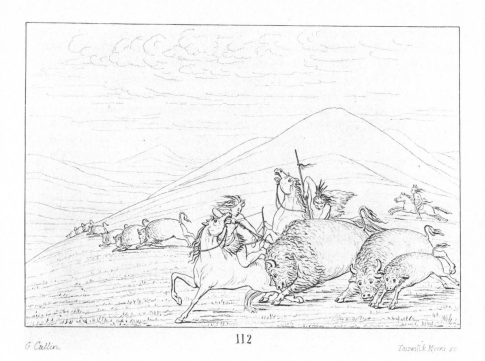

112

G. Catlin.   *Tasswill & Myers sc*

Untitled engraving (1841). George Catlin, in *Letters and Notes on the Manners, Customs and Conditions of the North American Indians* (London, 1841).

in fact, because in this version the horse is being gored! Apparently, Darley changed the stance of the buffalo to improve the composition. He also removed the other two buffalo in the foreground as well as the second Indian—again, presumably for aesthetic reasons. Catlin, on the other hand, included the extra figures for a purpose, as the text of his account makes clear:

> During the season of the year whilst the calves are young, the male seems to stroll about by the side of the dam [the female parent], as if for the purpose of protecting the young, at which time it is exceedingly hazardous to attack them, as they are sure to turn upon their pursuers, who have often to fly to each other's assistance. (Fig. 112).

Thus, while Darley has drawn on Catlin for inspiration, he has changed dramatically the import and narrative content of the picture.

Closer study reveals that other minor changes further tarnish Darley's authenticity. While the Indian's physique, posture, and anatomy have been refurbished, so has his wardrobe, with less commendable results. Catlin's riders appear to be either barefoot or wearing ankle-length moccasins; Darley's stylish brave wears moccasin-boots that cover the calf. The brave also sports a strange pair of skin-tight striped shorts the likes of which no Plains Indian ever wore. Equally foreign is Darley's tall, agitated, wheatlike vegetation. Catlin's landscape more accurately reflects the typical short grass of the Plains.

Because so few artists led the double life of an explorer, the pictures drawn by those who did were often copied, just as Darley relied on Catlin. The scarcity of authentic drawings is even more marked for the early stages of European exploration of North America. One artist whose work inspired many copies was John White, a member of the two English expeditions to the Carolinas financed by Sir Walter Raleigh. (The second expedition comprised the famous "lost colony" of Roanoke, whose fate still remains a mystery.) When White returned home in 1586 from the first expedition, he brought with him a graphic series of watercolors portraying the Carolina natives, their villages, religious ceremonies, and domestic customs, as well as examples of New World flora and fauna. (The latter included a flying fish, the exotic pelican, and "a flye which in the night seemeth a flame of fyer.")

Although White himself disappeared from the historical record by 1593, his watercolors secured his reputation—or perhaps more accurately, the reputation of Theodore De Bry, the man who popularized White's works through engraved copies. De Bry, a Flemish goldsmith and engraver who had come to England in 1588, quickly recognized that the public would be eager to see pictures of the strange New World. He arranged to issue his own engravings of White's drawings along with a previously published narrative of the first Roanoke voyage by Thomas Hariot, the expedition's official scientist. The book enjoyed an immediate success and, in turn, De Bry's engravings became sources for other hopeful artists.

On page 126 and 127, John White's figure of "an aged man in his winter garment" is juxtaposed with De Bry's engraved copy. Compare the two figures and assess the variations.

Most obviously, De Bry has added an elaborate background. Is it authentic? De Bry never visited the New World but a researcher would quickly discover that most of the background is based on White's other watercolors. The circular village is from a sketch of Pomeiock, an Indian settlement located in the area of present-day Hyde County, North Carolina. Its cornfields are provided with a small "scarecrow" hut (also from White), where an Indian watcher makes noise to keep away birds and animals. The river's canoeists are borrowed from yet another drawing. The Indian himself has one obvious addition which cannot be found in White: a pair of strange-looking moccasins. Perhaps De Bry felt that a winter outfit surely warranted footgear and so threw in the moccasins for good measure.

De Bry has changed John White's Indian in more subtle ways which, to the untrained observer, are at first more difficult to pin down. Somehow, the engraved Indian appears not quite "foreign" enough. He seems rather as if a European had been gotten up in Indian garb for the occasion. Much of the discrepancy has to do with the face. By modern standards of portraiture, neither White nor De Bry can remotely approach Bodmer's ability to capture facial character. Yet in De Bry's work, even more than in White's, the faces of the subjects appear uniform and unchanging. No doubt that occurs partly because De Bry was working secondhand. Since he never actually saw a Native American, let alone White's subjects, his engravings tended to homogenize facial characteristics.

De Bry, in other words, relied even more than usual on certain artistic conventions to portray his subject. All artists, like writers or composers, have their own characteristic patterns of composition, habitual techniques that are evident in their work. It follows that a historian using pictorial evidence should be aware of those conventions and understand how they may distort reality through their idiosyncratic re-creation of a situation. Such constraints are less obvious in discussing an artist like Karl Bodmer because so many of his artistic conventions coincide with the goals of the historian. Bodmer was aiming at realistic portraiture. He wished to paint Homach-Ksachkum not as a representative type—"Plains Indian"—but as an individual. He sought to make the face capture the subject's character. Bodmer also reflected Maximillian's ethnological interests by accurately recording the details of Indian dress and decoration. For De Bry, on the other hand, Indians were indeed "types" whose faces and individual character did not matter. Beyond that, he had absorbed many of the stylized artistic conventions of Mannerism, a school of art that flourished in sixteenth-century Europe.

Mannerist painters shared aspirations and goals that often conflicted with the canons of realistic portraiture. Mannerism takes its name from the Italian *maniera,* which, freely translated, means "style;" not style so much in the artistic sense of the word as style in behavior—proper manners. As one art historian has noted, style in the lavish world of the

Renaissance court meant "savoir-faire, effortless accomplishment and sophistication; [style] was inimical to revealed passion, evident effort and rude naiveté. It was, above all, courtly grace." Mannerist painters attempted to exhibit style in every facet of their lives, from the extravagant parties they attended to the elegance exhibited in their paintings or sculptures. Many of the artistic conventions that contributed to style in Mannerist painting are reflected in Theodore De Bry's portraits.

As much as anything else, Mannerists strove to display consummate technical skill in their creations. The human figure, for instance, was

An aged man in his winter garment. Watercolor by John White.

An aged man in his winter garment. Engraving by Theodore de Bry.

often rendered in difficult or unusual poses, with great attention paid to human anatomy and musculature. When De Bry's engraving of the old man is compared with John White's original watercolor, we can immediately see that De Bry has heightened the figure's musculature, especially in the area of the forearm. An extreme example of this technique can be seen in De Bry's engraving of a child clinging to his mother's back (page 128). This is a muscular babe indeed!

Because Mannerists wished to display technical proficiency, naturalism was not a quality they sought; in fact, quite the contrary. They praised a painting if it was "artificial," in the archaic sense of exhibiting qualities achieved through constructive skill, rather than spontaneity. Today, "artificial" has a derogatory connotation, but Mannerists gloried in the term and strove to demonstrate artifice, dexterity, and cleverness in the smallest of details. Notice, for example, that De Bry has slightly altered the position of the old man's right hand as it holds the cloth. The fifth finger curves outward in a somewhat unnatural but—to the Mannerist—highly elegant and artificial pose. So too the digits of the left hand are gracefully separated one from another.

Of course, the Mannerist conventions raise questions about what John White himself introduced into his original drawings. Did he ask the old man to stand as portrayed, one hand on his shawl, the other pointing outwards? Or did the old man himself choose that pose? Often, such information is hard to come by, but literary evidence can sometimes supply a clue. We know that White faithfully recorded a young Indian woman with her hands on her shoulders, covering her breasts "as a sign of maidenly modesty," because Thomas Hariot mentioned the custom in his account of the Roanoke voyage. White painted another woman resting one arm in a sling of pearls, a custom Hariot also indicated was common among the noblewomen of Carolina. Perhaps the pose was a Native American form of *maniera,* for once entirely appropriate to the style of the Mannerists. Note once again, however, that De Bry (page 129) has artificially separated one finger from the others on each hand

Their manner of carrying their children. Engraving by Theodore de Bry.

and, indeed, has done the same with the woman's big toes. (Try to stand naturally, sometime, with your big toes separated. This is artificial elegance with a vengeance!)

One last note on John White's old man in winter clothes: alert readers may have noticed that we have already met the old man in this book, in yet a third artistic reincarnation. When Robert Vaughan prepared engravings to accompany Captain John Smith's history of Virginia, he too borrowed from White, or more likely, De Bry. As the engraving reproduced on page 5 indicates, Vaughan himself admitted that he had "inserted those figures [of the Roanoke Indians] in this place because of the conveniency." The old man, it turns out, is used as a "convenient" model for none other than Pocahontas, probably because his winter garment allowed Vaughan to dress the Indian heroine a bit more mod-

A chief lady of Pomeioc.
Engraving by Theodore
de Bry.

estly than De Bry's bare-breasted female models. Thus with the deft aid of an engraver's tool, an old man is rejuvenated, thirdhand, to become a young Indian princess.

THE ARTIST'S CANVAS AS A LOOKING GLASS

Thus far we have examined pictorial evidence using the artist as the historian's natural ally. Bodmer, Catlin, White, and De Bry all recognized the value of preserving a record of Native American civilization. Yet the distortions and artistic conventions that are a part of every drawing suggest another tactic. A picture may be used to focus the historian's attention on its creator. Just as John Smith's account of Indian religion revealed as much about Smith and his culture as it did about Native American customs, so pictorial evidence may shed light on an artist's motivations, feelings, and preconceptions. Under these circumstances, the artist becomes less an ally than an unwitting subject.

That the artist's canvas may serve as a looking glass is neatly demonstrated in the Indian paintings of Charles Bird King. Unlike the wandering Catlin or Bodmer, King let his subjects come to him, at his studio in Washington, D.C. By the time he set up shop there in 1819, the drawing skills learned as a young boy in Rhode Island had been supplemented by training in England under the prominent American artist Benjamin West. After unsuccessful attempts to settle in Philadelphia, Baltimore, and Richmond, King moved to the bustling capital of America, where the congressmen were a little vainer and the portrait business, consequently, a bit brisker. Those who sat for King included young John Calhoun and Henry Clay.

Unexpected work came to the artist in 1821, when a delegation of Indians from the Missouri regions arrived at the capital to meet with President Monroe. The government encouraged these visits, in fact even subsidized them as part of a policy of conciliation toward the frontier tribes. It also wished to impress its visitors with the power of white civilization. The Indian delegates seemed to enjoy the visits for their novelty but with equal diplomatic aplomb refused to betray any wonderment or excitement when cannons were shot off for their benefit or navy-yards and forts displayed. When President Monroe offered to provide the benefits of civilization and religion, they politely declined. "It is too soon to send those good men [missionaries] among us—we are not starving yet," replied one delegate. "We have everything we want—we have plenty of land, if you will keep your people off it."

Prairie Wolf. Oil by Charles Bird King.
(The Warner Collection of Gulf States Paper Corporation)

Thomas L. McKenney, the government's superintendent of Indian trade, arranged to have King paint the portraits of the delegation, including an Oto representative, Shaumonekusse (Prairie Wolf) and his wife, Hayne Hudjihini (Eagle of Delight), the only female member of the delegation. Charles King did not have Karl Bodmer's advantage of observing his subjects in their home country; nor is his technique as polished. Yet the drawings do succeed as realistic portraiture and render facial expression and character far more accurately than the works of

Eagle of Delight. Oil by Charles Bird King.
(The Warner Collection of Gulf States Paper Corporation)

either White or De Bry. At first glance both paintings tell us more about their subjects than they do about King or his culture.

Still, there is one suggestive feature that distinguishes the two portraits. Prairie Wolf is painted wearing traditional Indian dress, while Eagle of Delight, although still holding her robe, wears a ruffled frock of white origin. If we look at other portraits King painted of Plains

Indians, we find a similar pattern: men in traditional costumes, women wearing European dress.* And in fact, this difference reflects a conscious perception on King's part of how males or females ought properly to be presented. Increasingly, women in nineteenth-century American society were being thought of as creatures of refined sensibility; their place was in the home with the family. It was not thought proper for them to exhibit assertiveness or aggression. Artistic convention dictated that women be depicted as graceful, while men could be shown in the full force of their character. Since white culture stereotyped the Plains cultures as savage, primitive, "completely in a state of nature," as one Washington paper noted in heralding the delegation's arrival, it seemed quite proper to paint the men in their "savage" attire. After all, one of the popular attractions of an Indian visit was the performance of a war dance, Indians "painted horribly . . . scalping and tomahawking in fine style" and "in a state of perfect nudity, except a piece of red flannel round the waist and passing between the legs."

Literary accounts of the visit reinforce this distinction. Note, for instance, the description of Eagle of Delight recorded by a male observer at the White House ceremony where President Monroe and the male members of the Indian delegation made speeches:

> When our lordly sex had finished their speeches, which they seemed as fond of making as are the members of some other great councils, the squaw, a comely young woman of eighteen, urged by some of them, apparently in sport, approached the President, and hanging her head on one side, with a pleasing smile and even yet more pleasing timidity, said that her Great Father had given the red men new clothes like white men, and they looked very well in them; and that those who had no silver medals would look still better if they had them, and that she too would like to be dressed as a white woman if her great Father would give her a new dress. I suspected that the first part of her speech was suggested by others, and the last was as natural as her blushes and smiles. You see that the love of finery is not created by civilization; it merely becomes more chaste and discriminating.

*King painted several other portraits of Eagle of Delight, in which she wore the same costume. Portraits of two other women from later delegations (Rantchewaine; Mahongo and child) pictured quite similar dresses of the same color. King, it is true, did paint Indian men wearing varying amounts of European dress, but virtually all of them were from eastern tribes (Cherokee, Seneca, etc.) which had maintained ties with white culture for longer periods of time.

Here is sweet modesty personified: Eagle of Delight measures up perfectly to the male observer's expectations.

Yet we may wonder whether the writer was in part seeing what he wanted to see. The Indian braves, after all, had not the spunk to speak for a medal themselves and left the task for an eighteen-year-old girl. Perhaps even more plausibly, Eagle of Delight may have been performing as she knew she was expected to perform. We should remember that, despite her supposed shyness, she was the only woman who chose to join the delegation and that her willingness to make a several-thousand-mile trek into the unknown indicates considerable initiative. She showed similar persistence during a visit to a local Washington physician, when her husband Prairie Wolf was shown a skeleton. Prairie Wolf "looked slyly in," noted an observer, "and the wife wanted to look, but he put himself in an attitude to represent a dead person and said 'no good, no good.' She still wanted to see, but he would not let her." Eagle of Delight persisted, however, and some time later the couple returned to the doctor, were both given a view of the skeleton, and went away "very well pleased." In 1824 another Indian squaw demonstrated similar determination when her delegation forbade her to accompany them and she secretly followed, appearing openly only when it was too late to send her home.*

None of the Indian women's personal traits are reflected in King's straightforward portraits—and they are spectacularly absent in the one extant Indian painting where he permitted his fantasy free rein. Unfortunately, readers of this book will have to employ their own fantasies with considerable free rein, for they will not find the picture, *Indian Girl at Her Toilet,* anywhere within these pages. In our own research for this chapter we found the oil painting reproduced in *The Paintings of Charles Bird King,* by Andrew Cosentino. But correspondence with the author revealed that the present owners of the portrait wished to remain anonymous and had only reluctantly permitted reproduction of the painting in Cosentino's volume, a comprehensive catalogue of King's work published by the Smithsonian Institution. Despite numerous letters and

---

*In all fairness we should note that the male account of Eagle of Delight's speech might also be used to argue against our case, since it indicates that Eagle of Delight had to make a special request for her dress, whereas the male Indians were given white clothes upon their arrival. (According to historian Herman Viola, Eagle of Delight had already been given scarlet pantaloons and a green cambric cloak.) All the same, King did not paint the men in their new European clothes as he easily might have, and as he did Eagle of Delight.

phone calls, we made no headway in obtaining the needed permission
to reproduce the painting. In a book about historical methods, this tale
may serve as a ruefully appropriate demonstration that a researcher's
hunt for materials is by no means invariably blessed with success.

So, in order to contrast King's realistic portraiture with the romantic
rendering of *Indian Girl at Her Toilet,* our readers, must either borrow
a copy of *The Paintings of Charles Bird King* or else study the outline
drawing shown below and do a bit of vivid imagining. For indeed, the
romantic painting tells us more about King than about his subject. You
will imagine, first, a young maiden sitting in a secluded forest glade.

Adorning her head is a delicate headdress, and from her ears hang ringlets much like Eagle of Delight's. Teepees in the background indicate a tribe's encampment nearby, but the girl pays heed only to her own delicate reflection in a mirror that she holds. A fur robe is draped about her in alluring fashion, although King, a perennial bachelor, has become discreetly indistinct in the brushwork delineating the rounded contours of the maiden's breasts.

Interestingly, the woman bears a strong resemblance to Eagle of Delight. In addition to the similar facial features, each woman has a blue spot on her forehead, and the romantic maiden wears arm bracelets like the ones in Prairie Wolf's portrait. The kinship of the two paintings suggests where the true historical value of King's romantic work lies— not in its ethnographic information about the life of an Oto woman, but in King's own wishful conception of how his young Indian acquaintance spends her days. The picture conjures up the popular eastern stereotype of the noble savage, a tradition that stood side by side, often incongruously, with the notion of Indians as primitive, warlike beasts. If the Indian war dance embodied for white audiences the beastly side of the Indian nature, King's innocent maiden represents the contrasting stereotype. The picture shows her living a simple life, unspoiled by the corruption of civilization. The erotic overtones of the picture may be discreetly enjoyed by the civilized male audience, all the while justified by the maiden's natural innocence. Like Eve, she is unaware of the need to cover her nakedness.

King's *Indian Maiden at Her Toilet* is a far cry from Bodmer's ethnographic studies of the upper Missouri tribes. Yet both sorts of pictorial evidence can be invaluable, so long as we remember that the apparent directness of pictorial communication is often deceptive. Eyewitness drawings no more necessarily record an event "as it really happened" than do written eyewitness accounts. In evaluating pictorial evidence, historians must establish the historical context of a painting just as they would establish the context of any document. They must be sensitive to the artistic conventions that shape or even distort a painting's subject matter. And they must be prepared to acknowledge that some paintings provide more information about their creator than about the subject being portrayed. When visual clues are combined with other printed source materials, whether they be the pedestrian trading inventories of blue glass beads or the literary fantasies of novelists, pictorial evidence can vivify historical narrative and deepen our understanding of American culture.

Additional Reading

Thanks to the wonder of modern printing techniques, excellent color reproductions of many of the paintings discussed in this chapter make it possible for readers to engage in their own pictorial sleuthing without visiting galleries first-hand.

The general public of Bodmer's day did not have the benefit of seeing his breathtaking watercolors reproduced, only aquatints based on them. Modern readers will find excellent reproductions of the watercolors (now located at the Joslyn Art Museum, Omaha, Nebraska) in Davis Thomas and Karin Ronnefeldt, eds., *People of the First Man* (New York, 1976). This edition also contains selections from Prince Maximillian's published account of his travels as well as from his field journals; a fuller reprinting of his published account can be found in Ruben Thwaites, ed., *Early Western Travels, 1748–1846,* vols. 22–24 (Cleveland, 1904–1907). (It was the industrious Thwaites, incidentally, who delivered the oration on early lead-mining in Wisconsin, mentioned in Chapter 4, at the Chicago World's Fair Congress where Turner presented his frontier thesis.)

For additional background on the trading patterns that contributed to wardrobes like that of Makuie-Poka, see John C. Ewers, *Indian Life on the Upper Missouri* (Norman, Okla., 1968), Chapter 7. Like the nomadic people of the Plains under his scrutiny, John Ewers has ranged far and wide, leaving the benefit of his scholarship and insights on diverse topics. For a more general background on painters of Indians, see his *Artists of the Old West* (Garden City, 1965). Joslyn Art Museum, *Catlin, Bodmer, Miller: Artist Explorers of the 1830s* (Omaha, Neb., 1967) covers George Catlin and Alfred Jacob Miller, two other artists who crossed the Plains.

Readers wishing to learn more about the adventures, a good many of them imaginary, of Felix Darley's Indians, should consult John C. Ewers, "Not Quite Redmen: The Plains Indian Illustrations of Felix O. C. Darley," *American Art Journal,* III, no. 2 (Fall 1971), 88–98. John I. H. Baur discusses Darley's reliance on George Catlin in "After Catlin," *Brooklyn Museum Bulletin,* X, no. 1 (1948), 17–20.

The most readily available reproductions of John White's watercolors are in Stefan Lorant, *The New World,* rev. ed. (New York, 1965), which also includes De Bry's engravings for easy comparison, as well as Thomas Hariot's account of the Roanoke Indians. White's drawings are also available in Paul H. Hulton and David B. Quinn, *The American Drawings of John White, 1577–1590* (Chapel Hill, N.C., 1964). John Shearman's *Mannerism* (Hammondsworth, 1967) is a convenient introduction for a newcomer to the field; see also Craig Hugh Smyth, *Mannerism and Maniera* (Locust Valley, N.Y., 1963) and Jacques Bosquet's lavish *Mannerism* (New York, 1964). For further instructive examples of how artistic conventions can transform reality, see William Goetzmann's discussion of Western landscape painters in *Exploration and Empire* (New York, 1966).

Charles Bird King has been treated in two excellent recent studies. Andrew J. Cosentino, *The Paintings of Charles Bird King* (Washington, D.C., 1977) provides an overview of King's career as well as a catalogue of his paintings. Herman J. Viola, *The Indian Legacy of Charles Bird King* (Washington, D.C., 1976), supplies valuable background on the Indian delegations King painted. A briefer treatment can be found in John C. Ewers, "Charles Bird King, Painter of Indian Visitors to the Nation's Capital," *Smithsonian Institution Annual Report for 1953* (Washington, 1954), 463–473.

White perceptions of Indian culture have been discussed by many historians. A few useful jumping-off points are Roy Harvey Pearce, *Savagism and Civilization,* rev. ed. (Baltimore, 1965), which treats the conflicting ideas of Indians as primitive beasts and noble savages. Hoxie Neale Fairchild discusses the same subject in *The Noble Savage* (New York, 1928). Elwood Parry uses pictorial evidence to discuss white–Indian themes in *The Image of the Indian and the Black Man in American Art* (New York, 1974), while Joshua C. Taylor, *America as Art* (Washington, D.C., 1976), includes a chapter by John G. Cawelti on "The Frontier and the Native American," 133–184.

SIX

The Madness of John Brown

For over two months the twenty-one men had hidden in the cramped attic. They were mostly idealistic young men in their twenties, bound together during the tedious waiting by a common hatred of slavery. Now, on October 16, 1859 their leader, Old John Brown, revealed to them his final battle plan. The group comprised five blacks and sixteen whites, including three of the old man's sons, Owen, Oliver, and Watson. For years Brown had nurtured the idea of striking a blow against the southern citadel of slavery. Tomorrow, he explained, they would move into Harpers Ferry, Virginia, and capture the town and its Federal arsenal. As they gathered arms, slaves would pour in from the surrounding countryside to join their army. Before the local militia organized, they would escape to the nearby hills. From there, they would fight a guerilla war until the curse of slavery had been exorcised and all slaves freed from bondage. No one among them questioned Brown or his plan.

An autumn chill filled the air, and a light rain fell as the war party made its way down the dark road toward Harpers Ferry. Three men had remained behind to handle supplies and arm slaves who took up the fight. A sleepy stillness covered the small town nestled in the hills where the Shenandoah joined the Potomac sixty miles from Washington, D.C. It was a region of small farms and relatively few slaves. Most likely, the presence of the arsenal and an armory explain why Brown chose to begin his campaign there.

The attack began without a hitch. Two raiders cut telegraph lines running east and west from the town. The others seized a rifle works, the armory, and three hostages, including a local planter descended from

George Washington. Soon the sounds of gunfire drew the townspeople from their beds. Amid the confusion, the church bell pealed the alarm dreaded throughout the South—slave insurrection! By late morning the hastily joined militia and armed farmers had trapped Brown and his men in the engine house of the Baltimore and Ohio Railroad. One son had been killed and another lay dying at his father's side. Drunken crowds thronged the streets crying for blood and revenge. When news of the raid reached Washington, President Buchanan dispatched federal troops under Colonel Robert E. Lee to put down the insurrection.

Thirty-six hours after the first shot, John Brown's war on slavery had ended. By any calculation the raid had been a total failure. Not a single slave had risen to join Brown's army. Ten of the raiders lay dead or dying; the rest had been scattered or captured. Though himself

John Brown, the revolutionary man of action: After the Pottawatomie Massacre, Brown grew a beard to disguise his appearance. His eastern backers were impressed with the aura he radiated as a western man of action. The image was not hurt by the fact that Brown hinted darkly of vigorous actions soon to be taken, or that he carried a bowie knife in his boot and regularly barricaded himself nights in his hotel rooms as a precaution against proslavery agents.

wounded, Brown had miraculously escaped death. The commander of the assault force had tried to kill him with his dress sword, but it merely bent double from the force of the blow. Seven other people had been killed and nine more wounded during the raid.

Most historians would agree that the Harpers Ferry raid was to the Civil War what the Boston Massacre had been to the American Revolution: an incendiary event. In an atmosphere of aroused passions, profound suspicions, and irreconcilable differences, Brown and his men put a match to the fuse. Once their deed had been done and blood shed, there seemed to be no drawing back for either North or South. The shouts of angry men overwhelmed the voices of compromise.

From pulpits and public platforms across the North leading abolitionists leapt to Brown's defense. No less a spokesman than Ralph Waldo Emerson pronounced the raider a "saint. . . . whose martyrdom, if it shall be perfected, will make the gallows as glorious as the cross." Newspaper editor Horace Greeley, who directed a generation of young men to the West, called the raid "the work of a madman" for which he had nothing but the highest admiration. At the same time the defenders of national union and of law and order generally condemned Brown and his violent tactics. Such northern political leaders as Abraham Lincoln, Stephen Douglas, and William Seward spoke out against Brown. The Republican party in 1860 went so far as to adopt a platform censuring the Harpers Ferry raid.

Reasoned northern voices were lost, however, on southern hotheads, to whom all abolitionists and Republicans were potential John Browns. Across the South angry mobs attacked northerners regardless of their views on the slave question. Everywhere the specter of slave insurrection fed irrational fears and the uproar strengthened the hand of secessionists who argued that the South's salvation lay in expunging all traces of northern influence.

THE MOTIVES OF A FANATIC

And what of the man who triggered all those passions? Had John Brown foreseen that his quixotic crusade would reap such a whirlwind of violence? On that issue both his contemporaries and historians have been sharply divided. Brown himself left a confusing and often contradictory record of his objectives. To his men, and to Frederick Douglass, the former slave and black abolitionist, Brown made clear he intended nothing less than to provoke a general slave insurrection. His preparations all pointed to that goal. He went to Harpers Ferry armed for such a task, and the choice of the armory as the raid's target left little doubt he intended to equip a slave army. But throughout the months of preparation, Brown had consistently warned the co-conspirators financing his scheme that the raid might fail. In that event, he told them, he still hoped the gesture would so divide the nation that a sectional crisis would ensue, leading to the destruction of slavery.

From his jail cell and at his trial Brown offered a decidedly contradictory explanation. Ignoring the weapons he had accumulated, he suggested that the raid was intended as an extension of the underground railroad work he had previously done. He repeatedly denied any intention to commit violence or instigate a slave rebellion. "I claim to be here in carrying out a measure I believe perfectly justifiable," he told a skeptical newspaper reporter, "and not to act the part of an incendiary or ruffian, but to aid those [slaves] suffering great wrong." To Congressman Clement Vallandigham of Ohio who asked Brown if he expected a slave uprising, the old man replied, "No, sir; nor did I wish it. I expected to gather them up from time to time and set them free." In court with his life hanging in the balance, Brown once again denied any violent intent. He sought only to expand his campaign for the liberation of slaves.

Brown's contradictory testimony has provoked much speculation over the man and his motives. Was he being quite rational and calculating in abruptly changing his story after capture? Certainly Brown knew how much his martyrdom would enhance the abolitionist movement. His execution, he wrote his wife, would "do vastly more toward advancing the cause I have earnestly endeavored to promote, than all I have done in my life before." On the other hand, perhaps Brown was so imbued with his own righteousness that he deceived himself into believing he had not acted the part of "incendiary or ruffian," but only meant to aid those slaves "suffering great wrong." "Poor old man!" commented Republican presidential hopeful Salmon Chase. "How sadly misled by his own imaginations!"

Yet for every American who saw Brown as either a calculating insurrectionist or a genuine if somewhat self-deluded martyr, there were those who thought him insane. How else could they explain the hopeless assault of eighteen men against a Federal arsenal and the state of Virginia —where slaves were "not abundant" and where "no Abolitionists were ever known to peep"? Who but a "madman" (to quote Greeley) could have concocted, much less attempted, such a wild scheme?

Nor was the issue of John Brown's sanity laid to rest by his execution on December 2, 1859. Brown had become a symbol, for both North and South, of the dimensions of the sectional struggle, condensing the issues

A PREMATURE MOVEMENT.

JOHN BROWN. "Here! Take this, and follow me. My name's Brown."
CUFFEE. "Please God! Mr. Brown, dat is onpossible. We ain't done seedin' yit at our house."

John Brown, the impractical idealist: "The old idiot—the quicker they hang him and get him out of the way, the better." So wrote the editor of a Chicago paper to Abraham Lincoln. Many contemporaries shared the view of the cartoon reprinted here, that Brown was a foolish dreamer. Yet Brown had other ideas. "I think you are fanatical!" exclaimed one southern bystander after Brown had been captured. "And I think you are fanatical," Brown retorted. "'Whom the Gods would destroy they first made mad,' and you are mad."

of the larger conflict in his own actions. Inevitably, the question of personal motivation becomes inextricably bound to historians' interpretations of the root causes of sectional and social conflict. Was Brown a heroic martyr— a white man in a racist society with the courage to lay

John Brown, the martyr of freedom:
  John Brown of Ossawatomie, they led him out to die;
  And lo! a poor slave-mother with her little child pressed nigh,
  Then the bold, blue eye grew tender, and the harsh face grew mild,
  And he stooped between the jeering ranks and kissed the Negro's child!
John Greenleaf Whittier based this incident in his poem, "Brown of Ossawatomie," (December 1859) on an erroneous newspaper report. Apparently Brown
did kiss the child of a white jailer he had befriended. Brown also remarked to
the same jailer that "he would prefer to be surrounded in his last moments by
a poor weeping slave mother with her children," noting that this "would make
the picture at the gallows complete."

down his life on behalf of his black brothers and the principles of the Declaration? Or was he an emotionally unbalanced fanatic whose propensity for wanton violence propelled the nation toward avoidable tragedy?

During the middle years of the twentieth century the view of Brown as an emotional fanatic gained ground. John Garraty, in a currently popular college text, describes Brown as so "deranged" that rather than hang him for his "dreadful act. . . . It would have been far wiser and more just to have committed him to an asylum. . . ." Allen Nevins defined a middle ground when he argued that on all questions except slavery, Brown could act coherently and rationally. "But on this special question of the readiness of slavery to crumble at a blow," Nevins thought, "his monomania . . . or his paranoia as a modern alienist [psychoanalyst] would define it, rendered him irresponsible."

Brown's most recent academic biographer, Stephen Oates, while recognizing in Brown much that was in no sense "normal," rejected the idea that insanity could either be adequately demonstrated or used in any substantive way to explain Brown's actions. That Brown had an "excitable temperament" and a single-minded obsession with slavery Oates conceded. He concluded, too, that Brown was egotistical, an overbearing father, an often inept man worn down by disease and suffering, and a revolutionary who believed himself called to his mission by God.

But having said all that, Oates demanded that before they dismissed Brown as insane, historians must consider the context of Brown's actions. To call him insane, Oates argued, "is to ignore the tremendous sympathy he felt for the black man in America. . . ." And, he added, "to label him a 'maniac' out of touch with 'reality' is to ignore the piercing insight he had into what his raid—whether it succeeded or whether it failed—would do to sectional tensions. . . ."

Given such conflicting views on the question of John Brown's sanity, it makes sense to examine more closely the evidence of his mental state. The most readily available material, and the most promising at first glance, was presented after the original trial by Brown's attorney, George Hoyt. As a last-minute stratagem, Hoyt submitted nineteen affidavits from Brown's friends and acquaintances, purporting to demonstrate Brown's instability.

Two major themes appear in those affidavits. First, a number of people testified to a pronounced pattern of insanity in the Brown family, particularly on his mother's side. In addition to his maternal grandmother and numerous uncles, aunts, and cousins, Brown's sister, his brother Salmon, his first wife Dianthe, and his sons Frederick and John Jr. were all said to have shown evidence of mental disorders. Second, some respondents described certain patterns of instability they saw in Brown himself. Almost everyone agreed he was profoundly religious and that he became agitated over the slavery question. A few traced Brown's insanity back through his years of repeated business failures. The "wild and desperate" nature of those business schemes and the rigidity with which he pursued them persuaded several friends of his "unsound" mind and "monomania."

Many old acquaintances thought that Brown's controversial experiences in Kansas had unhinged the man. There, in May 1856, proslavery forces had attacked the antislavery town of Lawrence. In retaliation, Brown led a band of seven men (including four of his sons) in a midnight raid on some of his proslavery neighbors at Pottawatomie Creek. Although the Pottawatomie residents had taken no part in the attack on faraway Lawrence, Brown's men, under his orders, took their broadswords and hacked to death five neighbors. That grisly act horrified free state and proslavery advocates alike. John Jr., one of Brown's sons who had not participated in the raid, suffered a nervous breakdown from his

John Brown, the terrorist: Mahala Doyle, the wife of James P. Doyle, one of those Brown killed at Pottawatomie, testified of Brown, "He said if a man stood between him and what he considered right, he would take his life as cooly as he would eat his breakfast. His actions show what he is. Always restless, he seems never to sleep. With an eye like a snake, he looks like a demon."

own personal torment and from the abuse he received after being thrown in prison. Another of Brown's sons, Frederick, had been murdered a few months later in the civil war that swiftly erupted in Kansas.

Thus a number of acquaintances testified in 1859 that from the time of the Pottawatomie killings onward, Brown had been mentally deranged. E. N. Sill, an acquaintance of both Brown and his father, admitted that he had once had considerable sympathy for Brown's plan to defend antislavery families in Kansas. "But from his peculiarities," Sill recalled, "I thought Brown an unsafe man to be commissioned with such a matter. . . ." It was Sill who suggested the idea, which Allen Nevins later adopted, that on the slavery question alone Brown was insane. "I have no confidence in his judgment in matters appertaining to slavery," he asserted. "I have no doubt that, upon this subject . . . he is surely as monomaniac as any inmate in any lunatic asylum in the country." David King, who talked to Brown after his Kansas experience, observed that "on the subject of slavery he was crazy" and that Brown saw himself as "an instrument in the hands of God to free slaves."

Such testimony seems to support the view that Harpers Ferry was the outcome of insanity. Yet even then and ever since many people have rejected that conclusion. Confronted with the affidavits, Governor Henry Wise of Virginia thought to have Brown examined by the head of the state's insane asylums. Upon reflection he changed his mind. Wise believed Brown perfectly sane and had even come to admire begrudgingly the old man's "indomitable" spirit. Wise once described Brown as "the gamest man I ever saw."

For what it is worth, Brown himself rejected any intimation that he was anything but sane. He refused to plead insanity at his trial and instead adopted the posture of the self-sacrificing revolutionary idealist. For him, slavery constituted an unethical and unconstitutional assault of one class of citizens against another. Under that assault acts which society deemed unlawful—dishonesty, murder, theft, or treason—could be justified in the name of a higher morality.

Furthermore, Oates and other historians have attacked the affidavits presented by Hoyt as patently unreliable. Many people had good reason to have Brown declared insane. Among those signing the affidavits were friends and relatives who hoped Governor Wise would spare Brown's life. Might they not have exaggerated the instances of mental disorders in his family to make their case more convincing? Most had not taken Brown's fanaticism seriously until his raid on Harpers Ferry. That event, as much as earlier observation, had shaped their opinions. Just as important, none of them had any medical training or experience that would qualify them to determine with any expertise whether Brown or any member of his family could be judged insane. Only one affidavit came from a doctor, and, like most physicians of the day, he had no particular competence in psychological observation.

Though it would be foolish to suggest that we in the twentieth century are better judges of character than our forefathers, it is fair to say that at least we have a better clinical understanding of mental disorders. Many symptoms which the nineteenth century lumped together under the term insanity have been since identified as a variety of very different diseases, each with its own distinct causes. Among those "crazy" Brown relatives were those who, based on the descriptions in the affidavits, may have suffered from senility, epilepsy, Addison's disease, or brain tumors. Thus the "preponderance" of insanity in Brown's family could well have been a series of unrelated disorders. Even if the disorders were related, psychologists today still hotly debate the extent to which psychological disorders are inheritable.

The insanity defense also had considerable appeal to political leaders. Moderates from both North and South, seeking to preserve the Union, needed an argument to soften the divisive impact of Harpers Ferry. Were Brown declared insane, northern abolitionists could not so easily portray him as a martyr. Southern secessionists could not treat Brown as typical of all northern abolitionists. As a result, their argument that the South would be safe only outside the Union would have far less force. Historian C. Vann Woodward has pointed out that the Republicans were eager to dissociate their abolitionist rhetoric from Brown's more radical tactics. During the 1859 Congressional elections, the Democrats tried to persuade voters that Harpers Ferry resulted inevitably from the Republicans' appeal to the doctrine of "irresistible conflict" and "higher law" abolitionism. To blunt such attacks, leading Republicans regularly attributed the raid to Brown's insanity.

Clearly, the affidavits provide only the flimsiest basis for judging the condition of Brown's mental health. But some historians have argued that the larger pattern of Brown's life demonstrated his imbalance. Indeed, even the most generous biographers must admit that Brown botched miserably much that he attempted to do. In the years before moving to Kansas, Brown had tried his hand at tanning, sheepherding, surveying, cattle-driving, and wool-merchandising—all with disastrous results. By 1852 he had suffered fifteen business failures in four different states. Creditors were continually hounding him. "Over the years before his Kansas escapade," John Garraty concluded, "Brown had been a drifter, horse thief and swindler, several times a bankrupt, a failure in everything he attempted."

But this evidence, too, must be considered with circumspection. During the period Brown applied himself in business, the American economy went through repeated cycles of boom and bust. Many hardworking entrepreneurs lost their shirts in business despite their best efforts. Brown's failures over the years may only suggest that he did not have an aptitude for business. His schemes were usually ill-conceived, and he was too inflexible to adapt to the rapidly changing business climate. But to show that Brown was a poor businessman and that much of his life he pursued the wrong career hardly proves him insane. Under those terms, much of the adult population in the United States would belong in asylums.

To call Brown a drifter is once again to condemn most Americans. Physical mobility has been such a salient trait of this nation that one respected historian has used it to distinguish the national character. During some periods of American history as much as twenty percent of the population has moved *each year!* In the 1840s and 1850s, a whole generation of Americans shared Brown's dream of remaking their fortunes in a new place. Many like him found the lure of new frontiers irresistible. And just as many failed along the way, only to pack up and try again.

The accusation that Brown was a swindler and horse thief, while containing a measure of truth, convicts him on arbitrary evidence. After several of his many business disasters, creditors hounded him in the courts. A few accused him of fraud. Yet Simon Perkins, an Ohio businessman who lost more money to Brown and who was more familiar with his business practices than anyone else, never accused Brown of swindling, even when the two dissolved their partnership in 1854. Again, it was poor business sense rather than a desire to swindle that led Brown into his difficulties.

The horse thievery charge hinges on the observer's point of view. During the years of fighting in Kansas, Brown occasionally "confiscated" horses from proslavery forces. Those who supported his cause treated the thefts as legitimate acts of war. Brown's enemies never believed he was sincere in his convictions. They accused him of exploiting the tensions in Kansas to act like a brigand. But in any case, it is far from clear that Brown ever stole for personal gain. Whatever money he raised, save for small sums he sent his wife, went toward organizing his crusade against slavery. Besides, it is one thing to establish Brown's behavior as antisocial and quite another to find him insane.

From the point of view of the "facts of the case," the question of insanity cannot be easily resolved. The issue becomes further muddled when we consider its theoretical aspects. Theory, as we saw when examining Andrew Jackson, will inevitably affect any judgment in the case. The question, "Was John Brown insane?" frames our inquiry and determines the kind of evidence being sought. And in this case, the question is particularly controversial because it remains unclear just exactly what we are asking. What does it mean, after all, to be "insane"?

Modern psychologists and psychiatrists have given up using the concept of insanity diagnostically because it is a catch-all term and too unspecific to have definite meaning. The only major attempt to define the concept more precisely has been in the legal world. In civil law insanity refers to the inability of individuals to maintain contractual or other legal obligations. Thus, to void a will, an injured party might try to demonstrate at the time of composition its author was not "of sound mind"—that is, not responsible for his or her actions. Insanity is considered sufficient grounds to commit an individual to a mental hospital. But since it involves such a curtailment of rights and freedom, it is extremely difficult to prove and generally requires the corroboration of several disinterested professionals.

Insanity has been widely used as a defense in criminal cases. By demonstrating that at the time of the crime a client could not distinguish right from wrong or was incapable of determining the nature of the act committed, a lawyer can protect the accused from some of the legal consequences of the act. To find Brown insane, as attorney Hoyt attempted to have the court do, would have been to assert Brown's inability to understand the consequences of his actions at Harpers Ferry. The raid would represent the irrational anger of a deranged man, deserving pity rather than hatred or admiration.

In the legal sense, then, Brown would have to be considered fit to stand trial. He may have been unrealistic in estimating his chance of success at Harpers Ferry, but he repeatedly demonstrated that he knew the consequences of his actions: that he would be arrested and punished if caught; that large portions of American society would condemn him; that, nevertheless, he believed himself in the right. In the legal sense, Brown was quite sane and clear-headed about his actions.

THE MOTIVES OF A SON—AND A FATHER

Yet the court's judgment, accurate as it may have been, is likely to leave us uneasy. To have Brown pronounced "sane" or "insane," in addition to "guilty" or "not guilty," does little to explain, deep down, why the man acted as he did. The verdict leaves us with the same emptiness that impelled psychologists to reject the whole concept of insanity. What drove John Brown to crusade against slavery? to execute in cold blood five men along a Kansas creek? to lead twenty-one men to Harpers Ferry? Many other northerners abhorred the institution of slavery. Yet only John Brown acted with such vehemence. In that sense he was far from being a normal American; far, even, from being a normal abolitionist. How can we begin to understand the intensity of his deeds?

Here we approach the limits of explanations based upon rational motives. To describe John Brown simply by referring to his professed —and undoubtedly sincere—antislavery ideology; or to explain his actions in terms of consciously held plans, is to leave unexplored the fire in the man. It focuses too much on rationalistic explanations of behavior, assuming that consciously expressed motivations can be taken largely at face value. Yet we have already seen, in the cases of the bewitched at Salem and the strong-willed Andrew Jackson, that unconscious motivations play a crucial role in human behavior. If it is not possible even for ostensibly "normal" people fully to explain or understand their behavior, how much less satisfying such rational explanations must seem in explaining people like Brown.

The discipline of psychoanalysis, pioneered by Sigmund Freud, offers the historian one way of understanding and discussing unconscious motivations. Freud assumed that everybody inevitably experiences intensely personal conflicts in life, which are extremely difficult to deal with. When a person resists coming to terms with such situations in an open and direct manner, he represses the conflict; that is, he is *unable* to think about it consciously. At this level, the conflict comes to be expressed unconsciously and indirectly—perhaps disguised in dreams or fantasies, or else resolved in actions which have significance beyond the apparent, or manifest, reasons for being performed.

Freud called special attention to two areas of life he thought were the source of much tension and conflict: instinctual sexual drives and the formative experiences of infancy and childhood. By exploring a patient's life history through a process of free association, the psychoanalyst takes the fragments of evidence presented by the patient and guides him toward a recognition of the unconscious forces that have shaped the personality. Thus the analyst seeks to explore the territory of the unconscious much as the historian seeks to make sense out of the jumble of documentary evidence.

In order to gain some concrete sense of how psychoanalytic theory might be used to understand a historical figure like John Brown, we will do well to concentrate on just one of Freud's concepts—what he called the oedipal stage of a child's development. The concept draws its name from Sophocle's *Oedipus Rex,* a Greek tragedy in which Oedipus unknowingly commits incest with his mother. For this "crime" he suffers blindness and exile. Psychoanalysis contends that somewhere between the age of three and six, boys normally pass through the oedipal phase. As their demand for erotic gratification intensifies, it is directed toward the mother. Strong attraction for a forbidden love object is fraught with psychic peril. It invites in the child's fears his father's jealous and destructive wrath.

Resolution of the oedipal conflict occurs when the child relinquishes his erotic impulses toward the mother and identifies with the father as the adult role model. The prohibitions against sexual gratification become internalized in normal individuals as the superego. The superego in turn acts as an ethical monitor controlling instinctual impulses as the child matures. Successful resolution of oedipal conflicts leads to increased self-control, improved capacity to test external reality, and reduced dependence on maternal response.

Failure to resolve the intense guilt, fears, and ambivalence associated with the oedipal phase can block formation of an integrated adult personality. Symptoms of unresolved conflict may take physical forms such as nervous twitches, tics, impaired bodily functions, or stammering. Phobias and compulsive rituals are neurotic symptoms linked to oedipal conflict. Some socially unacceptable behaviors may also result—sadistic cruelty or masochistic submission, stealing, lying, insatiable demanding, and excessive selfishness. Sexual intimacy in adulthood may become difficult or impossible. Some people go through life with intense feelings of guilt or inferiority. Other people assume personality traits that are mutually incompatible or even self-destructive. So we sometimes find people who are simultaneously conceited and desperate for positive reinforcement.

John Brown is, of course, more than a hundred years out of reach of the analyst's couch. Yet even if it is impossible to obtain further evidence from the man himself, psychoanalytic theory provides historians with a new perspective that can be used to reinterpret long-familiar records. Because Freudian insight depends so much on the experiences of infancy and childhood, one document of Brown's deserves especially close examination, a long letter written by him at the age of fifty-seven. The letter was addressed to thirteen-year-old Harry Stearns, the son of one of Brown's wealthy financial supporters. In it, Brown told the story of "a certain boy of my acquaintance" who, "for convenience," he called John. This was especially convenient since the boy was none other than

Brown himself. This letter, a revealing portrait of Brown's early years, is one of the few surviving sources of information about his childhood.

And yet, even before we begin to approach the letter from a psychoanalytic perspective, it is important to understand the limits of such an exercise. No matter how much this story of childhood is analytically dissected, it cannot provide a full explanation of why John Brown became an abolitionist. Another person with an essentially similar psychic profile but a different career might become—no doubt did become—a southern fire-eater. Nor can psychoanalytic theory provide a sufficient explanation of how John Brown came to attack Harpers Ferry in October 1859. To do so would be to ignore specific and crucial historical events that affected Brown over the years and that had nothing to do with his early childhood experiences.

But if psychoanalytic theory cannot explain *what* John Brown did, it can at least suggest *why* he did things the *way* he did them. It can do so by exploring some of the early emotional currents in his personality and by examining how these forces affected his behavior in later life. Such an exploration is particularly useful in John Brown's case because, as we have seen, Brown's "mad" behavior at Harpers Ferry seems to be grounded in several seemingly contradictory elements of his personality. On the one hand, Brown identified himself with black slaves—the most helpless and weak members of American society. On the other hand, he claimed for himself a mission and a power that was really vast: the God-given right to defy the laws of the United States, free and arm the slaves, and lead a rebellion designed to spread chaos throughout the South. How can we account for this peculiar combination of humility and arrogance, submission and aggression, murder and martyrdom?

At first, Brown's tale of simple boyhood recollections would seem to be of little help. The letter is reprinted here with only a few omissions of routine biographical data:

> I can not tell you of anything in the first Four years of John's life worth mentioning save that at that *early age* he was tempted by Three large Brass Pins belonging to a girl who lived in the family & *stole them.* In this he was detected by his Mother; & after having a full day to think of the wrong; received from her a thorough whipping. When he was Five years old his Father moved to Ohio; then a wilderness filled with wild beasts, & Indians. During the long journey, which was performed in part or mostly with an *ox-team;* he was called on by turns to assist a boy Five years older (who had been adopted by his Father & Mother) & learned to think he could accomplish *smart things* by driving the Cows; & riding the horses. Some-

times he met with Rattle Snakes which were very large; & which some of the company generally managed to kill. After getting to Ohio in 1805 he was for some time rather afraid of the Indians, & of their Rifles; but this soon wore off: & he used to hang about them quite as much as was consistent with good manners; & learned a trifle of their talk. His father learned to dress Deer Skins, & at 6 years old John was installed a young Buck Skin. He was perhaps rather observing as he ever after remembered the entire process of Deer Skin *dressing;* so that he could at any time dress his own leather such as Squirel, Raccoon, Cat, Wolf and Dog Skins, and also learned to make Whip Lashes, which brought him some change at times, & was of considerable service in many ways. At Six years old he began to be a rambler in the wild new country finding birds and squirrels and sometimes a wild Turkey's nest. But about this period he was placed in the school of *adversity;* which my young friend was a most necessary part of his early training. You may *laugh* when you come to read about it; but these were *sore trials* to John: whose earthly treasures were very *few & small.* These were the beginning of a severe but *much needed course* of discipline which he afterwards was to pass through; & which it is to be hoped has learned him before this time that the Heavenly Father sees it best to take all the little things out of his hands which he has ever placed in them. When John was in his Sixth year a poor *Indian boy* gave him a Yellow Marble the first he had ever seen. This he thought a great deal of; & kept it a good while; but at last *he lost it* beyond recovery. *It took years to heal the wound* & I *think* he cried at times about it. About Five months after this he caught a young Squirrel tearing off his tail in doing it; & getting severely bitten at the same time himself. He however held on *to the little bob tail Squirrel;* & finally got him perfectly tamed, so that he almost idolized his pet. *This too he lost;* by its wandering away; or by getting killed; & for a year or two John was *in mourning;* and looking at all the Squirrels he could see to try & discover Bobtail, *if possible.* I must not neglect to tell you of a verry *bad and foolish* habbit to which John was somewhat addicted. I mean *telling lies;* generally to screen himself from blame; or from punishment. He could not well endure to be reproached; & I now think had he been oftener encouraged to be entirely frank; *by making frankness a kind of atonement* for some of his faults; he would not have been so often guilty of this fault; nor have been (in after life) obliged to struggle *so long* with *so mean* a habit.

John was never *quarelsome;* but was *excessively* fond of the *hardest & roughest* kind of plays; & could *never get enough* [of] them. Indeed when for a short time he was sometimes sent to School the opportunity it afforded to wrestle & Snow ball & run & jump & knock off old seedy Wool hats;

offered to him almost the only compensation for the confinement, & restraints of school. I need not tell you that with such a feeling & but little chance of going to school *at all:* he did not become much of a schollar. He would always choose to stay at home & work hard rather than be sent to school; & during the warm season might generally be seen *barefooted & bareheaded:* with Buck skin Breeches suspended often with one leather strap over his shoulder but sometimes with Two. To be sent off through the wilderness alone to very considerable distances was particularly his delight; & in this he was often indulged so that by the time he was Twelve years old he was sent off more than a Hundred Miles with companies of cattle; & he would have thought his character much injured had he been obliged to be helped in any such job. This was a boyish kind of feeling but characteristic however.

At Eight years old, John was left a Motherless boy which loss was complete and pearmanent for notwithstanding his Father again married to a sensible, intelligent, and on many accounts a very estimable woman; yet he never *adopted her in feeling;* but continued to pine after his own Mother for years. This opperated very unfavourably upon him; as he was both naturally fond of females; &, withall, extremely diffident; & deprived him of a suitable connecting link between the different sexes; the want of which might under some circumstances, have proved his ruin. . . .

During the war with England [in 1812] a circumstance occured that in the end made him a most *determined Abolitionist:* & led him to declare, or *Swear: Eternal war* with Slavery. He was staying for a short time with a very gentlemanly landlord since a United States Marshall who held a slave boy near his own age very active, inteligent and good feeling; & to whom John was under considerable obligation for numerous little acts of kindness. *The master* made a great pet of John: brought him to table with his first company; & friends; called their attention to every little smart thing he *said or did:* & to the fact of his being more than a hundred miles from home with a company of cattle alone; while the *negro boy* (who was fully if not more than his equal) was badly clothed, poorly fed; & *lodged in cold weather;* & beaten before his eyes with Iron Shovels or any other thing that came first to hand. This brought John to reflect on the wretched, hopeless condition, of *Fatherless & Motherless* slave *children:* for such children have neither Fathers or Mothers to protect, & provide for them. He sometimes would raise the question *is God their Father?* . . .

I had like to have forgotten to tell you of one of John's misfortunes which set rather hard on him while a young boy. He had by some means *perhaps* by gift of his father become the owner of a little Ewe Lamb which did finely till it was about Two Thirds grown; & then sickened & died. This brought another protracted *mourning season:* not that he felt the pecuniary loss so much: for that was never his disposition; but so strong & earnest were his attachments.

John had been taught from earliest childhood to "fear God and keep his commandments;" & though quite skeptical he had always by turns felt much serious doubt as to his future well being; & about this time became to some extent a convert to Christianity & ever after a firm believer in the divine authenticity of the Bible. With this book he became very familiar, & possessed a most unusual memory of its entire contents.

Now some of the things I have been *telling of;* were just such as I would recommend to you: & I would like to know that you had selected these out; & adopted them as part of your own plan of life; & I wish you to have some *deffinite plan.* Many seem to have none; & others never stick to any that they do form. This was not the case with John. He followed up with *tenacity* whatever he set about so long as it answered his general purpose; & hence he rarely failed in some good degree to effect the things he undertook. This was so much the case that he *habitually expected to succeed* in his undertakings. With this feeling *should be coupled;* the consciousness that our plans are right in themselves.

During the period I have named, John had acquired a kind of ownership to certain animals of some little value but as he had come to understand that the *title of minors* might be a little imperfect: he had recourse to various means in order to secure a more *independent;* & perfect right of property. One of those means was to exchange with his Father for something of far less value. Another was by trading with others persons for something his Father had never owned. Older persons have some times found difficulty with *titles.*

From Fifteen to Twenty years old, he spent most of his time working at the Tanner & Currier's trade keeping Bachelors hall; & he officiating as Cook; & for most of the time as foreman of the establishment under his Father. During this period he found much trouble with some of the bad habits I have mentioned & with some that I have not told you off: his conscience urging him forward with great power in this matter: but his close attention to *business;* & success in its management; together with the way he got along with a company of men, & boys; made him quite a favorite with the serious & more inteligent portion of older persons. This was so much the case; & secured for him so many little notices from those he esteemed; that his vanity was very much fed by it: & he came forward to manhood quite full of self-conceit; & self-confident; notwithstanding his *extreme* bashfulness. A younger brother used sometimes to remind him of this: & to repeat to him *this expression* which you may somewhere find, "A

King against whom there is no rising up." The habit so early formed of being obeyed rendered him in after life too much disposed to speak in an imperious or dictating way. From Fifteen years & upward he felt a good deal of anxiety to learn; but could only read & studdy a little; both for want of time; & on account of inflammation of the eyes. He however managed by the help of books to make himself tolerably well acquainted with common arithmetic; & Surveying; which he practiced more or less after he was Twenty years old. . . .

Before exploring the letter's significance in psychoanalytic terms, it may be worth reminding ourselves what a straightforward reading of the document provides. Attention would naturally center on Brown's striking tale of how, as a twelve year old, he was first roused to oppose slavery. Shocked by the cruel treatment of his young black friend, John was further incensed by the unfair and contrasting treatment he benefited from simply because he was white. Here is a vivid, emotional experience that seems to go a good way toward explaining why the evil of slavery weighed so heavily on Brown's mind. In writing an article on the motivations behind the raid at Harpers Ferry, this anecdote is quite clearly the one piece of evidence worth extracting from the long letter. The additional material on Brown's childhood, which often seems to ramble incoherently, might be included in a book-length biography of Brown, but hardly seems relevant to an article which must quickly get to the heart of the man's involvement with abolition.

Yet when we look more closely, Brown's story of the mistreated young slave does not go very far toward explaining Brown's motives. In a land where slavery was central to the culture, hundreds, even thousands of young white boys must have had similar experiences, where black playmates were unfairly whipped, degraded, and treated as inferiors. Nonetheless, many of those boys went on to become slaveholders. Furthermore, although some undoubtedly developed a strong dislike of slavery (Abraham Lincoln among them*), none felt compelled to mount the kind of campaigns Brown did in Kansas and at Harpers Ferry. Why did Brown's rather commonplace experience make such a strong impression on him?

Psychoanalytic theory suggests that the answer to that question may be learned if we do not dismiss the other portions of Brown's childhood experiences as irrelevant but instead examine them for clues to his psy-

---

*As a young man, Lincoln was reputed to have been strongly moved by the sight of slaves being auctioned in New Orleans.

chological development. So let us turn, for a moment, from a direct examination of Brown's abolitionism to the other elements of the letter to Harry Stearns. In doing so we must consider each of Brown's stories, illustrations, and comments with care, keeping in mind Freud's stress on unconscious motivations. In previous chapters we have seen that historians must always treat primary sources skeptically, identifying the personal perspectives and biases which may influence the writer. Psychoanalytic theory requires us to take that skepticism one step further, assuming not only that the evidence may be influenced by unstated motivations (such as Brown's wishing to impress Harry Stearns's father with his virtue) but also that some, even the most powerful of Brown's motivations, may be unconscious—hidden even from Brown himself.

At first glance the narrative appears to recount fairly ordinary events in a child's life. Who, after all, has not cried one time or another at the loss of a pet, or has been proud of accomplishments like driving cows and riding horses? Yet we must remember that these are only a few events selected from among thousands in Brown's childhood; events meaningful enough to him that he has remembered and related them over fifty years later. Why did Brown retain these memories rather than others? What suggestive images and themes recur? Because psychoanalytic theory emphasizes the importance of parental relationships, we may begin by examining Brown's relationship with his mother and father.

Of the two parents, John's mother is the most visible of the two in this letter, and it is clear that Brown loved her dearly. Notice the language describing his mother's death. John "was left a Motherless boy," he writes—not the simpler and less revealing, "John's mother died," which places the emphasis on the mother rather than on the loss incurred by the "Motherless boy." Furthermore, the loss was "complete & pearmanent." Brown never grew to love his new mother and "continued to pine after his own Mother for years." The phrase, "pine after" (which the Oxford English Dictionary defines as being "consumed with longing," or languishing "with intense desire") has erotic overtones, which are made even more manifest by the sentence that follows. Brown moves directly from his love for his mother to the erotic temptations young women had for him, implicitly linking the two: "This opperated very unfavourably uppon him; as he was both naturally fond of females; & withall extremely diffident; & deprived him of a suitable connecting link between the different sexes; the want of which might under some circumstances have proved his ruin."

John's father, at first glance, appears to have taken a less prominent role in the letter, either positively or negatively. True, Owen Brown does teach John the art of dressing skins (and also, John takes care to note, of making "Whip lashes"); but the attention centers not on the father's devoted teaching so much as John's remarkable ability to learn by watching his father only once. Perhaps most revealing, however, is an ambiguous passage in which Brown's father does *not* appear, yet plays a substantial, hidden role. The relevant paragraph begins by noting that John had "acquired a kind of ownership to certain animals of some little value. . . ." From earlier parts of the letter, we are aware how much these pets meant to him—the loss of the squirrel "Bob tail" (which he "almost idolized") and later the ewe lamb (which he had *"perhaps"* by gift of his father become the owner). Now, Brown indicates that he had owned other animals, but apparently not completely. He is curiously circumspect about explaining why: the ownership, he says, was incomplete because "the *title of minors*" was "a little imperfect." Apparently, animals which he thought he owned were taken away from him, on the grounds that he did not have "title" to them as a minor. So John, being extremely strong-willed despite his bashfulness, determinedly set out to "secure a more independent; & perfect right of property." Significantly, this question of ownership appears to have occurred more than once, for Brown noted that he devised "various means" to deal with it.

What is happening here? Brown's evasive language makes the situation difficult to reconstruct, but certain outlines emerge. The only logical person who might repeatedly prevent John from obtaining full "title" to his pets was his father Owen. Why Owen objected is never stated, but several ideas suggest themselves. Conceivably the elder Brown needed one of John's "pet" sheep or cows to feed the family or to sell for income. Furthermore, in a frontier settlement where unfenced woodlands merged with small farms, wild or stray domestic animals might have roamed onto the Brown farm from time to time. If young John Brown found them, he would likely have claimed them as pets, only to discover that the animal was on father Owen's land—and duly appropriated for food or income.

Whatever the specific situations, young Brown repeatedly attempted to secure his property through one of two means. "One of those means was to exchange with his Father for something of far less value." The implication is that in some cases Owen Brown allowed John to treat animals as pets if they were formally "purchased" from his father for a token fee ("something of far less value"). In such cases, Owen Brown acted kindly toward his son, though rigorously insisting that the formalities of "property" and "title" be observed. But on other occasions John apparently could not convince his father to spare such pets, for the letter indicates that another means of obtaining them "was by trading with others persons for something his Father had never owned." If Owen would not give him pets, John would be able to get them from more willing neighbors.

The conflict of ownership between father and son obviously left a strong imprint. More than forty years later, Brown still vividly remembered how Owen confiscated his pets, as well as the means he worked out to satisfy, or in some cases, actually to evade his father's authority. Even more important, the evasive language in the passage demonstrates that Brown still remained unable to acknowledge his anger openly. In effect, the paragraph reveals a concealed hostility which Brown was still carrying toward his father. The last sentence amounts to a condemnation, but the son could only express his anger indirectly, through use of a generality: "Older persons have some times found difficulty with titles."

Unconsciously, Brown may have been applying the last phrase to himself as well. For the crucial message of the passage is not Brown's hostility toward his father, but the issues through which the hostility is

John Brown, the kindly father: Brown's daughter Ruth remembered the following incident from her childhood: "When I first began to go to school, I found a piece of calico one day behind one of the benches,—it was not large, but seemed quite a treasure to me, and I did not show it to any one until I got home. Father heard me then telling about it, and said, 'Don't you know what girl lost it?' I told him I did not. 'Well, when you go to school to-morrow take it with you, and find out if you can who lost it. It is a trifling thing, but always remember that if you should lose anything *you* valued, no matter how small, you would want the person that found it to give it back to you.''

expressed: that is to say, title and ownership. Indeed, a psychoanalytic interpretation of Brown's childhood suggests that throughout his life, Brown never fully resolved the question of "titles" of his own identity. The more the letter is probed, the more it reveals a patterned obsession with property and title. Brown continually describes himself as finding some piece of "property," forming strong attachments to it, and then losing it and severely mourning the loss.

What, after all, is the very first experience in Brown's life which he can recall? Before the age of four, John steals three brass pins, discovers that his title to them is imperfect, has them taken away, and is severely whipped. At six, John receives a treasured yellow marble, loses it, and mourns for "years." Soon afterwards, John catches a squirrel, pulling its tail out in the process; then tames and idolizes it; then loses it and mourns another year or two. At eight, John loses another precious possession—his mother—and pines after her for years. Then comes the story of the lamb; and later, his conflicts with his father over the ownership of other pets. The religious moral drawn from these lessons ("a severe but *much needed course* of discipline,") was that "the Heavenly Father sees it best to take all the little things out of his hands which he has ever placed in them." Clearly, the process of becoming an independent adult was for John Brown a continuing effort to reconcile his guilt and anger over losing property with his fierce desire to become truly independent, to possess clear title to his own pets, to become a "propertied" father like Owen and—dare we say it? even like God the father himself. Paradoxically, only when Brown internalized and accepted the authority of his "fathers" could he then act the part of a stern loving parent himself. Submission to his father's authority made it possible for him to accept as legitimate his own authority over his own "pets."

The pattern of Brown's struggle for autonomy is reflected in the role he played as father to his own children. Owen Brown had been a stern disciplinarian, in part because he had felt the lack of a strong hand in his own childhood. John internalized and emulated this severe approach early on. When his younger brother, Salmon, had been pardoned for some misdeed by a boarding-school teacher, John went to the teacher and told him that "if Salmon had done this thing at home, father would have punished him. I know he would expect you to punish him now for doing this—and if you don't, I shall." When the schoolmaster persisted in his lenience, John was reported to have given Salmon a "severe flogging." As a parent, Brown's discipline was equally harsh. When his three-year-old son Jason claimed that a certain dream actually had occurred, Brown felt obliged to whip the boy for lying. The father's immense ambivalence in such a situation was evidenced by the tears that welled up in his eyes as he performed the whipping.

For Brown, even sins took on an aspect of property. The father kept a detailed account book of his son John Jr.'s transgressions, along with the number of whiplashes each sin deserved. Recalled the son:

> On a certain Sunday morning he invited me to accompany him from the house to the tannery, saying that he had concluded it was time for a settlement. We went into the upper or finishing room, and after a long and tearful talk over my faults, he again showed me my account, which exhibited a fearful footing up of *debits*. . . . I then paid about one-third of the debt, reckoned in strokes from a nicely-prepared blue-beech switch, laid on 'masterly.' Then, to my utter astonishment, father stripped off his shirt, and, seating himself on a block, gave me the whip and bade me 'lay it on' to his bare back. I dared not refuse to obey, but at first I did not strike hard. 'Harder!' he said; 'harder, harder!' until he received the *balance of the account.* Small drops of blood showed on his back where the tip end of the tingling beech cut through. Thus ended the account and settlement, which was also my first practical illustration of the Doctrine of Atonement.

In this astonishing tableau, Brown's personal conflicts are vividly reflected. The father punishes the son as justice demands; yet Brown also plays the wayward son himself. And as John Brown, Jr. recognized only later, his father was consciously assuming the mantle of Christ, whom the heavenly father had permitted mankind to crucify and punish, in order that his other children's sins would be forgiven.

The upshot of such discipline was that Brown's sons harbored a similar ambivalence toward their father—an intense feeling of loyalty and submission countered by a strong desire for independence. The contradiction of such training became apparent to one of Brown's sons, Watson, during the raid on Harpers Ferry. "The trouble is," Watson remarked to his father, "you want your boys to be brave as tigers, and still afraid of you." "And that was perfectly true," agreed Salmon Brown, another son.

Psychoanalytic insight has thus helped to reveal some of John Brown's most intense personal conflicts: his ambivalence toward his father's strict discipline; the paradox of his struggle to internalize and accept his father's authority in order to become independent himself; and his excessive concern with property and "pets" as a means of defining his independence. Having exposed these themes, let us now return to the

John Brown, the stern father: Brown was influenced in his harsh discipline by his father Owen (left) and in turn influenced his own son, John, Jr. (right). The father kept a detailed account book of John, Jr.'s sinful acts, along with the number of whiplashes each sin deserved. Recalled the son: "On a certain Sunday morning he invited me to accompany him from the house to the tannery, saying that he had concluded it was time for a settlement. We went into the upper or finishing room, and after a long and tearful talk over my faults, he again showed me my account, which exhibited a fearful footing up of *debits*. . . . I then paid about *one-third* of the debt, reckoned in strokes from a nicely-prepared blue-beech switch, laid on 'masterly.' Then, to my utter astonishment, father stripped off his shirt, and, seating himself on a block, gave me the whip and bade me 'lay it on' to his bare back. I dared not refuse to obey, but at first I did not strike hard. 'Harder!' he said; 'harder, harder!' until he received the *balance of the account.*"

starting point of our original analysis of the letter—the anecdote about Brown and the young slave. Suddenly, what had seemed a straightforward tale is filled with immensely suggestive vocabulary, whose overtones reveal a great deal. The passage is worth reading once again:

During the war with England a circumstance occurred that in the end made him a most *determined Abolitionist:* & led him to declare, or *Swear: Eternal war* with Slavery. He was staying for a short time with a very gentlemanly landlord since a United States Marshall who held a slave boy near his own age very active, inteligent and good feeling; & to whom John was under considerable obligation for numerous little acts of kindness. *The master* made a great pet of John: brought him to table with his first company; & friends; called their attention to every little smart thing he *said or did:* & to the fact of his being more than a hundred miles from home with a company of cattle alone; while the *negro boy* (who was fully if not more than his equal) was badly clothed, poorly fed; & *lodged in cold weather;* & beaten before his eyes with Iron Shovels or any other thing that came first to hand. This brought John to reflect on the wretched, hopeless condition, of *Fatherless & Motherless* slave *children:* for such children have neither Fathers or Mothers to protect, & provide for them. He sometimes would raise the question *is God their Father?*

Upon this second reading, it becomes evident that Brown's language and metaphors here are full of references to parental relationships, dependence, and authority. John stayed with a "very gentlemanly landlord" who "made a great pet of John," treating the boy just as John treated his own pets. At the same time, however, this gentlemanly father acted like no father at all to the negro boy, beating him unmercifully. This led John to reflect "on the wretched, hopeless condition, of *Fatherless & Motherless* slave *children. . . ."* "*Is God their Father?*" he asked himself.

The situation confronted young Brown with two starkly contrasting models of a father, corresponding with the boy's own ambivalent feelings toward Owen. Naturally, John wanted his own father to discipline him less harshly. He wanted to be treated as a "pet;" as his own animals were treated; as this gentleman treated him. Similarly, he identified with the negro boy, an innocent lad who was being punished just as Owen Brown punished John. Yet like all boys, he also identified with his own father. He desired as well as hated the power Owen wielded over him, and that this gentleman wielded over the negro boy. He thus felt the tug of two conflicting loyalties. To use the religious imagery so familiar to that age, John Brown wanted to grow up and act both as God the merciful Father and as God the righteous Judge.

This ambivalent father–son relationship suggests that Brown's intense lifelong identification with black slaves might well have sprung from the struggle he experienced with paternal discipline. Helping slaves was ultimately a means of helping himself without consciously recognizing the source of his emotions and convictions. He could channel the repressed hostility toward his father into a more acceptable form—hatred of the slaveholders, another class of paternalistic oppressors who cruelly whipped their charges. In attacking the planters, Brown relieved the sense of guilt he harbored for secretly wishing to destroy his father. After all, God the implacable Father and Judge was using Brown as his instrument for bringing justice to the world. At the same time, by protecting and defending the helpless slaves, Brown carried out God's will as a merciful father. In liberating the black nation, he could free himself. In some indirect yet significant way, the raid at Harpers Ferry involved the working out of psychological turmoil that had troubled Brown since childhood.

Does all this speculation lead us then to assume that childhood neuroses rather than moral conviction dictated Brown's actions? No responsible historian or psychoanalyst would jump to such a conclusion. To do so would be to take a reductionist view of history, explaining major events by tracing them to infantiie conflicts. Such an approach assumes that the explanation for what has happened in the past lies in the psychic turmoil of great men. We might then conclude that had John Brown not been abused by his father, the raid on Harpers Ferry would never have occurred. Since Harpers Ferry led directly to the Civil War, even the war might have been avoided. How much more peaceful history would be in a world where all boys and girls enjoyed a childhood free of trauma!

No, a full explanation of any person's actions and beliefs must, in the end, be multicausal if it is to reflect the complexity of real life. We cannot minimize the sincerity—nor the nobility—of Brown's belief in the brotherhood of blacks and whites. Yet the stirrings of deeply rooted unconscious forces can no more be neglected than the more rational components of behavior.

This psychoanalytic interpretation, then, is not offered as a definitive or an exclusive one. And our brief exposition of one letter constitutes only one small part of what should properly be a much larger analysis of Brown's personality and career. But the exposition is ample enough to suggest how fruitful a psychoanalytical approach can be. As Michael Rogin suggested in the case of Andrew Jackson, it provides historians with a theory which sensitizes them to profitable themes, motifs, and vocabularies. An awareness of recurring tensions stemming from Brown's childhood makes it possible to appreciate how his personal sufferings incorporated the larger events of the period. Erik Erikson, the psychologist who has done the most to introduce psychoanalytic insight into history, has at the same time stressed the need to root psychology firmly in contemporary historical context. What Erikson said of such great men as Martin Luther or Mahatma Gandhi could easily be said of Brown. All three shared a "grim willingness to do the dirty work of their ages." They achieved a spiritual breakthrough by translating their inner conflicts into behaviors that spoke to the consciousness of their generations. Or as Erikson said of Luther, Brown had to strike his blow against slavery "to lift his individual patienthood to the level of a universal one, and to try to solve for all what he could not solve for himself alone."

At the moment Brown transcended his life of failure, he forced his generation to identify either positively or negatively with the action he took to liberate black Americans. His act of violence was appropriate to what Oates described as "the violent, irrational, and paradoxical times in which he lived." Given his profoundly religious nature and commitment to human liberty and equality, Brown could not be at peace until his society recognized the contradiction between its religious and political ideals and the existence of slavery. Within Erikson's historical scheme Brown's angry messianism on the slave question intersected with the collective history of the racist, slave society in which he lived.

In the end, John Brown turned the tables on society. His raid on Harpers Ferry pressed his fellow Americans to consider whether it was not actually their values, and society's, which were immoral and "abnormal." The outbreak of civil war, after all, demonstrated that American society was so maladjusted and so divided that it could not remain a "normal," integrated whole without violently purging itself. If Brown's raid was an isolated act of a disturbed man, why did it drive an entire generation to the brink of war? Why did Brown's generation find it impossible to agree about the meaning of Harpers Ferry? As C. Vann Woodward concluded, the importance lay not so much in the man or event, but in the use made of them by northern and southern hotheads. For every Emerson or Thoreau who pronounced the raid the work of a saint, a southern fire-eater condemned the venture as the villainy of all northerners.

None of these partisans paid much attention to evidence. A crisis mentality thwarted any attempts at understanding or reconciliation. In the fury of mutual recrimination, both sides lost sight of the man who had provoked the public outcry and propelled the nation toward war. In such times it will always be, as abolitionist Wendell Phillips remarked, "hard to tell who's mad."

Additional Reading

John Brown's truth goes marching on, and so do the books about him. In the 1970s, four full-scale biographies were issued, the best of which is Stephen Oates, *To Purge This Land with Blood* (New York, 1970). Oates's treatment is even-handed, scholarly, and stirring in its narrative. (Other biographies available are by Jules C. Abels, Truman Nelson, and Richard O. Boyer.) Oswald Garrison Villard, *John Brown, 1800–1859: A Biography Fifty Years After* (Boston, 1910) is an older work worth reading. It draws upon and excerpts many primary sources. C. Vann Woodward, "John Brown's Private War," is one of the best short interpretive essays available on the raid and can be found in his *Burden of Southern History* (Baton Rouge, La., 1968). For a detailed account of Brown's earlier doings in Kansas, see James C. Malin, *John Brown and the Legacy of Fifty-six* (Philadelphia, 1942).

Readers wishing to see for themselves the evidence and conflicting interpretations of Brown will do well to begin with Jonathan Fanton and Richard Warch, eds., *John Brown* (Englewood Cliffs, N.J., 1973). This well-edited collection of primary and secondary materials concentrates on documenting the Harpers Ferry raid and its preparations. It also provides evidence relating to Brown's personality and previous career. Franklin B. Sanborn, *The Life and Letters of John Brown* (Boston, 1891), unabashedly sympathetic to Brown, contains many valuable personal letters for those wishing to pursue psychoanalytic (or other) interpretations. The fullest collection of materials on the raid and trial is *The Life, Trial and Execution of John Brown* (New York, 1859).

The field of psychohistory is broad and diverse. Not only is applying psychiatric theory to historical situations a delicate task, psychology and psychoanalysis are fields undergoing continuous revision. With so little space available in this chapter, we chose to avoid the intricacies of debate over the validity of psychoanalytic methods and have concentrated on giving readers a taste of the kinds of evidence that psychohistorians habitually examine and the kinds of deductions they make. Psychoanalysis can be an arcane discipline, and it harbors more than its share of dogmatists and true-believers. We would argue, as critic Frederick Crews once noted, that it is possible to "dissent" from the rigid orthodoxy of psychoanalytic theory "without forsaking the most promising aspects of psychoanalysis—its attentiveness to signs of conflict, its hospitality to multiple significance, its ideas of ambivalence, identification, repression, and projection." Those readers who wish further introduction to psychoanalytic theory may consult Franz Alexander and Helen Ross, *The Impact of Freudian Psychiatry* (Chicago, 1961) and J. A. C. Brown, *Freud and the Post-Freudians* (London, 1960).

The promise of psychoanalytic techniques for doing history received widespread attention when William L. Langer used his presidential address to the American Historical Association to call for further efforts in the genre. Langer's address, "The Next Assignment," is reprinted in the *American Historical Review*, LXIII (January 1958), 283–304. A more recent "state of the art" evaluation is Robert J. Lifton, ed., *Explorations in Psychohistory* (New York, 1974), which includes essays by eminent practitioners of the craft such as Lifton himself, Erik Erikson, Bruce Mazlish, Philip Rieff, and Robert Coles. Also useful is George M. Kren and Leon H. Rappoport, eds., *Varieties of Psychohistory* (New York, 1976) and Bruce Mazlish, *Psychoanalysis and History,* rev. ed. (New York, 1971).

For an example of responsible psychohistory, see Erik Erikson's excellent biographies, *Young Man Luther* (New York, 1958) and *Gandhi's Truth* (New York, 1969). On John Brown himself, Alan Nevins provides a psychological interpretation in *The Emergence of Lincoln,* vol. 2 (New York, 1950) 5–27 and 70–97. On the other hand, the excesses of the trade are lamentably demonstrated in a book co-authored by Sigmund Freud himself and William Bullitt, *Thomas Woodrow Wilson* (Boston, reprinted 1968). Skeptics who believe that psychohistory is by its very nature flawed will find comforting reinforcement in *Shrinking History* (New York, 1980), an incisive critique of the discipline by a friend and colleague of ours, David Stannard, who most emphatically had nothing to do with the present chapter.

Finally, as professed amateurs in the psychoanalytic field, we would like to thank Dr. David Musto, able psychiatrist and historian, whose graduate seminar at Yale provided a fine introduction to the territory. Our specific evaluation of John Brown's motives was substantially guided by consultation with two practicing psychiatrists, both aware of the possibilities and limitations of their discipline. Dr. Geoff Linburn of the M.I.T. mental health staff outlined the interpretive limits of what our evidence might sustain. Dr. Eric Berger of Yale's psychiatric faculty unlocked many of the possible meanings to be found in John Brown's autobiographical letter. In addition, our friend Dr. John Rugge brought into clear focus Brown's striking concern for property and ownership. None of these gentlemen, we should stress, is responsible for the final results exhibited here. It is we who wrestled Brown to the couch and, perforce, we take full responsibility for the consequences.

SEVEN

❖

The View from the Bottom Rail

Thunder. From across the swamps and salt marshes of the Carolina coast came the distant, repetitive pounding. Thunder out of a clear blue sky. Down at the slave quarters, young Sam Mitchell heard the noise and wondered. In Beaufort, the nearby village, planter John Chaplin heard too, and dashed for his carriage. The drive back to his plantation was as quick as Chaplin could make it. Once home, he ordered his wife and children to pack; then looked for his slaves. The flatboat must be made ready, he told them; the family was going to Charleston. He needed eight men at the oars. One of the slaves, Sam Mitchell's father, brought the news to his wife and son at the slave quarters. "You ain't gonna row no boat to Charleston," the wife snapped, "you go out dat back door and keep a-going." Young Sam was mystified by all the commotion. How could it thunder without a cloud in the sky? "Son, dat ain't no t'under," explained the mother, "dat Yankee come to gib you freedom."

The pounding of the guns came relatively quickly to Beaufort—November of 1861, only seven months after the first hostilities at Fort Sumter. Yet it was only a matter of time before the thunder of freedom rolled across the rest of the south, from the bayous and deltas of Louisiana in 1862 to the farms around Richmond in 1865. And as the guns of the Union spoke, thousands of Sam Mitchells experienced their own unforgettable moments. Freedom was coming to a nation of four million slaves.

To most slaves, the men in the blue coats were foreigners. As foreigners, they were sometimes suspect. Many southern masters painted the

prospect of Northern invasion in deliberately lurid colors. Union soldiers, one Tennessee slave was told, "got long horns on their heads, and
tushes in their mouths, and eyes sticking out like a cow! They're mean
old things." A terrified Mississippi slave refused to come down out of
a tree until the Union soldier below her took off his cap and demonstrated he had no horns. Many slaves, however, took such tales with
more than a grain of salt. "We all hear 'bout dem Yankees," a Carolina
slave told his overseer. "Folks tell we they has horns and a tail . . . W'en
I see dem coming I shall run like all possess." But as soon as the overseer
fled, leaving the plantation in the slaves' care, the tune changed: "Good-
by, ole man, good-by. That's right. Skedaddle as fast as you kin. . . . We's

This slave family lived on a plantation at Beaufort, South Carolina, not far from
the plantation where Sam Mitchell heard the thunder of northern guns in 1861.
The photograph was taken after northern forces had occupied the Sea Island
area.

gwine to run sure enough; but we knows the Yankees, an' we runs that way."

For some slaves, the habit of long years, the bond of loyalty, or the fear of alternatives led them to side with their masters. Faithful slaves hid valuable silver, persuaded Yankees that their departed masters were actually Union sympathizers, or feigned contagious illness in order to scare off marauding soldiers. One pert slave even led Yankees right to the plantation beehives. "De Yankees forgot all about de meat an' things dey done stole," she noted with satisfaction; "they took off down de road at a run." But in many cases, the conflict between loyalty and freedom caused confusion and anguish. An old Georgia couple, both over sixty, greeted the advance of Sherman's soldiers calmly and with apparent lack of interest. They seemed entirely content to remain under the care of their master instead of joining the mass of slaves flocking along behind Sherman's troops. As the soldiers prepared to leave, however, the old woman suddenly stood up, a "fierce, almost devilish" look in her eyes, and turned to her husband. "What you sit dar for?" she asked vehemently. "You s'pose I wait sixty years for nutten? Don't yer see de door open? I'se follow my child; I not stay. Yes, anudder day I goes 'long wid dese people; yes, sar, I walks till I drop in my tracks."

Other slaves felt no hesitation about choosing freedom; indeed, they found it difficult to contain the joy within them. One woman, who overheard the news of emancipation just before she was to serve her master's dinner, asked to be excused because she had to get water from a nearby spring. Once she had reached the seclusion of the spring, she allowed her feelings free rein.

> I jump up and scream, "Glory, glory hallelujah to Jesus! I'se free! I'se free! Glory to God, you come down an' free us; no big man could do it." An' I got sort o' scared, afeared somebody hear me, an' I takes another good look, an' fall on de groun' an' roll over, an' kiss de groun' fo' de Lord's sake, I's so full o' praise to Masser Jesus.

To the newly freed slaves, it seemed as if the world had been turned upside down. Rich and powerful masters were fleeing before Yankees, while freed slaves were left with the run of the plantation. The situation was summed up succinctly by one black soldier who was surprised—and delighted—to find that his former master was among the prisoners he was guarding. "Hello, massa!" he said cheerfully, "bottom rail top dis time!"

IN SEARCH OF THE FREEDMEN'S POINT OF VIEW

The freeing of four million blacks surely ranks as one of the major events in American history. Yet the story has not been an easy one to tell. To understand the personal trials and triumphs of the newly liberated slaves, or freedmen as they came to be called, the historian must draw upon the personal experiences of those at the center of the drama. He must recreate the freedman's point of view. But slaves had occupied the lowest level of America's social and economic scale. They sat, as the black soldier correctly noted, on the bottom rail of the fence. For several reasons, that debased position has made it unusually difficult for historians to recover the freedman's point of view.

In the first place, most histories suffer from a natural "top-rail" bias. They tend to take as their subjects members of the higher social classes. Histories cannot be written without the aid of documentary raw material, left in the historical record by participants. The more detailed the records, the easier it is to write a history. By and large, those on the top rails of society produce the best and most voluminous records. Having been privileged to receive an education, they are more apt to publish memoirs, keep diaries, or write letters. As leaders of society who make decisions, they are the subjects of official minutes and records. They are more often written about and commented on by their contemporaries.

At the other end of the social spectrum, "bottom-rail" people lead lives that are commonly repetitious. While a political leader involves himself in what appears to be one momentous issue after another, a farmer most often plants the same crop and follows the ritual of the seasons year after year. Furthermore, the individual actions of the anonymous majority seem to have little effect on the course of history. Biographical details of such people appear both uninspiring and unavailable, at first glance anyway, when compared to the bustling lives of the powerful. Thus the elites of any society have long been the natural subjects of historians.

The decade of the 1970s saw an increasing interest by historians in the writing of social histories that would shed greater light on the activities and feelings of bottom rail people. We saw, for example, that a knowledge of the social and economic position of the serving class was essential to understanding the volatile society of early Virginia. Similarly, we turned to the social tensions of ordinary farmers in order to explain the alliances behind the witchcraft controversy at Salem. Often enough, social historians have found it difficult to piece together the lives of any anonymous class of Americans; yet reconstructing the perspective of the black slave or freedman has proved particularly challenging, simply because few written source materials are available. Black slaves were not only discouraged from learning to read and write, southern legislatures passed slave codes which flatly forbade whites to teach them.

The laws were not entirely effective; a few blacks employed as drivers on large plantations learned to read and correspond so that their absent masters might send them instructions. Some black preachers were also literate. Still, most reading remained a clandestine affair, done out of sight of the master or other whites. During the war, a literate slave named Squires Jackson was eagerly scanning a newspaper for word of northern victories when his master unexpectedly entered the room and demanded to know what the slave was doing. The surprised reader deftly turned the newspaper upside down, put on a foolish grin, and said, "Confederates done won the war!" The master laughed and went about his business.

Even though most slaves never wrote letters, kept diaries, or left any other written records, it might at first seem easy enough to learn about slave life from accounts written by white contemporaries. Slavery, after all, was an institution whose faults and alleged virtues were hotly debated by nineteenth-century Americans. Any number of letters, books, travellers' accounts, and diaries survive, full of descriptions of life under slavery and of the experiences of freedmen after the war. Yet here too, the question of perspective raises serious problems. The vantage point of white Americans observing slavery was emphatically not that of slaves who lived under the "peculiar institution," nor of those freedmen forced to cope with their dramatically changed circumstances. The marked differences between the social and psychological positions of blacks and whites makes it extremely difficult to reconstruct the black point of view solely from white accounts.

Consider, first, the observations of whites who associated most often and most closely with black slaves: their masters. The relation between master and slave was inherently unequal. Blacks were at the mercy of their owners' whims. Slaves could be whipped for trifling offenses; they could be sold or separated from their families and closest friends; even under "kind" masters, they were bound to labor as ordered if they wanted their ration of food and clothing. With slaves so dependent on the master's authority, they were hardly likely to reveal their true feelings; the dangerous consequences of such indiscretion were too great.

In fact, we have already encountered an example where a black was forced to deceive his master, the case of Squires Jackson and his newspaper. A moment's reflection will indicate that we narrated that story from Jackson's point of view, not the master's. Our impression of the slave's conduct would have been remarkably different if we had access only to a diary kept by Jackson's master. "A humorous incident occurred today," the entry might have read.

> While entering the woodshed to attend some business, I came upon my slave Squires. His large eyes were fixed with intense interest upon an old copy of a newspaper he had come upon, which alarmed me some until I discovered the rascal was reading its contents upside down. "Why Squires," I said innocently. "What is the latest news?" He looked up at me with a big grin and said, "Massa, de 'Federates jes' won de war!" It made me laugh to see the darkey's simple confidence. I wish I could share his optimism.

This entry is fictional, but having Jackson's version of the story serves to cast suspicion on similar entries in real planter diaries. One Louisiana slaveowner, for instance, marvelled that his field hands went on with their Christmas party apparently unaware that Yankee raiding parties had pillaged a nearby town. "We have been watching the negroes dancing for the last two hours. . . . They are having a merry time, thoughtless creatures, they think not of the morrow." It apparently never occurred to the planter that the "thoughtless" merriment may have been especially great because of the Northern troops nearby.*

The harsh realities of the war brought many southerners to realize for the first time just how little they really knew about their slaves. In areas where Union troops were near, slaves ran for freedom—often the very servants masters had deemed most loyal. Mary Chestnut, whose house was not far from Fort Sumter, sought in vain to penetrate the blank expressions of her slaves. "Not by one word or look can we detect any

---

*Readers who review the opening narrative of this chapter will discover that they have already encountered quite a few other examples of blacks concealing their true feelings. In fact, except for the black soldier's comment about the bottom rail being top, every example of white–black relations cited in the opening section has some element of concealment or deception, either by blacks toward whites, or by whites toward blacks. It may be worth noting that we did not select the opening incidents with that fact in mind. The preponderance of deception was noted only when we reviewed the draft several days after it had been written.

"They are having a merry time, thoughtless creatures, they think not of the morrow." This scene of a Christmas party, similar to the one described by the Louisiana planter, appeared with an article written by a northern correspondent for *Frank Leslie's Illustrated Newspaper* in 1857. The picture, reflecting the popular stereotype of slaves as cheerful and ignorantly content with their lot, suggests that the social constraints of the times made it as difficult for southern blacks to be completely candid with their northern liberators as it had been to be candid with their southern masters.

change in the demeanor of these Negro servants. . . . You could not tell that they even hear the awful noise that is going on in the bay [at Fort Sumter], though it is dinning in their ears night and day. . . . Are they stolidly stupid, or wiser than we are, silent and strong, biding their time?"

It is tempting to suppose that northerners, as liberators of the slaves, might provide more sympathetic or accurate accounts of freedmen's attitudes. But that is a dangerous assumption to make. Although virtually all northern slaves had been freed by 1820, race prejudice remained overwhelmingly evident. Antislavery forces often combined a vehement dislike of slavery with an equally vehement desire to keep blacks out of the North. For blacks who did live there, most housing and transportation facilities were segregated. Whites and blacks had much less contact than afforded by the easy, if unequal, familiarity common in the South.

Consequently, while some Union soldiers went out of their way to be kind to the slaves they encountered, many more looked upon blacks with distaste and open hostility. Many Yankees strongly believed that they were fighting a war to save the Union, not to free the "cursed Nigger," as one recruit put it. Even white officers who commanded black regiments could be remarkably unsympathetic. "Any one listening to your shouting and singing can see how grotesquely ignorant you are," one officer lectured his troops, when they refused to accept less than the pay promised them upon enlistment. Missionaries and other sympathetic northerners who came to occupied territory understood the slaves better, but even they had preconceptions to overcome. "I saw some very low-looking women who answered very intelligently, contrary to my expectations," noted Philadelphia missionary Laura Towne. Where she was serving, in the Carolina sea-islands near Beaufort, she observed that "some, indeed most of [the slaves], were the real bullet-headed negroes." Another female missionary, much less sympathetic than Laura Towne, bridled when a black child greeted her with too much familiarity. "I say good-mornin' to my young missus," recounted the child to a friend, "and she say, 'I slap your mouth for your impudence, you nigger.' " Such callousness underlines the need for caution when dealing with northern accounts.

Indeed, the more perceptive northern observers recognized that blacks would continue to be circumspect around whites. Just as the slave had been dependent on his southern masters, so the freedman found himself similarly vulnerable to the new class of conquerors. Blacks often responded to questions with answers carefully designed to please. "One of these blacks, fresh from slavery, will most adroitly tell you precisely what you want to hear," noted northerner Charles Nordhoff.

> To cross-examine such a creature is a task of the most delicate nature; if you chance to put a leading question he will answer to its spirit as closely as the compass needle answers to the magnetic pole. Ask if the enemy had fifty thousand men, and he will be sure that they had at least that many; express your belief that they had not five thousand, and he will laugh at the idea of their having more than forty-five hundred.

Samuel Gridley Howe, a wartime commissioner investigating the freedmen's condition, saw the situation clearly. "The negro, like other men, naturally desires to live in the light of truth," he argued, "but he hides in the shadow of falsehood, more or less deeply, according as his safety or welfare seems to require it. Other things equal, the freer a people, the more truthful; and only the perfectly free and fearless are perfectly truthful.'"

Even sympathetic northerners were at a disadvantage in recounting the freedmen's point of view, simply because black culture was so foreign to them. The world of the southern field hand, black religious culture, surviving African folk customs and songs—all these were unfamiliar to northern observers. Black dialect too created problems. Charles Nordhoff noted that often he had the feeling that he was "speaking with foreigners." The slaves' phrase "I go shum" puzzled him until he discovered it to be a contraction of "I'll go see about it." Another missionary was "teaching the little darkies gymnastics and what various things were for, eyes, etc. He asked what ears were made for, and when they said, 'To yer with,' he could not understand them at all."

If black dialect was difficult to understand, black culture and religion could appear even more unfathomable. Although most slaves nominally shared with northerners a belief in Christianity, black methods of worship shocked more than one staid Unitarian. After church meetings, slaves often participated in a singing and dancing session known as a "shout," where the leader would sing out a line of song and the chorus respond, dancing in rhythm to the music. As the night proceeded, the music became more vocal and the dancing more vigorous. "Tonight I have been to a 'shout,'" reported Laura Towne, "which seems to me certainly the remains of some old idol worship . . . I never saw anything so savage." Another missionary noted, "It was the most hideous and at the same time the most pitiful sight I ever witnessed."

Thus, as sympathetic as many northerners wished to be, significant obstacles prevented them from fully appreciating the freedman's point of view. With race prejudice so prevalent, with blacks in such a vulnerable position, with black culture so much at odds with white, it is not surprising that perceptive observers like Nordhoff felt as if they were speaking with "foreigners." The nature of slave society and the persistence of race prejudice made it virtually impossible for blacks and whites to deal with one another in open, candid ways.

THE FREEDMEN SPEAK

Given the scarcity of first-person black accounts, how can we fully recover the freedman's point of view? From the very beginning, some observers recognized the value that black testimony would have and worked to collect it. If few blacks could write, their stories could be written down by others and made public. Oral testimony, transcribed by literate editors, would allow blacks to speak out on issues that affected them most closely.

The tradition of oral evidence began even before the slaves were freed. Abolitionists recognized the value of firsthand evidence against the slave system. They took down the stories of fugitive slaves who had safely made their way North, and published the accounts. During the war, Congress also established the Freedman's Inquiry Commission, which collected information about blacks that might aid the government in formulating policies toward the newly freed slaves.

In the half-century following Reconstruction, however, interest in preserving black history generally languished. An occasional journalist or historian travelled through the South to interview former slaves. Educators at black schools, such as the Hampton Institute, published a few recollections. But a relatively small number of subjects were interviewed. Often the interviews were published in daily newspapers whose standards of accuracy were not high and where limitations of space required that the interviews be severely edited.

Furthermore, the vast majority of professional historians writing about Reconstruction ignored these interviews, as well as the freedmen's perspective in general. They most often relied on white accounts which, not unexpectedly, painted a rather partial picture. William A. Dunning, a historian at Columbia University, was perhaps the most influential scholar in setting forth the prevalent viewpoint. He painted the freedmen as childish, happy-go-lucky creatures who failed to appreciate the responsibilities of their new status. "As the full meaning of [emancipation] was grasped by the freedmen," Dunning wrote, "great numbers of them abandoned their old homes, and, regardless of crops to be cultivated, stock to be cared for, or food to be provided, gave themselves up to testing their freedom. They wandered aimless but happy through the country. . . ." At the same time Dunning asserted that Confederate soldiers and other southern whites had "devoted themselves with desperate energy to the procurement of what must sustain the life of both themselves and their former slaves." Such were the conclusions deduced without the aid of the freedmen's perspectives.

Only in the twentieth century were systematic efforts made to question blacks about their experiences as slaves and freedmen. Interest in the black heritage rose markedly during the 1920s, in great part spurred by the efforts of black scholars like W. E. B. DuBois, Charles Johnson, and Carter Woodson, the editor and founder of the *Journal of Negro History*. Those scholars labored diligently to overturn the Reconstruction stereotypes promoted by the Dunning school. Moreover, the growth of both sociology and anthropology departments at American universities encouraged scholars to analyze Southern culture using the tools of the new social sciences. By the beginning of the 1930s historians at Fisk and Southern universities had instituted projects to collect oral evidence.

Ironically, it was the economic adversity of the Depression that sparked the greatest single effort to gather oral testimony from the freedmen. One of the many alphabet-soup agencies chartered by the Roosevelt administration was the Federal Writers' Project (FWP). Primarily, the project sought to compile cultural guides to each of the forty-eight states, using unemployed writers and journalists to collect and edit the information. But under the direction of folklorist John Lomax, the FWP also organized staffs in many states to interview former slaves.

Although Lomax's project placed greatest emphasis on collecting black folklore and songs, the FWP's directive to interviewers included a long list of historical questions that interviewers were encouraged to ask. The following sampling gives an indication of the project's interests:

> What work did you do in slavery days? Did you ever earn any money? What did you eat and how was it cooked? Any possums? Rabbits? Fish? Was there a jail for slaves? Did you ever see any slaves sold or auctioned off? How and for what causes were the slaves punished? Tell what you saw.
> What do you remember about the war that brought you your freedom? When the Yankees came what did they do or say?
> What did the slaves do after the war? What did they receive generally? What do they think about the reconstruction period?

The results of these interviews are remarkable, if only in terms of sheer bulk. More than 2,300 were recorded and edited in state FWP offices and then sent to Washington, assembled in 1941, and published in typescript. A facsimile edition, issued during the 1970s, takes up nineteen volumes. Supplementary materials, including hundreds of interviews never forwarded to Washington during the project's life, comprise another twelve volumes, with additional materials forthcoming. Benjamin Botkin, the series' original editor, recognized the collection's importance:

> These life histories, taken down as far as possible in the narrator's words, constitute an invaluable body of unconscious evidence or indirect source material, which scholars and writers dealing with the South, especially,

social psychologists and cultural anthropolgists, cannot afford to reckon without. For the first and last time, a large number of surviving slaves (many of whom have since died) have been permitted to tell their own story, in their own way.

At first glance, the slave narrative collection would appear to fulfill admirably the need for a guide to the freedmen's point of view. But even Botkin, for all his enthusiasm, recognized that the narratives could not simply be taken at face value. Like other primary source materials, they need to be viewed in terms of the context in which they originated.

To begin with, no matter how massive the nineteen volumes of interviews may appear on the library shelf, they still constitute a small sampling of the original four million freedmen. What sort of selection bias might exist? Geographic imbalance comes quickly to mind. Are the slave interviews drawn from a broad cross-section of southern states? Counting the number of slaves interviewed from each state, we discover that there are only 155 interviews from blacks living in Virginia, Missouri, Maryland, Delaware, and Kentucky—about 6 percent of the total number of interviews published. Yet in 1860, 23 percent of the southern slave population lived in those states. Thus the upper South is underrepresented in the collection. For researchers who wished to investigate whether conditions varied from the border states to the deep south, this geographic bias would have to be taken into account.*

What about age? Since the interviews took place primarily between 1936 and 1938, ex-slaves were fairly old: fully two-thirds of them were over 80. The predominance of elderly interviewees raises several questions. Most obviously, the Civil War was already seventy years in the past. How sharp were the informants' memories? Ability to recall accurately varies from person to person, but common sense suggests that the further away from an event, the less detailed one's memory is likely to be. In addition, age may have biased the *type* of recollections as well as their accuracy. Historian John Blassingame has noted that the average life-expectancy of a slave in 1850 was less than 50 years. Those who lived to a ripe old age might well have survived because they were treated better than the average slave. If so, their accounts would reflect some of the milder experiences of slaves.

Secondly, if those interviewed were predominantly old in 1936, they

*Statistics quoted are for the original slave narrative interviews only. They do not include materials issued in the supplementary volumes, which are helping to rectify the imbalance.

were predominantly young during the Civil War. Almost half (43 percent) were less than ten years old in 1865. Sixty-seven percent were under fifteen years old, and 83 percent were under twenty. Thus, many remembered slavery as it would have been experienced by a child. Since the conditions of bondage were relatively less harsh for a child than for an adult slave, once again the FWP narratives may be somewhat skewed toward an optimistic view of slavery. (On the other hand, it might be argued that since children are so impressionable, memories both good and bad might have been vividly magnified.)

Other possible sampling biases come to mind—the sex of the subjects or the kinds of labor they performed as slaves. But distortions may be introduced into the slave narratives in ways more serious than sample bias. Interviewers, simply by choosing their questions, define the kinds of information a subject will volunteer. We have already seen that sensitive observers, such as Charles Nordhoff, recognized how important it was not to ask leading questions. But even Nordhoff may not have realized how many unconscious cues the most innocent questions carry.

Social scientists specializing in interviewing have pointed out that even the grammatical form of a question will influence a subject's response. Take, for example, the following questions:

Where did you hear about this job opening?
How did you hear about this job opening?
So you saw our want ad for this job?

Each question is directed at the same information, yet each suggests to the subject a different response. The first version (*"Where* did you hear . . .") implies that the interviewer wants a specific, limited answer. ("Down at the employment center.") The second question, by substituting *how* for *where,* invites the subject to offer a longer response. ("Well, I'd been looking around for a job for several weeks, and I was over at the employment office when. . . .") The final question signals that the interviewer wants only a yes or no confirmation to a question whose answer he believes he already knows.

Interviewers, in other words, constantly communicate to their subjects the kinds of evidence they want, the length of the answers, and even the manner in which answers ought to be offered. If such interviewing "cues" influence routine conversations, they prove even more crucial when a subject as controversial as slavery is involved, and where relations between blacks and whites continue to be strained. In fact, the most important cue an interviewer was likely to have given was one presented before any conversation took place. Was the interviewer white or black? William Ferris, a sociologist obtaining oral folklore in the Mississippi Delta region in 1968 discussed the problem. "It was not possible to maintain rapport with both Whites and Blacks in the same community," he noted,

> for the confidence and cooperation of each was based on their belief that I was 'with them' in my convictions about racial taboos of Delta society. Thus when I was 'presented' to Blacks by a white member of the community, the informants regarded me as a member of the white caste and therefore limited their lore to noncontroversial topics. . . .

Such tensions were even more prevalent throughout the South during the 1930s. In hundreds of ways, blacks were made aware that they were still considered inferior to whites, and that they were to remain within strictly segregated and subordinate bounds. From 1931 to 1935, more than 70 blacks were lynched in the South, often for minor or nonexistent crimes. Blacks in prison found themselves forced to negotiate grossly unfavorable labor contracts if they wished to be released. Many share-croppers and other poor farmers were constantly in debt to white property owners.

Smaller matters of etiquette reflected the larger state of affairs. A southern white would commonly address adult blacks by their first names, or as "boy," "auntie," "uncle," regardless of the black person's status and even if the white knew the black's full name. Blacks were required to address whites as "ma'am" or "mister." Such distinctions were maintained even on the telephone. If a black placed a long-distance call for "Mr. Smith" in a neighboring town, the white operator would ask, "Is he colored?" The answer being yes, her reply would be, "Don't you say 'Mister' to me. He ain't 'Mister' to me." Conversely, an operator would refuse to place a call by a black who did not address her as "Ma'am."

In such circumstances, most blacks were naturally reticent about volunteering information to white FWP interviewers. "Lots of old slaves closes the door before they tell the truth about their days of slavery," noted one Texas black to an interviewer. "When the door is open, they tell how kind their masters was and how rosy it all was. . . ." Samuel S. Taylor, a skilled black interviewer in Arkansas, found that he had to reassure informants that the information they were giving would not be used against them. "I've told you too much," one subject concluded. "How come they want all this stuff from the colored people anyway. Do you take any stories from the white people? They know all about it. They know more about it than I do. They dont need me to tell it to them."

Often the whites who interviewed blacks lived in the same town and were long acquaintances. "I 'members when you was barefoot at de bottom," one black told his white (and balding) interviewer; "now I see you a settin' dere, gittin' bare at de top, as bare as de palm of my hand." Another black revealed an even closer relationship when he noted that his wife Ellen " 'joy herself, have a good time nussin' [nursing] white folks chillun. Nussed you; she tell me 'bout it many time." In such circumstances blacks could hardly be expected to speak frankly. One older woman summed up the situation quite cheerfully. "Oh, I know your father en your granfather en all of dem. Bless Mercy, child, I don't want to tell you nothin' but what to please you."

Although such statements put a researcher on guard, readers who are new to this field may still find it difficult to appreciate the varying responses that different interviewers might elicit. In order to bring home the point more forcibly, it may be helpful to analyze an interview that we came across during our own research in the slave narrative collection. The interview is with Susan Hamlin, a black who lived in Charleston, and we reprint it below exactly as it appears in typescript.

Interview With Ex-Slave

On July 6th, I interviewed Susan Hamlin, ex-slave, at 17 Henrietta street, Charleston, S. C. She was sitting just inside of the front door, on a step leading up to the porch, and upon hearing me inquire for her she assumed that I was from the Welfare office, from which she had received aid prior to its closing. I did not correct this impression, and at no time did she suspect that the object of my visit was to get the story of her experience as a slave. During our conversation she mentioned her age. "Why that's very interesting, Susan," I told her, "If you are that old you probably remember the Civil War and slavery days." "Yes, Ma'am, I been a slave myself," she said, and told me the following story:

"I kin remember some things like it was yesterday, but I is 104 years old now, and age is starting to get me, I can't remember everything like I use to. I getting old, old. You know I is old when I been a grown woman when the Civil War broke out. I was hired out then, to a Mr. McDonald, who lived on Atlantic Street, and I remembers when de first shot was fired, and the shells went right over de city. I got seven dollars a month for looking after children, not taking them out, you understand, just minding them. I did not got the money, Mausa got it." "Don't you think that was fair?" I asked. "If you were fed and clothed by him, shouldn't he be paid

"I've told you too much. How come they want all this stuff from the colored people anyway? Do you take any stories from the white people? . . . They don't need me to tell it to them." This Georgia woman, like many of the subjects interviewed for the Federal Writers' Project, was still living in the 1930s on the plantation where she had grown up as a slave child. The plantation was still owned by descendants of her former master. Under such conditions suspicion toward Project interviewers was a predictable reaction, even if the interviewer was black; doubly so if he or she was white and a resident of the community.

for your work?" "Course it been fair," she answered, "I belong to him and he got to get something to take care of me."

"My name before I was married was Susan Calder, but I married a man name Hamlin. I belonged to Mr. Edward Fuller, he was president of the First National Bank. He was a good man to his people till de Lord took him. Mr. Fuller got his slaves by marriage. He married Miss Mikell, a lady what lived on Edisto Island, who was a slave owner, and we lived on Edisto on a plantation. I don't remember de name cause when Mr. Fuller got to be president of de bank we come to Charleston to live. He sell out the plantation and say them (the slaves) that want to come to Charleston with him could come and them what wants to stay can stay on the island with his wife's people. We had our choice. Some is come and some is stay, but my ma and us children come with Mr. Fuller.

We lived on St. Philip street. The house still there, good as ever. I go 'round there to see it all de time; the cistern still there too, where we used to sit 'round and drink the cold water, and eat, and talk and laugh. Mr. Fuller have lots of servants and the ones he didn't need hisself he hired out. The slaves had rooms in the back, the ones with children had two rooms and them that didn't have any children had one room, not to cook in but to sleep in. They all cooked and ate downstairs in the hall that they had for the colored people. I don't know about slavery but I know all the slavery I know about, the people was good to me. Mr. Fuller was a good man and his wife's people been grand people, all good to their slaves. Seem like Mr. Fuller just git his slaves so he could be good to dem. He made all the little colored chillen love him. If you don't believe they loved him what they all cry, and scream, and holler for when dey hear he dead? 'Oh, Mausa dead my Mausa dead, what I going to do, my Mausa dead.' Dey tell dem t'aint no use to cry, dat can't bring him back, but de chillen keep on crying. We used to call him Mausa Eddie but he named Mr. Edward Fuller, and he sure was a good man.

"A man come here about a month ago, say he from de Government, and dey send him to find out 'bout slavery. I give him most a book, and what he give me? A dime. He ask me all kind of questions. He ask me dis and he ask me dat, didn't de white people do dis and did dey do dat but Mr. Fuller was a good man, he was sure good to me and all his people, dey all like him, God bless him, he in de ground now but I ain't going to let nobody lie on him. You know he good when even the little chillen cry and holler when he dead. I tell you dey couldn't just fix us up any kind of way when we going to Sunday School. We had to be dressed nice, if you pass him and you ain't dress to suit him he send you right back and say tell your ma to see dat you dress right. Dey couldn't send you out in de cold barefoot neither. I 'member one day my ma want to send me wid some milk for her sister-in-law what live 'round de corner. I fuss cause it cold and say 'how you going to send me out wid no shoe, and it cold?' Mausa hear how I talkin and turn he back and laugh, den he call to my ma to gone in de house and find shoe to put on my feet and don't let him see me barefoot again in cold weather.

When de war start going good and de shell fly over Charleston he take all us up to Aiken for protection. Talk 'bout marching through Georgia, dey sure march through Aiken, soldiers was everywhere.

"My ma had six children, three boys and three girls, but I de only one left, all my white people and all de colored people gone, not a soul left but me. I ain't been sick in 25 years. I is near my church and I don't miss service any Sunday, night or morning. I kin walk wherever I please, I kin walk to de Battery if I want to. The Welfare use to help me but dey shut down now, I can't find out if dey going to open again or not. Miss (Mrs.) Buist and Miss Pringle, dey help me when I can go there but all my own dead."

"Were most of the masters kind?" I asked. "Well you know," she answered, "times den was just like dey is now, some was kind and some was mean; heaps of wickedness went on just de same as now. All my people was good people. I see some wickedness and I hear 'bout all kinds of t'ings but you don't know whether it was lie or not. Mr. Fuller been a Christian man."

"Do you think it would have been better if the Negroes had never left Africa?" was the next question I asked. "No Ma'am," (emphatically) dem heathen didn't have no religion. I tell you how I t'ink it is. The Lord made t'ree nations, the white, the red and the black, and put dem in different places on de earth where dey was to stay. Dose black ignoramuses in Africa forgot God, and didn't have no religion and God blessed and prospered the white people dat did remember Him and sent dem to teach de black people even if dey have to grab dem and bring dem into bondage till dey learned some sense. The Indians forgot God and dey had to be taught better so dey land was taken away from dem. God sure bless and prosper de white people and He put de red and de black people under dem so dey could teach dem and bring dem into sense wid God. Dey had to get dere brains right, and honor God, and learn uprightness wid God cause ain't He make you, and ain't His Son redeem you and save you wid His precious blood. You kin plan all de wickedness you want and pull hard as you choose but when the Lord mek up His mind you is to change, He can change you dat quick (snapping her fingers) and easy. You got to believe on Him if it tek bondage to bring you to your knees.

You know I is got converted. I been in Big Bethel (church) on my knees praying under one of de preachers. I see a great, big, dark pack on my back, and it had me all bent over and my shoulders drawn down, all hunch up. I look up and I see de glory, I see a big beautiful light, a great light, and in de middle is de Sabior, hanging so (extending her arms) just like He died. Den I gone to praying good, and I can feel de sheckles (shackles) loose up and moving and de pack fall off. I don't know where it went to, I see de angels in de Heaven, and hear dem say 'Your sins are forgiven." I scream and fell off so. (Swoon.) When I come to dey has laid me out straight and I know I is converted cause you can't see no such sight and go on like you is before. I know I is still a sinner but I believe in de power of God and I trust his Holy name. Den dey put me wid de seekers but I know I is already saved."

"Did they take good care of the slaves when their babies were born?" she was asked. "If you want chickens for fat (to fatten) you got to feed dem," she said with a smile, "and if you want people to work dey got to be strong, you got to feed dem and take care of dem too. If dey can't work it come out of your pocket. Lots of wickedness gone on in dem days, just as it do now, some good, some mean, black and white, it just dere nature, if dey good dey going to be kind to everybody, if dey mean dey going to be mean to everybody. Sometimes chillen was sold away from dey parents. De Mausa would come and say "Where Jennie," tell um to put clothes on dat baby, I want um. He sell de baby and de ma scream and holler, you know how dey carry on. Geneally (generally) dey sold it when de ma wasn't dere. Mr. Fuller didn't sell none of us, we stay wid our ma's till we grown. I stay wid my ma till she dead.

"You know I is mix blood, my grandfather bin a white man and my grandmother a mulatto. She been marry to a black so dat how I get fix like I is. I got both blood, so how I going to quarrel wid either side?"

SOURCE: Interview with Susan Hamlin, 17 Henrietta Street.

NOTE * Susan lives with a mulatto family of the better type. The name is Hamlin not Hamilton, and her name prior to her marriage was Calder not Collins. I paid particular attention to this and had them spell the names for me. I would judge Susan to be in the late nineties but she is wonderfully well preserved. She now claims to be 104 years old.

From the beginning, the circumstances of this conversation arouse suspicion. The white interviewer, Jessie Butler, mentions that she allowed Hamlin to think she was from the welfare office. Evidently, Butler thought Hamlin would speak more freely if the real purpose of the visit was hidden. But surely the deception had the opposite effect. Hamlin, like most of the blacks interviewed, was elderly, unable to work, and dependent on charity. If Butler appeared to be from the welfare office, Hamlin would likely have done whatever she could to ingratiate herself. Many blacks consistently assumed that their white interviewers had influence with the welfare office. "You through wid me now, boss? I sho' is glad of dat," concluded one subject. "Help all you kin to git me dat pension befo' I die and de Lord will bless you, honey. . . . Has you got a dime to give dis old nigger, boss?"

Furthermore, Butler's questioning was hardly subtle. When Hamlin noted that she had to give her master the money she made from looking after children, Butler asked, "Don't you think that was fair?" "Course it been fair," came the quick response. Hamlin knew very well what was expected, especially since Butler had already answered the question herself: "If you were fed and clothed by him, shouldn't he be paid for your work?"

Not surprisingly, then, the interview paints slavery in relatively mild colors. Hamlin describes in great detail how good her master was and how she had shoes in the winter. When asked whether most masters were kind, Hamlin appears eminently "fair"—"some was kind and some was mean." She admits hearing "all kinds of t'ings but you don't know whether it was lie or not." She does note that slave children could be sold away from parents and that black mothers protested; but she talks as if that were only to be expected. ("De ma scream and holler, you know how dey carry on.")

Equally flattering is the picture Hamlin paints of relations between the races. "Black ignoramuses" in Africa had forgotten about God, she explains, just as the Indians had; but "God sure bless and prosper de white people." So blacks and the Indians are placed under white supervision, "to get dere brains right, and honor God, and learn uprightness." Those were not exactly the words proslavery apologists would have used to describe the situation, but they were the same sentiments. Defenders of slavery constantly stressed that whites served as benevolent models ("parents," Andrew Jackson might have said) leading blacks and Indians on the slow upward road to civilization.

All these aspects of the interview led us to be suspicious about its content. Moreover, there were several additional clues in the document that puzzled us. Hamlin had mentioned a man who visited her "about a month ago, say he from de Government, and dey send him to find out 'bout slavery." Apparently her interview with Jessie Butler was the second she had given. Butler, for her part, made a fuss at the end of the

transcript over the spelling of Hamlin's name. ("I paid particular attention to this.") It was "Hamlin not Hamilton" and her maiden name was
"Calder not Collins." The phrasing indicates that somewhere else Butler
had seen Hamlin referred to as "Susan Hamilton." If someone had
interviewed Hamlin earlier, we wondered, could Hamilton have been
the name on that original report?

We found the answer when we continued on through the narrative
collection. The interview following Butler's was conducted by a man
named Augustus Ladson, with a slave named "Susan Hamilton." When
compared with Jessie Butler's interview, Augustus Ladson's makes ab-
sorbing reading. Here it is, printed exactly as it appears in the collection:

Ex-Slave 101 Years of Age

Has Never Shaken Hands Since 1863
Was on Knees Scrubbing when Freedom Gun Fired

I'm a hund'ed an' one years old now, son. De only one livin' in my
crowd frum de days I wuz a slave. Mr. Fuller, my master, who was
president of the Firs' National Bank, owned the fambly of us except my
father. There were eight men an' women with five girls an' six boys
workin' for him. Most o' them wus hired out. De house in which we stayed
is still dere with de sisterns an' slave quarters. I always go to see de old
home which is on St. Phillip Street.

My ma had t'ree boys an' t'ree girls who did well at their work. Hope
Mikell, my eldest brodder, an' James wus de shoemaker. William Fuller,
son of our Master, wus de bricklayer. Margurite an' Catharine wus de
maids an' look as de children.

My pa b'long to a man on Edisto Island. Frum what he said, his master
was very mean. Pa real name wus Adam Collins but he took his master'
name; he wus de coachman. Pa did supin one day en his master whipped
him. De next day which wus Monday, pa carry him 'bout four miles frum
home in de woods an' give him de same 'mount of lickin' he wus given
on Sunday. He tied him to a tree an' unhitched de horse so it couldn't git
tie-up an' kill e self. Pa den gone to de landin' an' cetch a boat dat wus
comin' to Charleston wood fa'm products. He (was) permitted by his
master to go to town on errands, which helped him to go on de boat
without bein' question'. W'en he got here he gone on de water-front an'

ax for a job on a ship so he could git to de North. He got de job an' sail'
wood de ship. Dey search de island up an' down for him wood houndogs
en w'en it wus t'ought he wus drowned, 'cause dey track him to de river,
did dey give up. One of his master' friend gone to New York en went
in a store w'ere pas wus employed as a clerk. he reconize' pa is easy is pa
reconize' him. He gone back home an' tell pa master who know den dat
pa wusn't comin' back an' before he died he sign' papers dat pa wus free.
Pa' ma wus dead an' he come down to bury her by de permission of his
master' son who had promised no ha'm would come to him, but dey wus'
fixin' plans to keep him, so he went to de Work House an' ax to be sold
'cause any slave could sell e self if e could git to de Work House. But it
wus on record down dere so dey couldn't sell 'im an' told him his master'
people couldn't hold him a slave.

People den use to do de same t'ings dey do now. Some marry an' some
live together jus' like now. One t'ing, no minister nebber say in readin'
de matrimony "let no man put asounder" 'cause a couple would be
married tonight an' tomorrow one would be taken away en be sold. All
slaves wus married in dere master house, in de livin' room where slaves
an' dere missus an' mossa wus to witness de ceremony. Brides use to wear
some of de finest dress an' if dey could afford it, have de best kind of
furniture. Your master nor your missus objected to good t'ings.

I'll always 'member Clory, de washer. She wus very high-tempered. She
was a mulatto with beautiful hair she could sit on; Clory didn't take
foolishness frum anybody. One day our missus gone in de laundry an' find
fault with de clothes. Clory didn't do a t'ing but pick her up bodily an'
throw 'er out de door. Dey had to sen' fur a doctor 'cause she pregnant
an' less than two hours de baby wus bo'n. Afta dat she begged to be sold
fur she didn't [want] to kill missus, but our master ain't nebber want to
sell his slaves. But dat didn't keep Clory frum gittin' a brutal whippin'.
Dey whip' 'er until dere wusn't a white spot on her body. Dat wus de
worst I ebber see a human bein' got such a beatin'. I t'ought she wus goin'
to die, but she got well an' didn't get any better but meaner until our
master decide it wus bes' to rent her out. She willingly agree' since she
wusn't 'round missus. She hated an' detest' both of them an' all de fambly.

W'en any slave wus whipped all de other slaves wus made to watch. I
see women hung frum de ceilin' of buildin's an' whipped with only supin
tied 'round her lower part of de body, until w'en dey wus taken down,
dere wusn't breath in de body. I had some terribly bad experiences.

Yankees use to come t'rough de streets, especially de Big Market,
huntin' those who want to go to de "free country" as dey call' it. Men an'
women wus always missin' an' nobody could give 'count of dere disap-
pearance. De men wus train' up North fur sojus.

De white race is so brazen. Dey come here an' run de Indians frum dere own lan', but dey couldn't make dem slaves 'cause dey wouldn't stan' for it. Indians use to git up in trees an' shoot dem with poison arrow. W'en dey couldn't make dem slaves den dey gone to Africa an' bring dere black brother an' sister. Dey say 'mong themselves, "we gwine mix dem up en make ourselves king. Dats d only way we'd git even with de Indians."

All time, night an' day, you could hear men an' women screamin' to de tip of dere voices as either ma, pa, sister, or brother wus take without any warnin' an' sell. Some time mother who had only one chile wus separated fur life. People wus always dyin' frum a broken heart.

One night a couple married an' de next mornin' de boss sell de wife. De gal ma got in in de street an' cursed de white woman fur all she could find. She said: "dat damn white, pale-face bastard sell my daughter who jus' married las' night," an' other t'ings. The white man tresten' her to call de police if she didn't stop, but de collud woman said: "hit me or call de police. I redder die dan to stan' dis any longer." De police took her to de Work House by de white woman orders an' what became of 'er, I never hear.

W'en de war began we wus taken to Aiken, South Ca'lina w'ere we stay' until de Yankees come t'rough. We could see balls sailin' t'rough de air w'en Sherman wus comin'. Bumbs hit trees in our yard. W'en de freedom gun wus fired, I wus on my 'nees scrubbin'. Dey tell me I wus free but I didn't b'lieve it.

In de days of slavory woman wus jus' given time 'nough to deliver dere babies. Dey deliver de baby 'bout eight in de mornin' an' twelve had to be back to work.

I wus a member of Emmanuel African Methodist Episcopal Church for 67 years. Big Zion, across de street wus my church before den an' before Old Bethel w'en I lived on de other end of town.

Sence Lincoln shook hands with his assasin who at de same time shoot him, frum dat day I stop shakin' hands, even in de church, an' you know how long dat wus. I don't b'lieve in kissin' neider fur all carry dere meannesses. De Master wus betrayed by one of his bosom frien' with a kiss.

SOURCE Interview with (Mrs.) Susan Hamilton, 17 Henrietta Street, who claims to be 101 years of age. She has never been sick for twenty years and walks as though just 40. She was hired out by her master for seven dollars a month which had to be given her master.

Susan Hamlin and Susan "Hamilton" are obviously one and the same; yet by the end of Ladson's interview, we are wondering if we

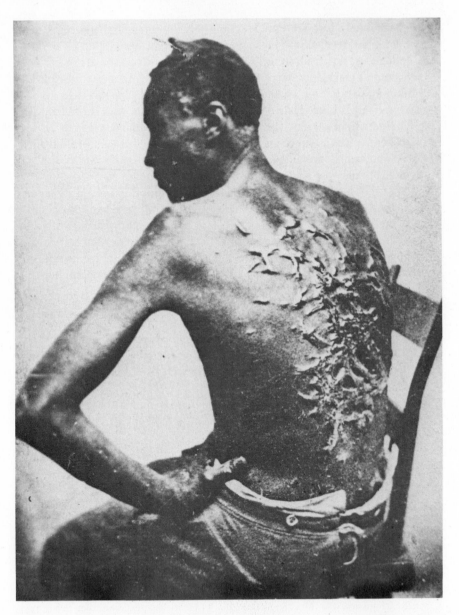

"W'en any slave wus whipped all de other slaves was made to watch. . . . I had some terribly bad experiences." The scars from whippings on this slave's back were recorded in 1863 by an unknown photographer travelling with the Union army.

have been listening to the same person! Kindness of the masters? We hear no tales about old Mr. Fuller; only vivid recollections of whippings so harsh "dere wusn't a white spot on her body." To Butler, Hamlin had mentioned only cruelties that she had heard about second-hand ("you don't know whether it was lie or not"); to Ladson, she recounts firsthand experiences ("I see women hung from de ceilin' of buildin's an' whipped with only supin tied 'round her lower part of de body.")

Discussions of happy family relations? Instead of tales about shoes in the winter, we hear of Hamlin's father, whipped so severely, he rebels and flees. We hear of family separations, not downplayed with a "you know how dey carry on," but with all the bitterness of mothers whose children had been taken "without any warnin'." We hear of a couple married one night, then callously separated and sold the next day. In the Butler account, slave babies are fed well, treated nicely; in the Ladson account, the recollection is of mothers who were given only a few hours away from the fields in order to deliver their children.

Benevolent white paternalism? This time Hamlin's tale of three races draws a different moral. The white race is "brazen," running the Indians off their land. With a touch of admiration, she notes that the Indians "wouldn't stan' for" being made slaves. White motives are seen not as religious but exploitative and vengeful: "Dey say 'mong themselves, 'we gwine mix dem up and make ourselves king. Dats de only way we'll git even with de Indians.'" The difference between the two interviews, both in tone and substance, is astonishing.

How do we account for this? Nowhere in the South Carolina narratives is the race of Augustus Ladson mentioned, but internal evidence would indicate he is black. In a culture where blacks usually addressed whites respectfully with a "Sir," "Ma'am," or "Boss," it seems doubtful that Susan Hamlin would address a white man as "son." ("I'm a hund'ed an' one years old now, son.") Furthermore, the content of the interview is just too consistently anti-white. Hamlin would never have remarked, "De white race is so brazen," if Ladson had been white, especially given the reticence demonstrated in her interview with Butler. Nor would she have been so specific about the angry mother's curses ("damn white, pale-face bastard"). It would be difficult to conceive of a more strikingly dramatic demonstration of how an interviewer can affect the responses of a subject.

FREEDOM AND DECEPTION

The slave narrative collection, then, is not the direct, unfiltered perspective that it first appears to be. In fact, interviews like the ones with Susan Hamlin seem to suggest that the search for the "true" freedmen's perspective is bound to end in failure and frustration. We have seen, first, that information from planters and other white sources must be treated with extreme skepticism; second, that northern white sources deserve similar caution. Finally, it appears that even the oral testimony of blacks themselves must be questioned, given the circumstances under which much of it was gathered. It is as if a detective discovered that all the clues he had carefully pieced together were hopelessly biased, leading his investigation down the wrong path.

The seriousness of the problem should not be underestimated. It is fundamental. We can try to ease out of the dilemma by noting that there are doubtless differing degrees of bias—that some accounts, relatively speaking, are likely to be less deceptive than others. It can be argued, for instance, that Susan Hamlin's interview with Ladson is a more accurate portrayal of her feelings than the interview with Butler. In large measure that is probably true. But does that mean we must reject all of the Butler interview? Presumably, Susan Hamlin's master did give her a pair of shoes one cold winter day. Are we to assume, because of Ladson's interview, that the young child felt no gratitude or obligation to "kind old" Mr. Fuller? Or that the old woman did not look back on those years with some ambivalence? For all her life, both slave and free, Susan Hamlin lived in a world where she was required to "feel" one set of emotions when dealing with some people and a different set when dealing with other people. Can we rest completely confident in concluding that the emotions she expressed to Ladson were her "real" feelings, while the ones to Jessie Butler were her "false" feelings? How can we possibly arrive at an objective conclusion about "real" feelings in any social situation where such severe strains existed?

Yet putting the question in this light offers at least a partial way out of the dilemma. If so many clues in the investigation are hopelessly "biased"—that is, distorted by the social situation in which they are set —then the very pervasiveness of the distortion may serve as a key to understanding the situation. The evidence in the case is warped precisely because it accurately reflects a distortion in the society itself. The elements of racism and slavery determined a culture where personal relations were necessarily grounded in mistrust and deception; where slaves could survive only if they remained acutely conscious of the need to adapt their feelings to the situation. The distortion in the evidence, in other words, speaks eloquently of the hurt inflicted in a society where personal behavior routinely operated under an economy of deception.

The deception was mutual—practiced by both sides upon each other. Susan Hamlin was adapting the story of her past to the needs of the moment, at the same time that Jessie Butler was letting Hamlin believe her to be a welfare agent. White masters painted lurid stories of Yankee devils with horns while slaves, playing roles they were expected to play, rolled their eyes in fear until they had the chance to run straight for Union lines. The deceptions fed upon each other and were compounded, becoming an inextricable part of daily life.

It would be tempting, given our awareness of this situation, simply to turn previous historical interpretations on their heads. Where William Dunning and his disciples took most of their primary sources at face value and thus saw only cheerful, childlike Sambos, an enlightened history would read the documents upside down, so to speak, stripping away the camouflage to reveal slaves who, quite rationally, went about the daily business of "puttin' on ole massa." And of course we have already seen abundant evidence that slaves did use calculated deception in order to protect themselves.

But simply to replace one set of feelings with another is to ignore the intricate and tense relationships between them. It drastically underestimates the strains that arose out of an economy of deception. The longer and more consistently masters and slaves were compelled to live false and inauthentic lives, the easier it must have been for them to mislead themselves as well as others. Where whites and blacks alike engaged in daily dissimulation, some of the deception was inevitably directed inward, simply to preserve the fiction of living in a tolerable, normally functioning society.

When the war came, shattering that fiction, whites and blacks were exposed in concrete and vivid ways to the deception that had been so much a part of their lives. For white slaveholders, the revelation usually came when Union troops entered a region and slaves deserted the plantations in droves. Especially demoralizing was the flight of blacks whom planters had believed most loyal. "He was about my age and I had always treated him more as a companion than a slave," noted one planter, of the first defector from his ranks. Mary Chestnut, the woman near Fort Sumter who had tried to penetrate the blank expressions of her slaves, discovered how impossible the task had been. "Jonathan, whom we trusted, betrayed us," she lamented, while "Claiborne, that black rascal who was suspected by all the world," faithfully protected the plantation.

Many slaveholders, when faced with the truth, refused to recognize the role that deception had played in their lives, so deceiving themselves further. "The poor negroes don't do us any harm except when they are put up to it," concluded one Georgia woman. A Richmond newspaper editor demanded that a slave who had denounced Jefferson Davis "be whipped every day until he confesses what white man put these notions in his head." Yet the war brought painful insight to others. "We were all laboring under a delusion," confessed one South Carolina planter. "I believed that these people were content, happy, and attached to their masters. But events and reflection have caused me to change these opinions. . . . If they were content, happy and attached to their masters, why did they desert him in the moment of his need and flock to an enemy, whom they did not know . . . ?"

For black slaves, the news of emancipation brought an entirely different reaction, but still one conditioned by the old habits. We have already seen how one old Georgia slave couple remained impassive as Sherman's troops passed through, until finally the wife could restrain herself no longer. Even the servant who eloquently shouted the praises of freedom at a secluded brook instinctively remembered the need for caution: "I got sort o' scared, afeared somebody hear me, an' I takes another good look. . . ." Although emancipation promised a society founded upon equal treatment and open relations, slaves could not help wondering whether the new order would fully replace the old. That would occur only if the freedmen could forge relationships that were no longer based on the customs of deception nor rooted in the central fiction of slavery —that blacks were morally and intellectually incapable of assuming a place in free society.

No historian has more vividly conveyed the freedmen's attempts to achieve that goal than Leon Litwack. Having recognized the substantial value of the slave narrative collection, Litwack drew upon its evidence as well as the standard range of primary sources to recreate the freedmen's perspectives as they sought the real meaning of their new freedom. Certainly that meaning was by no means evident once the first excitement of liberation had passed. James Lucas, a slave of Jefferson Davis, recalled the freedmen's confusion: "Dey all had diffe'nt ways o' thinkin' 'bout it. Mos'ly though dey was jus' lak me, dey didn' know jus' zackly what it meant. It was jus' somp'n dat de white folks an' slaves all de time talk 'bout. Dat's all. Folks dat ain' never been free don' rightly know de *feel* of bein' free. Dey don' know de meanin' of it." But blacks were not long in taking their first steps toward defining freedom. On the surface, many of these seemed small. But however limited, they served to distance the freedmen in significant ways from the old habits of bondage.

The taking of new names was one such step. As slaves, blacks often had no surname, or took the name of their master. Equally demeaning, given names were often casually assigned by their owners. Cicero, Pompey, and other Latin or Biblical names were commonly bestowed in jest. And whether or not slaves had a surname, they were always addressed familiarly, by their given names. Such customs were part of the symbolic language of deception, promoting the illusion that blacks were helpless and even laughable dependents of the planter's family.

Thus many freedmen took for themselves new names, severing the symbolic tie with their old masters. "A heap of people say they was going to name their selves over," recalled one freedman. "They named their selves big names. . . . Some of the names was Abraham an' some called their selves Lincum. Any big name 'ceptin' their master's name. It was the fashion." Even blacks who remained loyal to their masters recognized the significance of the change. "When you'all had de power you was good to me," an older freedman told his master, "an I'll protect you now. No niggers nor Yankees shall touch you. If you want anything, call for Sambo. I mean, call for Mr. Samuel—that's my name now."

Just as freedmen took new names to symbolize their new status, so also many husbands and wives reaffirmed their marriages in formal ceremonies. Under slavery, many marriages and family ties had been ignored through the convenient fiction that blacks were morally inferior. Black affections, the planters argued, were dominated by impulse and the physical desires of the moment. Such self-deception eased many a master's conscience when slave families were separated and sold. Similarly, many planters married slaves only informally, with a few words sufficing to join the couple. "Don't mean nuthin' less you say, "What God done jined, cain't no man pull asunder," noted one Virginia freedman. "But dey never would say dat. Jus' say, 'Now you married.'" For obvious reasons of human dignity, blacks moved to solemnize their marriage vows. There were practical reasons for an official ceremony too: it might qualify families for military pensions, or the division of lands that were widely rumored to be coming.

Equally symbolic for most blacks was the freedom to travel where they wished. As we have seen, historian William Dunning recognized this fact, but interpreted it from the viewpoint of his southern white sources as "aimless but happy" wandering. Black accounts make abundantly

clear how travel helped freedmen to rid themselves of the role they had
been forced to play during their bondage. Richard Edwards, a preacher
in Florida, explicitly described the symbolic nature of such a move:

> You ain't, none o' you, gwinter feel rale free till you shakes de dus' ob
> de Old Plantashun offen yore feet an' goes ter a new place whey you kin
> live out o' sight o' de gret house. So long ez de shadder ob de gret house
> falls acrost you, you ain't gwine ter feel lak no free man, an' you ain't
> gwine ter feel lak no free 'oman. You mus' all move—you mus' move clar
> away from de ole places what you knows, ter de new places what you don't
> know, whey you kin raise up yore head douten no fear o' Marse Dis ur
> Marse Tudder.

And so, in the spring and summer of 1865, southern roads were filled
with blacks, hiving off "like bees trying to find a setting place," as one
ex-slave recalled. Generally freedmen preferred to remain within the
general locale of family and friends, merely leaving one plantation in
search of work at another. But a sizeable minority travelled farther, to
settle in cities, move west, or try their fortunes at new occupations.

Many ex-slaves travelled in order to reunite families separated
through previous sales. Freedmen "had a passion, not so much for wandering, as for getting together," a Freedman's Bureau agent observed;
"and every mother's son among them seemed to be in search of his
mother; every mother in search of her children." Often, relatives had
only scanty information; in other cases, so much time had passed that kin
could hardly recognize each other, especially when young children had
grown up separated from their parents.

A change of name or location, the formalization of marriages, reunion
with relatives—all these acts demonstrated that freedmen wanted no part
of the old constraints and deceptions of slavery. But as much as these acts
defined black freedom, larger issues remained. How much would emancipation broaden economic avenues open to blacks? Would freedom
provide an opportunity to rise on the social ladder? The freedmen
looked anxiously for signs of significant changes.

Perhaps the most commonly perceived avenue to success was through
education. Slavery had been rationalized, in part, through the fiction that
blacks were incapable of profiting from an education. The myth of
intellectual inferiority stood side by side with that of moral inferiority.
Especially in areas where masters had energetically prevented slaves
from acquiring skills in reading, writing, and arithmetic, the freedmen's
hunger for learning was intense. When Northerners occupied the Caro-

lina Sea Islands during the war, Yankee plantation superintendents found that the most effective way to force unwilling laborers to work was to threaten to take away their schoolbooks. "The Negroes . . . will do anything for us, if we will only teach them," noted one missionary stationed on the islands.

After the war, when the Freedman's Bureau sent hundreds of northern school teachers into the South, blacks flocked enthusiastically to the makeshift schoolhouses. Often, classes could be held only at night, but the freedmen were willing. "We work all day, but we'll come to you in the evening for learning," Georgia freedmen told their teacher, "and we want you to make us learn; we're dull, but we want you to beat it into

"My Lord, ma'am, what a great thing larning is!" a freedman exclaimed to a white teacher. Many whites were surprised by the intensity of the ex-slaves' desire for an education. To say that the freedmen were "anxious to learn" was not strong enough, one Virginia school official noted; "they are *crazy* to learn." This woodcut, drawn in 1867, depicts several youngsters studying their lessons along a village street.

us!" Some white plantation owners discovered that if they wished to keep their field hands, they would have to provide a schoolhouse and teacher.

Important as education was, the freedmen were preoccupied even more with their relation to the lands they had worked for so many years. The vast majority of slaves were field hands. The agricultural life was the one they had grown up with, and as freedmen, they wanted the chance to own and cultivate their own property. Independent ownership would lay to rest the lie that blacks were incapable of managing their own affairs; but without land, the idea of freedom would be just another deception. "Gib us our own land and we take care ourselves; but widout land, de ole massas can hire us or starve us, as dey please," noted one freedman.

In the heady enthusiasm at the close of the war, many ex-slaves were convinced that the Union would divide up confiscated Confederate plantations. Each family, so the persistent rumor went, would receive forty acres and a mule. "This was no slight error, no trifling idea," reported one white observer, "but a fixed and earnest conviction as strong as any belief a man can ever have." Slaves had worked their masters' lands for so long without significant compensation, it seemed only fair that recompense should finally be made. Further, blacks had more than hopes to rely on. Ever since southern planters had fled from invading Union troops, some blacks had been allowed to cultivate the abandoned fields.

The largest of such occupied regions was the Sea Islands along the Carolina coast, where young Sam Mitchell had first heard the northern guns. As early as March 1863, freedmen were purchasing confiscated lands from the government. Then in January 1865, after General William Sherman completed his devastating march to the sea, he extended the area which was open to confiscation. In his Special Field Order No. 15, Sherman decreed that a long strip of abandoned lands, stretching from Charleston on the north to Jacksonville on the south, would be reserved for the freedmen. The lands would be subdivided into forty-acre tracts, which could be rented for a nominal fee. After three years, the freedmen had the option to purchase the land outright.

Sherman's order was essentially a tactical maneuver, designed to deal with the overwhelming problem of refugees in his path. But blacks widely perceived this order and other promises by enthusiastic northerners as a foretaste of Reconstruction policy. Consequently, when white planters returned to their plantations, they often found blacks who no longer bowed obsequiously and tipped their hats. Thomas Pinckney of South Carolina, having called his former slaves together, asked them if they would continue to work for him. "O yes, we gwi wuk! we gwi wuk all right . . . ." came the angry response. "We gwi wuk fuh ourse'ves. We ain' gwi wuk fuh no white man." Where would they go to work, Pinckney asked—seeing as they had no land? "We ain't gwine nowhar," they replied defiantly. "We gwi wuk right here on de lan' whar we wuz bo'n an' whar belongs tuh us."

Despite the defiance, Pinckney prevailed, as did the vast majority of southern planters. Redistribution of southern lands was an idea strongly supported only by more radical northerners. Thaddeus Stevens introduced a confiscation bill in Congress, but it was swamped by debate and never passed. President Johnson, whose conciliatory policies pleased southern planters, determined to settle the issue as quickly as possible. He summoned General O. O. Howard, head of the Freedman's Bureau, and instructed Howard to reach a solution "mutually satisfactory" to both blacks and planters. Howard, though sympathetic to the freedmen, could not mistake the true meaning of the President's order.

Regretfully, the general returned to the Sea Islands in October and assembled a group of freedmen on Edisto Island. The audience, suspecting the bad news, was restless and unruly. Howard tried vainly to speak, and made "no progress" until a woman in the crowd began singing, "Nobody knows the trouble I've seen." The crowd joined, then was silent while Howard told them they must give up their lands. Bitter cries of "No! No!" came from the audience. "Why, General Howard, why do you take away our lands?" called one burly man. "You take them from us who have always been true, always true to the Government! You give them to our all-time enemies! That is not right!"

Reluctantly, and sometimes only after forcible resistance, blacks lost the lands to returning planters. Whatever else freedom might mean, it was not to signify compensation for previous labor. In the years to come Reconstruction would offer freedom of another sort, through the political process. By the beginning of 1866, the radicals in Congress had charted a plan that gave blacks basic civil rights and political power. Yet even that avenue of opportunity was quickly sealed off. In the decades that followed the first thunder of emancipation, blacks would look back on their early experiences almost as if they were part of another, vanished world. The traditions of racial oppression and the daily deceptions that went with them were too strong to be thoroughly overturned by the war. It is perhaps significant that the term "freedman" uses a past participle. Despite the best efforts of blacks, American society found it impossible to define them without reference to the fictions of their past.

"I was right smart bit by de freedom bug for awhile," Charlie Davenport of Mississippi recalled.

> It sounded pow'ful nice to be tol: "You don't have to chop cotton no more. You can th'ow dat hoe down an' go fishin' whensoever de notion strikes you. An' you can roam 'roun' at night an' court gals jus' as you please. Aint no marster gwine a-say to you, 'Charlie, you's got to be back when de clock strikes nine.'" I was fool 'nough to b'lieve all dat kin' o' stuff.

Both perceptions—the first flush of the "freedom bug" as well as Davenport's later disillusionment—accurately reflect the black experience. Freedom had come to a nation of four million slaves, and it changed their lives in deep and important ways. But for many years after the war put an end to human bondage, the freedmen still had to settle for the view from the bottom rail.

Additional Reading

Leon Litwack's superb *Been In the Storm So Long: the Aftermath of Slavery* (New York, 1979) serves as an excellent starting point for background on the freedmen's experience after the war. Litwack supplies an interpretive framework that moves the book from topic to topic, but the material is kaleidoscopic in detail, story after story tumbling onto the page and threatening to overwhelm the book's structure. The result is a rich and vibrant portrait. Willie Lee Rose, *Rehearsal for Reconstruction: the Port Royal Experiment* (Indianapolis, Ind., 1964), tells the story of the Union occupation of the Carolina Sea Islands, where the North first attempted to forge a coherent Reconstruction policy. Black experiences can also be traced in state histories of Reconstruction, where more attention is given to grass-roots effects of the new freedom. Joel Williamson, *After Slavery* (Chapel Hill, N.C., 1965) covers South Carolina; Peter Kolchin, *First Freedom* (Westport, Conn., 1972) treats Alabama. William McFeely's *Yankee Stepfather* (New Haven, Conn., 1968) provides good coverage of the Freedman's Bureau in his biography of its leader, General O. O. Howard.

Contemporary white accounts of the slaves' first days of freedom abound. Litwack, cited above, has a helpful bibliography. Among those sources we found useful: Rupert S. Holland, ed., *Letters and Diary of Laura M. Towne* (Cambridge, Mass., 1912); Charles Nordhoff, *The Freedmen of South-Carolina* (New York, 1863); C. Vann Woodward, ed., *Mary Chestnut's Civil War* (New Haven, 1981); and Arney R. Childs, ed., *The Private Journal of Henry William Ravenel, 1859–1887* (Columbia, S.C., 1947). James L. Roark, *Masters Without Slaves* (New York, 1977) provides an account of the postwar perceptions of the planter class. In addition to the slave narrative collection discussed below, other sources for the freedmen's perspective include Octavia V. Rogers Albert, *The House of Bondage* (New York, 1891); Orland K. Armstrong, *Old Massa's People* (Indianapolis, Ind., 1931); M. F. Armstrong and Helen W. Ludlow, *Hampton and Its Students* (New York, 1875); and Laura Haviland, *A Woman's Life Work* (Cincinnati, 1881).

The Federal Writers' Project interviews are found in George P. Rawick, *The American Slave: A Composite Autobiography,* 19 vols. & supplements (Westport, Conn., 1972–). The collection invites use in many ways. Intriguing material is available on the relations between blacks and Indians, for example, especially in the Oklahoma narratives. Because one interviewer often submitted many interviews, readers may wish to analyze strengths and weaknesses of particular interviewers. The Library of Congress, under Benjamin Botkin's direction, began such an analysis; its records can be examined at the National Archives, catalogued under Correspondence Pertaining to Ex-Slave Studies, Records of the Federal Writers' Project, Records Group 69, Works Progress Administration.

Further information on the slave narratives may be found in Norman Yetman, "The Background of the Slave Narrative Collection," *American Quarterly*, 19 (Fall 1967), 534–553. John Blassingame has an excellent discussion of oral history and its pitfalls in "Using the Testimony of Ex-slaves: Approaches and Problems," *Journal of Southern History*, XLI (November 1975), 473–492, available in expanded form in his introduction to *Slave Testimony* (Baton Rouge, La., 1977). Paul D. Escott, *Slavery Remembered: A Record of Twentieth-Century Slave Narratives* (Chapel Hill, N.C. 1979) provides interested researchers with helpful data. Escott's quantitative analysis of the narratives includes the percentage of interviews with field hands, house servants, and artisans; the occupations they took up as freedmen, and the destinations of those who migrated. The race of many of the project's interviewers is also included (although not always accurately—see Jerrold Hirsch's review of the book in *Reviews in American History*, VIII (September 1980), 312–317).

Finally, those who wish to do their own oral history should consult Stephen A. Richardson et al., *Interviewing: Its Forms and Functions* (New York, 1965) for an introduction to that art. More specific, nuts-and-bolts information can be found in James Hoopes's excellent *Oral History: An Introduction for Students* (Chapel Hill, N.C., 1979). See also Cullom Davis et al., *Oral History: From Tape to Type* (Chicago, 1977) and Ramon I. Harris, et al., *The Practice of Oral History* (Glen Rock, N.J., 1975). The latter book has erred in at least one pertinent fact, however: in the area of libel, it blithely assures would-be publishers of oral history that truth is always a sufficient defense. Truth may suffice when it comes to history, but not invariably so in the courts of law.

Index

About the Authors

JAMES WEST DAVIDSON is a full-time writer, trained as a historian, who also teaches in the Department of History at Smith College. He was educated at Haverford College and at Yale University, where he was granted a Ph.D. in 1973. Davidson's earlier books include *The Complete Wilderness Paddler* (with John Rugge, 1977) and *The Logic of Millennial Thought* (1977).

MARK HAMILTON LYTLE is Associate Professor of History at Bard College. He received his Ph.D. from Cornell University and his Ph.D. from Yale University in 1973. He is co-author (with Davidson) of *The United States: A History of the Republic* (1981).

A Note on the Design of This Book

The text of this book was set via computer-driven cathode
ray tube in a type face known as Garamond.
Its design is based on letterforms
originally created by Claude Garamond, 1510-1561.
Garamond was a pupil of Geoffrey Troy and
may have patterned his letterforms on Venetian
models. To this day, the type face that
bears his name is one of the most attractive
used in book composition, and the intervening years
have caused it to lose little of its
freshness or beauty.